ANN GILLANDERS'
Compendium of Healing Points

This book is dedicated to all those who support the banner of healing the body the natural way, whichever discipline they may choose.
Ann Gillanders

**Ann Gillanders' Books
are available direct from
BSR Sales Ltd.**
Send for Mail Order Catalogue

**Reflexology, The Ancient Answer
to Modern Ailments**
Published by Ann Gillanders
ISBN 0 9511868 0 9
No Mean Feat – Autobiography
Published by Ann Gillanders
ISBN 0 9511868 1 7
**Reflexology – The Theory and
Practice**
Published by Ann Gillanders
ISBN 0 9511868 2 5
**Gateways to Health and Harmony
with Reflexology**
Published by Ann Gillanders
ISBN 0 9511868 4 1
**The Essential Guide to Foot and
Hand Reflexology**
Published by Ann Gillanders
ISBN 0 9511868 5 X
**Reflexology and the Intestinal
Link** (Book)
Published by Ann Gillanders
ISBN 0 9511868 9 2
**Reflexology and the Intestinal
Link Wall Chart**
(To complement book)
Published by Ann Gillanders
ISBN 0 9511868 8 4

ALSO AVAILABLE:
**Reflexology – A Step by Step
Guide**
Published by Gaia Books
ISBN 1 85675 081 7
The Family Guide to Reflexology
Published by Gaia Books
ISBN 1 85675 049 3
...and a video
**Reflexology – The Timeless Art
of Self Healing** *featuring Ann
Gillanders.*
*Produced by Wave
Communications.*

***Send for a full colour
Mail Order Catalogue***
Telephone: 01279 429060
Fax: 01279 445234
Email: sales@footreflexology.com
Website – shop online:
www.footreflexology.com

*BSR Sales Limited,
92 Sheering Road, Old Harlow,
Essex CM17 0JW*

**ANN GILLANDERS' COMPENDIUM OF HEALING POINTS
by Ann Gillanders
ISBN 0 9511868 7 6**

British Library Cataloguing in Publication Data.
A catalogue record for this book is available from the British Library.

Text & *Illustrations: Copyight ©Ann Gillanders 2001

Published by Ann Gillanders 2001

All rights reserved. No part of this publication may be reproduced, stored in a retrieval system, transmitted or published by any means available, including publication on the Internet, without the prior written permission of the publisher.

Book design and preparation by: Eleanor Tanner Design,
25 Godfrey Way, Great Dunmow, Essex CM6 2AY.
Tel: 01371 873449   Fax: 01371 873912
Illustrations by Eleanor Tanner

Typefaces: Times New Roman and CG Omega (text) with Garamond and CG Omega (headings).

Printed and bound in Great Britain by Alden Press, Oxford.

Copyright acknowledgement: The author has permission to use anatomy and physiology diagrams from 'The Sourcebook of Medical Illustration' whose copyright is held by The Medical College of St. Bartholomew's Hospital, London. Diagrams from this source are to be found on pages: 16,17,20,33,48,77,82, 90 &111.

**DISCLAIMER & CAUTIONARY ADVICE FROM
ANN GILLANDERS: SEE PAGE 6**

Contents

Contents

Contents

Dear Readers,

I hope you will gain further knowledge and support from the articles contained in my **Compendium of Healing Points.** *Many of these articles and features were published initially in* **Healing Points,** *the quarterly complementary health magazine which was founded by me, and I now present these for the first time in convenient paperback format for ease of reference and to bring these articles to as wide an audience as possible.*

Now revised, four NEW illustrated and detailed features on major health issues of our time have been added.

It is 25 years since I was introduced to reflexology and complementary medicines generally and, as you all know, not only does the study of learning how to treat the body 'the natural way' change the lives of many sick people, it also changes the lives of those who devote their lives to the 'caring professions'.

I have had the privilege of training and educating practitioners not only through reflexology but in the many books that I have written, and have seen such dramatic changes in people who decided to change the direction of their lives and study complementary medicines.

Women in particular, many of whom had traumatic lives, experienced serious health problems, overcame their mental and physical sufferings and took steps to study and help other people.

I have seen as many changes 'in patients' as I have 'in students' who evolved as positive, fulfilled individuals, gained self-worth and through their work enjoyed a 'Better Quality of Life'.

**'Remember, knowledge is like love –
the more you give out, the more you get back.'**

Sincerely yours, Ann Gillanders.

Introduction

Disease can only manifest in the body after there have been disturbances in the energy flow. You may hear this 'energy' referred to frequently as *ying* or *yang* by the Chinese, or *chi* which is the life force of the human body.

Once the life force leaves the human organism at death, we are just a jumbled mass of cells, blood, organs and structures: there is 'no energy' emanating to stimulate the body to activate all its functions. Human beings are mind, body and spirit complexes which exist in a constant dynamic, vibrational energy.

Vibrational medicines are usually tinctures, or substances charged with a particular frequency of subtle energy – as with homeopathy.

Dr Edward Bach was one of the most respected homeopathic practitioners and treated his patients successfully by using flower essences which contained minute quantities of a physical substance; yet they were considered to be pure vibrational remedies. Dr Bach linked stress, emotions and illness decades before most contemporary physicians had begun to address the connections.

Fear, and the way it has a depressing effect on our psyche, causes disharmony in our physical bodies and paves the way for 'bacterial' invasion. We do not 'catch' viruses and bacteria – they 'catch us' if the conditions are right within the body and the mind for them to flourish.

The use of 'healing hands' to relieve human suffering dates back thousands of years. Evidence of their use in Ancient Egypt is found in the Ebers Papyrus, circa 1552 BC. This document describes the laying on of hands for healing.

Centuries before the birth of Christ, the Greeks used 'touch therapies' in their temples for healing the sick, and there is evidence of the feet being used for healing at that time too.

Many miracles in the Bible refer to the laying on of hands for healing both spiritual and physical ailments.

In the future, healing will pass from the domain of physical methods for treating the physical body and recognise the need for the spirituality and mental attitude of the patient to be addressed.

By integrating harmony between the body, mind and spirit, we will be able to eradicate the very basic cause of disease.

CHAPTER 1

Healing the body, mind and spirit

We hear the word 'holistic' being referred to so frequently today: what does this actually mean? The simple truth of the matter is that 'holistic' means dealing with the emotional, physical and spiritual needs of the individual.

Life before birth

Life does not begin the day we are born: it begins nine months earlier when we are a minute speck of life, a single cell which is not visible to the human eye. I believe that children should inherit their mother's name since every child has far more of its mother in it than its father. A mother's egg is thousands of times larger than the father's sperm and it is directly from her egg that a new life will evolve. The female egg is a complete cell with its combination of protoplasm, its enzymes, and its mitochondria – the power stations which provide the cell's activity.

During the nine months of pregnancy, the mother transmits her emotions, whether happy or sad, to her child and these emotional experiences during pregnancy have a great impact on the child's neuronal network: the father's do not. The father's contribution to new life is half of the chromosomes. Apart from the emotional needs of the unborn child the human foetus requires a sufficient balance of vitamins and nutrients. If these are missing from the mother's diet the baby will suffer and the mother will have a more difficult birth than anticipated. Without a mother's care during the early weeks of birth, few babies would survive.

Foundations for health

Going back to the very grass roots of time, tribal life was always on the move and there was just no time to wait for women to have long, drawn-out labours: short labours, a strong vigorous baby and the ability to be active just as quickly as possible were needed – a very primitive inheritance.

If you consider laying down strong foundations in the human body and compare these needs to the skills of a successful gardener, who respects the need to prepare the soil with nitrogen, phosphorous and potassium – nitrogen for leaf growth, phosphorous to produce the flowers, plus strength to the root and stem – you will begin to realise how vital the months of pregnancy are. The mother, too, needs to lay down sound nutrition in order to produce a healthy offspring.

Healing from within

The human body has the most amazing healing principles. It heals from the inside out, repairs broken bones, and heals open wounds following, for example, an accident or surgical intervention, so that all you can see six weeks later is a fine white line, which we refer to as 'a scar' – quite amazing!

The body, therefore, has the ability to heal itself from disorder or disease provided it is given the right food, and that means a correct balance of vitamins and minerals which we do not get today in the de-mineralised environment in which we all live.

Fruit and vegetables wrapped in plastic should be avoided since plastic throws off excessive toxic substances; and you should never leave your food wrapped for long periods in a refrigerator. Our fruits have generally travelled great distances before reaching markets and have also been subjected to chemical sprays to prevent any insect invading the skins.

The housewife demands blemish-free fruit and vegetables because they 'look good'. Organic fruits and vegetables are not so attractive to the eye but are rich in the minerals and vitamins which our bodies crave.

Healthy heart and circulation

Our body adjusts to climatic changes quite remarkably: one day the skin is called upon to be a radiator, giving off heat, the next day it may have to be an insulator retaining body heat. This puts quite a strain on the heart and circulation.

The human heart is the motor of the human body, every single cell relies on the efficient functioning of this double pump which delivers six ounces of blood per heartbeat into the large artery leaving the heart, and yet this organ is only the size of its owner's fist and can, in many cases, pump effectively for one hundred years, or even longer!

Folk medicine includes ways to aid the heart, and natural honey is a great tonic to the heart muscle, the blood vessels and the general blood supply. Herbalism and old Folk Law remedies have been around from the very beginning of time and I sincerely believe that if 'Mother Nature' meant mankind to take drugs to heal its body, every baby would enter the world with a supply strapped to its back.

Understanding disease

We do not become diseased overnight. Disease attacks when the fundamental laws of nature are interfered with and when there is constant suppression of 'symptoms' which are the cries of help from the body saying 'all is not well here – I need some help'. When we become ill and when sickness appears we must support the activity of the body cells, which is why we are always encouraged to increase our intake of fluids, particularly juices such as apple, grape or cranberry.

A fever is not the 'alarming situation' that most people fear. A fever is a 'burn up' – a furnace the body produces to burn up the toxic waste matter that is not being eliminated through the correct channels. Toxins build up from bacteria and viruses, chemicals from our food stuffs, an overburdened liver because of too much alcohol, too many rich high protein foods that stress the liver's activities and poor elimination from our kidneys because of insufficient water in our diet and far too much intake of caffeine. Water is needed by the kidneys to flush the system: too little and toxins will be retained within the delicate nephrons.

We are forced to take to our beds when we have a fever and very few people have any appetite at all when the temperature is raised – all to the good! As we rest in bed our bodies can get to work burning up waste, and eliminating more toxins through our skin as we perspire heavily. As we rest in this 'fasting stage' all the body's energy will be directed to healing and stimulating the immune system to produce billions of white blood cells, called lymphocytes, which act as an army against the offending bacteria or virus infection.

A fever is a 'healing sign' not a major disaster. If the body was not able to produce a fever when required, we would be in big trouble as this would mean that our life energy was severely depleted and our immune system was failing.

When we fast we are not calling upon our body to direct energy into systems such as the digestive system and the functioning of our bowel, therefore the body can direct all its energies into healing.

There are two systems in the human body that have memory: one is the human brain and the other the immune system which comprises our spleen and thymus gland. If we constantly suppress unpleasant symptoms with antibiotics the body rapidly forgets how to heal. Anti-biotics (anti-life) work against the principles of healing.

Stress

We hear much about 'stress' as the cause of disease. Stress does not cause disease, it is how the body manages stress that causes it. Stress is perhaps the 'final straw that broke the camel's back' in a toxic-tired body that has been neglected for some time.

Many individuals absolutely thrive on stress. They cannot wait for the next challenge, thrive on deadlines that have to be met and, if they do not have stress in their life to 'jolly them along', they will encourage it. They enjoy getting up and accepting any challenge that presents itself each day and they do not become sick.

It is the 'dragging down' kind of stress that makes people ill: an ill-matched relationship that seems to be going nowhere; a boring job; constant care day in and day out for a disabled child or elderly parent; the constant 'giving out' and 'not getting back'.

Poor self image, the inability to communicate, a dead marriage, stresses of this nature are destructive to the immune system and, after all, if our immune systems were working correctly we would not become sick.

Individuals should seriously consider reducing their mind-created stress because of its connection with three debilitating and demylineating diseases: rheumatoid arthritis, multiple sclerosis and AIDS. All these diseases are on the increase.

Auto-immunity or auto allergy begins when the body decides to produce antibodies against its own cells. Stress and the efficiency of our immune system are very related. Trying to reduce exploiting life, and taking life at a slower pace is the safest medicine for helping these diseases. A similar reasoning could also be used for Addison's disease which is a disorder of the functioning of our adrenal glands. The adrenal glands are related to the hypothalamus which is very reactive to the mind's worries and stresses. Stress also affects ageing.

One of the most irritating symptoms of stress can be insomnia. A recent survey shows that a third of the population suffers from poor quality sleep: they either cannot get to sleep, sleep only a few hours and then awaken at two or three in the morning, or wake up eight or nine times during the night. Insomnia is usually created by an over activity of the pituitary-adrenal system, the emergency system of the body that is discharging large hormonal outputs, in particular adrenaline that is triggered by a racing mind

'My first responsibility to me is to do everything in my power to keep well and follow everyday commonsense rules of healthful living.'

and worries that invade us during the long periods of night.

Watching a video that is relaxing, or one that makes you laugh, can help. Laughing helps to discharge tension. Physical activity such as an enjoyable sport creates physical tiredness: this will encourage sleep. It is interesting to note that we are the only animal on the planet that suffers from insomnia.

Depression

Depression is common. We take billions of tons of antidepressant tablets in the fast track of the western world. The most usual feeling of a depressed person is the feeling of worthlessness which is reached when we realise that we are unable to achieve our aspirations.

By making our existence of value to another, we automatically reduce depression, even if we direct our caring to the needs of a pet. In extreme circumstances depressed people suffer from deep self-hate which can easily inspire the idea of suicide. Love for others implies sacrifice and sacrifice provides good feelings.

Much of the stress we suffer in this progressive world is what I refer to as 'invented stress'. Many of our habits such as drinking, smoking and drug abuse, as well as job selection and our passion for luxury and expensive gadgets, are dictated by man's search for importance, and women follow close behind.

The invention of the credit card, which invites you to 'have now – pay later', encourages the young to have little respect for anything as getting into debt to replace belongings is just a way of life.

The credit card is really rather like a cowboy with a gun in his holster, 'it just has to be used'!

There was some thrill years ago when we economised and saved for a new piece of furniture or holiday, went out with the money in our pocket, paid for it, and in return were handed over the goods.

Reflexology – how does it work?

There are so many theories on reflexology and its benefits and how it works. In my opinion reflexology works on a cell memory basis, difficult to understand but if we just stop a moment and consider that the human body is composed of billions of cells, and cells have memory. The cells produced at conception have knowledge and a memory, very much like a computer, that enables the cells to divide at intervals over a few days until the division is complete and the formation of the foetus begins.

The immune system is also composed of cells, white blood cells that register a memory when bacteria or viruses attack the body. The cells ward off the offending virus by surrounding it with millions of white blood cells in an attempt to destroy.

When we have an illness like measles, mumps, or chicken pox, our cell structure lays down in the memory bank knowledge that this foreign body has invaded the human form and produces an antibody to prevent further attack. This resistance to further infection is registered in the cells, or in the memory bank of the cell, so that we do not become subjected to this illness again. The immune system works efficiently and gives lifelong protection against contracting these illnesses a second time: vaccinations do not give lifelong protection.

As reflexology works through stimulation of nerve pathways, it must be connected to the nervous system, otherwise the patient would not experience a sensitive reaction in the feet!

When there is damage or disease in the body the organ produces a sensitivity in the nerve pathway which terminates in the feet, and carries a message via the cellular structure of that organ to the brain that all is not well. The patient experiences a sensitive reaction in the feet that we, the practitioners, stimulate through the nerve pathways to the organ and, in effect, change the message. We restore the balance of the cellular structure of that organ function or part.

Another example is the pain an amputee experiences when say, a foot has been removed by surgery and the patient still experiences often agonising pain in the phantom foot for months and sometimes years. The brain cells are still registering the image of the foot, even though it is missing. The medical profession refer to this experience as 'phantom pain'.

The feet are by far the most sensitive areas of the body and contain many thousands of nerve endings. Working on the feet is far more beneficial than working on the hands. Stimulation from the bases to the brain creates far more energy: all growth in nature is stimulated from the roots to the flower or leaf and our body works in a similar way.

Side effects following a reflexology treatment

It is not at all unusual to get a reaction following a treatment of reflexology. It is essential therefore that both the patient and practitioner are well aware of exactly what is going on within the body when these symptoms occur.

I must make it quite clear that this in no way means that the patient has 'become worse'. In fact, any reaction after treatment is something to be pleased about as it is proof indeed that the body has responded to the treatment and change is taking place.

In all forms of complementary medicine including herbalism,

homeopathy, acupuncture and even massage, the patient may sometimes experience a temporary worsening of their state.

The sinus problem from which you are suffering may become more blocked than ever, or your nose may start streaming after treatment. If you are a sufferer from migraine you may find that the treatment precipitates an attack. This is likely to be very short term in duration but may be a disappointing setback. Your back condition could feel even more uncomfortable and if you suffer from colitis or any urinary tract infection you may well find that your urine output increases, or you may well have several bowel movements.

I have known patients to come out in a rash following the treatment session. This certainly is a very positive sign: the body uses the skin as a first line of defence and creates an elimination. Any rashes or spots are in fact the body ridding itself of unwanted toxins.

One very good result following treatment with reflexology is that the patient makes a claim that they slept for many hours following a session and have never slept better. This is due to a total breakdown in the stress of the body, creating within the patient a feeling of harmony and relief.

A little advice as regards to side effects from reflexology can be given to the patient. Recommend that he or she drinks a large quantity of bottled pure spring water, combined with taking a gram of vitamin C. Vitamin C helps inflammation and will lessen the reactions from treatment. This is particularly vital when your patient is suffering from an organic condition.

It is unusual to continue having side effects with reflexology after the first couple of treatments. Thereafter all should be plain sailing and the patient should find that their condition improves little by little, week by week, until at the end of six or eight sessions they should have an excellent result from their particular disorder.

Reflexology is safe, efficient and highly effective: there are no dangers. Over the years people have complicated this science with viewpoints that suggest that there is 'danger' in treating cancer; 'danger' in treating diabetics and 'danger' in spreading disease.

Reflexology, above all, helps the immune system, and if our immune system worked efficiently we would not become ill.

Reflexology is effective in eliminating toxins that have built up in the body: detoxification must take place in order for healing to take place. Nature cannot heal over toxic waste and if we try to work against nature, the body will produce symptoms to get rid of unwanted substances. The symptoms will be vomiting, diarrhoea and skin rashes. Suppression leads to more disease.

Reflexology is a profession and, just as every chiropodist, acupuncturist or osteopath has regular appointments through the day, often seeing many patients, we too must get on with the job in hand and treat the patient professionally and properly, and then move on to the next one

We hear far too much about the 'practitioner picking up negative influences from the patient'. I believe that this is 'all in the mind'. If every doctor or surgeon considered this a possibility as they treated the general public in vast numbers daily, for all manner of acute or chronic states, few would be able to continue with their work.

There should be no concentration on negative energies. Why do we have to pick up negatives? Why could we not receive a positive energy from a patient?

Reflexology treatments introduced regularly give a great relief from both mental and physical stress as well as tension that encourages disease to manifest and has such a positive effect on the immune system.

Reflexology provides relaxation that encourages the balance of the body. Patients will become aware of a new feeling of well being which perhaps has been foreign to them until now.

And what about the Practitioner?

As he or she gains experience and confidence in the work, a great sense of self-satisfaction and reward will be experienced in seeing chronic conditions, which previously had not responded to conventional medicine, fade away and people enjoy a better quality of life than they had ever dreamed of. This is the greatest asset that this wonderful treatment can provide.

Did you know?
Colds and Sore Throats
There are so many different strains of the cold virus which breed in excess in our centrally heated houses with double glazed windows! We are, therefore, more likely to catch colds during the winter period.

Useful supplements
To boost your immune system:
Vitamin C This vitamin has been shown to shorten the duration of a cold.
Zinc or zinc lozenges for sore throats.
Vitamin A for mucous membrane health.
Garlic High Potency – garlic has antiviral and antibacterial properties.
Echinacea purpurea for three weeks to support the efficiency of the immune system.

An area explained – colon health

In the beginning....the first acidophilus implant is received from mother's milk. Nature gives females mammary glands which provide milk (lacto) and bacteria for their young infant's nourishment and immune system.

Mother's milk contains bifidus, a lacto bacteria and specific growth factors for bifidus along with important immunoglobulins. These all help establish the basis for a strong immune system in the child. Bifidus constitutes 99 per cent of the nursing infant's colon flora. The presence of this simplified bifidus flora is considered to be a major factor contributing to the greater resistance to infection and better health of breast-fed babies. The existence of the simplified lactobacteria in flora acts as a vital barrier to infections. The colon of the breast-fed infant is by nature slightly acidic due to the acid loving and acid secreting bifidus. This slightly acidified colon prevents the growth of any harmful bacteria which can only thrive in an alkaline environment. In addition to these acidic secretions other factors in acidophilus secretions have been found to exert antagonistic actions on the growth of specific harmful types of bacteria. It is primarily due to this action that acidophilus are now generally classified as probiotics.

When the infant begins to eat food other than mother's milk, more types of bacteria begin in the colon including L.Acidophilus and other beneficial bacteria along with some harmful types carried on foods of all kinds. This is the change from the healthy, colon flora of a breast-fed infant to a mixed, more complex flora. Healthy colon flora in an adult consists of an estimated 85 per cent protective lacto-bacteria with 15 – 20 per cent of other types. This balance should be maintained through proper diet and lifestyle to ensure the slightly acidic pH essential for a healthy colon and a strong immune system throughout life.

Living acidophilus

The word acidophilus means 'acid loving' in Greek. Since the acidophilus and bifidus families are very large, to simplify this text all types of beneficial bacteria in the colon will hereafter be referred to as acidophilus unless referring to specific research.

Flora means flower. In the colon bacteria are similar to flowers in a garden. Here, flora refers to the micro-environment of bacteria in the colon. All bacteria are living organisms with specific growth and nutrient requirements. Human acidophilus are very delicate. They are an anaerobic and can only live in dark, oxygen free environments. A plant will not grow in soil with a wrong pH even when given proper nutrients. pH refers to the degree of acidity or alkalinity of a substance and is measured in a range of 0 to 14. 7 is neutral. Anything below 7 is acid, and above 7 is alkaline.

Acidophilus growth is optimum at a slightly acidic pH within a range of 5.0 to 6.9. Beneath or above this range it will not survive. When taken orally, acidophilus must pass through the stomach whose digestive juices are very acidic. In the normal range of 0.9 to 1.5 this strong acidity serves to digest certain foods and to kill microorganisms ingested with the foods. In infancy strong acids are not yet active allowing the bifidus in mother's milk to pass through unharmed. In adults it is found that in many depleted or chronically ill persons the stomach acids are deficient and may allow the passage of not only acidophilus but harmful micro-organisms as well. Even if a few surviving acidophilus pass through the stomach to reach the colon there must be proper conditions in the colon for them to survive and implant there. Acidophilus is rendered ineffective in a predominantly alkaline colon, harbouring trillions of pathogens. A few million acidophilus are insufficient to acidify the colon and will be, therefore, overwhelmed.

Acidophilus have complex nutritional requirements. Their primary need is for carbohydrates. They are known as fermentative bacteria because they ferment specific carbohydrates, such as lactose, creating acidic secretions in the process. Acidophilus creates the very pH it requires.

Besides providing their human host with protection from harmful bacteria acidophilus synthesise valuable nutrients in the process of the metabolic growth of the body. These nutrients include the essential vitamins such as vitamin K, biotin, folic acid, B_{12} and other B complex members which are utilised by the healthy human host.

Acidophilus must be of human origin to implant in

a human colon. Strains of acidophilus from animals, birds or plants will not take up residency and live in the human colon. Growth factors for acidophilus found in milk vary from species to species as well because the bacterial strains differ. Many acidophilus products on the market are of bovine (cow) origin. Those that survive the strong stomach acids if any will pass through the colon as a transient. If such a product has a temporary effect it can usually be attributed to the presence of whey as a carrier. Even in an alkaline colon dominated by putrefactive bacteria there may be a few surviving acidophilus though they are rendered ineffective by being in the minority.

If these survivors are provided with four factors then these native acidophilus may be able to multiply and re-establish their dominance in the colon. Two of these factors are: **1.** Elimination of toxins and accumulated faecal matter from the colon. **2.** Re-establishment of a slightly acidic environment in the colon. These first two steps create favourable conditions for the growth of acidophilus: it is like weeding and preparing the garden soil for planting. The remaining two factors are: **3.** Rectal implantation of human strain acidophilus of sufficient live count: these are like the troops sent in to clean out the enemy and reclaim their territory. **4.** Provision of proper food for nourishment and growth of acidophilus: this assists implanted bacteria to be able to reproduce in the colon.

Bacteria multiply by a process called fission which means division: one bacterium divides to form two. When these two bacteria divide again, four are formed. Thus bacteria grow at a geometric rate. Every twenty minutes a normal bacterium divides into two. In just 24 hours this one bacterium is capable of becoming several million bacteria. Both alkaline and acid producing bacteria multiply in this manner: one towards health, the other towards disease. This natural law makes it imperative to maintain the normal acidophilus flora and acidic pH in the colon.

Colon health

The intestinal tract, part of the digestive system, is divided into two main parts: small intestine and large intestine (colon). The small intestine opens into the colon at the ileocaecal valve. Food enters the ascending colon, passes along the transverse colon, down the descending colon and out through the rectum. The appendix and caecum are beneath the ascending colon: see diagram above.

Our colon health depends primarily on three factors: **1.** Existence of a slightly acidic pH. **2.** Maintenance of a predominantly acidophilus colon flora. **3.** Regular elimination.

The small intestine has alkaline pH for digestion and assimilation of nutrients which takes place through the finger-like villi. Scientific data points out that in a healthy state the small intestine is sterile. It is not normally inhabited by a bacterial population as the colon is, and any bacteria are transient.

Two vital functions of the colon are: **1.** The absorption of fluid and electrolytes into the body in the process of eliminating the faeces. **2.** The colon serves as a fermentation chamber for acidophilus.

The caecum provides an

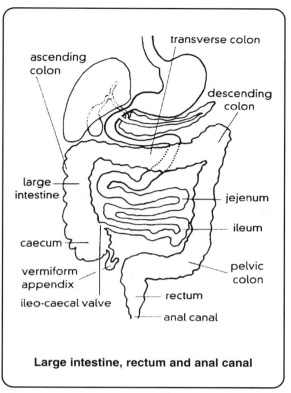

Large intestine, rectum and anal canal

important function in the colon, it is a tough, thick pouch to which the appendix is attached. When the small intestine empties into the ascending colon the caecum contracts, mixing the food and pushing it along. In the healthy colon faecal matter is pushed along by contractions of the muscular colon walls. These contractions are called peristalsis. When there are no acidophilus present the caecum becomes weak and sluggish. Faecal or food residues can remain in the caecum and may not be pushed along properly for elimination. In this small pouch, harmful bacteria and toxins can accumulate.

Far Eastern, nomadic tribes used leather containers with a pouch at the bottom to store their milk. This small pouch retains milk cultures to acidify fresh milk added to the container. Metchnikoff and others state: the caecum is intended to function in a similar manner as the leather milk container pouch. Bifidus implanted in a breast-fed baby multiplies in the caecum which is a reservoir for acidophilus. This is why any effort at re-implanting the colon with acidophilus must reach the caecum.

Studies show faeces contain 75 per cent water and 25 per cent solid matter. About 30 per cent of this solid matter is bacteria. Faecal bacteria are often indicative of bacteria inhabiting the colon. Because colonies are alive in the large intestine it is a natural process that dead 'waste' bacteria are eliminated along with live bacteria, both harmful and beneficial types. It is the ratio of harmful to beneficial that is most important.

When the colon is slightly acidic with a predominance of acidophilus the excess pathogenic bacteria are eliminated and balance is maintained within the colon chamber.

Factors such as antibiotics and other drugs, diet, stress and exposure to micro-organisms in food and the environment along with the constitution and health of the individual are all major factors in determining the condition and population of colon flora.

The prevalence of an alkali colon has led some health professionals and laypersons to the misconception that normal colon pH is slightly alkaline. It may be most common but is not normal. When the colon is at a pH of 5.7 – 6.0 this vital living part of our immune system is working as nature intended for optimum health.

Chronic constipation and diarrhoea are often eliminated when the colon is restored and maintained at a slightly acidic pH.

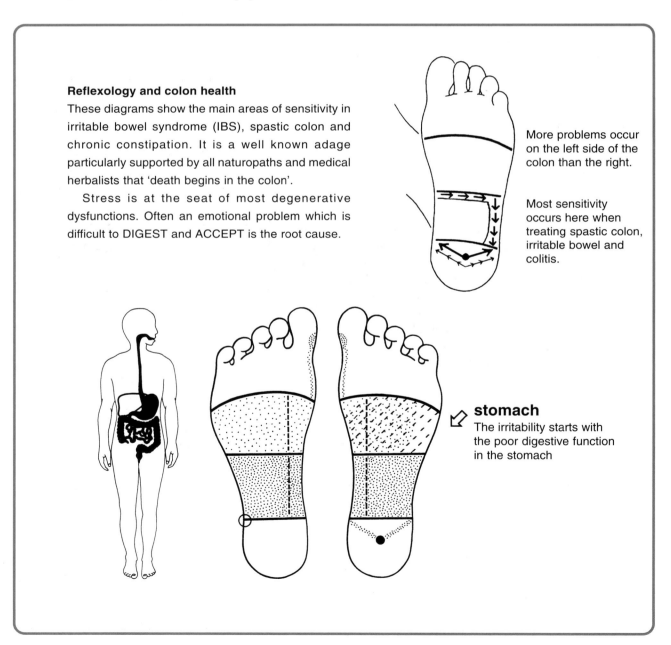

Reflexology and colon health
These diagrams show the main areas of sensitivity in irritable bowel syndrome (IBS), spastic colon and chronic constipation. It is a well known adage particularly supported by all naturopaths and medical herbalists that 'death begins in the colon'.

Stress is at the seat of most degenerative dysfunctions. Often an emotional problem which is difficult to DIGEST and ACCEPT is the root cause.

More problems occur on the left side of the colon than the right.

Most sensitivity occurs here when treating spastic colon, irritable bowel and colitis.

stomach
The irritability starts with the poor digestive function in the stomach

Q&A Colon health

Q. Why do I seem to get constipated when I take fibre like psyllium or bran every day? I thought they were supposed to act as a laxative.

A. First of all psyllium and bran are most effective for occasional short-term use. More importantly, be sure to drink sufficient water along with these – without water they are very dry substances that tend to clog the colon and make the condition even worse than it was. Liquid is vital to expand the fibre and help to push it through the colon.

Q. I never feel satisfied no matter how much I eat. I can't gain weight. Is this related to colon health?

A. These symptoms may be due to digestive enzyme imbalance or parasites. Microscopic parasite and/or worms are picked up easily from raw fish, poorly cooked meat, unwashed vegetables or improper hygiene. With the expansion of travel, parasites are also travelling and spreading around the planet. The presence of worms or parasites can cause weight loss by taking nutrients from the system. They thrive in an alkaline pH.

Q. Does mental and emotional stress affect the colon?

A. The lower left descending colon called the sigmoid flexure can become spastic and cause constipation. This is caused by stress and when the person relaxes the spasm is often relieved in most cases.

Many studies show the effect of emotions and stress on the whole digestive process. Food is not digested or assimilated properly when a person is angry, upset or under stress. This in turn affects the colon which becomes burdened with improperly digested substances. In the cases of extreme anxiety this stimulates the peristaltic action of the whole of the intestinal tract and can cause problems like irritable bowel syndrome and chronic diarrhoea.

Q. I get excessive attacks of wind which are most embarrassing and uncomfortable when I am under extreme stress. Is there anything that you can suggest I could take?

A. Charcoal tablets are excellent in helping to relieve the condition but obviously the stress which is the ultimate cause needs to be tackled as well.

Q. What is the difference between soluble and insoluble fibre?

A. Insoluble fibre is most beneficial to the colon and is the indigestible fibre found in vegetables and whole grains.

The insoluble fibres naturally occurring in whole foods contribute to colon health in many ways. They act as an intestinal broom giving bulk and softness to the stool and assisting in the movement of faeces through the colon. They help to give proper muscle tone to the muscular colon wall due to the slight stretching on the wall from the bulk.

Soluble fibre will dissolve in water and is found in fruits, legumes and grains such as oats.

The primary action of soluble fibres is to delay the emptying time of the stomach which assists blood/sugar problems. Soluble fibre is especially noted for its action in helping lower cholesterol in the body.

CHAPTER 3

The heart of the matter

The number of deaths from heart disease is reaching quite terrifying statistics. The American Heart Association's Heart and Stroke Statistics for 1999 translate into 400,000 Americans developing congestive heart failure each year. Of the 1.5 million people who suffer a heart attack in the USA just 350,000 live to tell the tale. The first attack is often the last.

We hear so much about the need 'to take aspirin to thin the blood, consume a low fat diet, exercise regularly', and we need to create activity in the body during exercise so that we aware of our heart beating rapidly, and we begin to perspire. It is no good just strolling around the block.

Whether your cholesterol levels are elevated are yet another cause for concern, and so we rush for low fat this, and low fat that, hoping that something we do will protect our hearts.

Cholesterol and atherosclerosis

Men and women with serum cholesterol levels of 256mg/dl or over have a five times greater risk of developing coronary artery disease than those whose levels are below 220mg/dl. LDL (low density lipoprotein) transports cholesterol to the tissues, whereas HDL transports cholesterol to the liver for metabolism and excretion.

In countries in which heart attacks are common, such as Britain and the USA, early signs of atherosclerosis can be seen in childhood. The damage does not develop in the whole blood vessel,

it is patchy. It is the lining that is affected known as atherosclerotic plaques and as these enlarge over the years they bulge into the cavity of the artery causing restriction of blood flow. See diagrams on page 21. Atherosclerosis begins when a particular form of white blood cell adheres to the lining of the artery. As these cells 'root' themselves below the surface of the artery they begin to attract droplets of fatty substances – in particular cholesterol – and it is this type of cholesterol which gives the cells a foamy appearance.

Cholesterol in the cells of the plaques comes from the cholesterol in the blood stream produced by the liver which is called low density lipoprotein or LDL. High density cholesterol levels are caused by an excess of LDL and the higher the levels become, the more rapidly cholesterol accumulates on the walls of the artery, and the thicker the plaques grow.

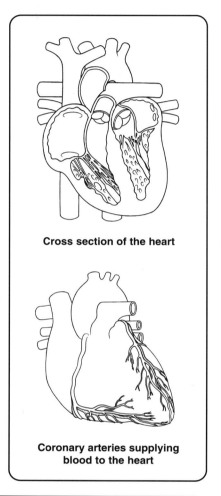

Cross section of the heart

Coronary arteries supplying blood to the heart

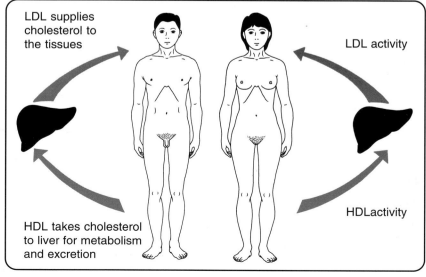

LDL supplies cholesterol to the tissues

LDL activity

HDL takes cholesterol to liver for metabolism and excretion

HDLactivity

Cholesterol has three distinct roles in the body. **1.** It is a necessary part of the membranes that surround the body's cells. **2.** The liver needs cholesterol to produce bile which helps to digest our food. **3.** It is used by hormone producing glands to make certain hormones.

Another cause for the thickening of the arterial walls is that large numbers of muscle cells accumulate also in the inner lining. These cells secrete a material called collagen. Collagen is a protein that is the principal constituent of white fibrous connective tissue (as occurs in tendons). Collagen can also be found in skin, bone, cartilage and ligaments. It is relatively inelastic but has a high tensile strength.

A heart attack in a man of say fifty years of age has its origin in the commencement of atherosclerosis that began thirty years or more earlier. Where there is a familial tendency to heart disease and where cholesterol levels are between 8 to 14 mmol/l there is a risk at least ten times greater than those whose levels are around 6 mmol/l.

There are higher levels of deaths from heart disease in Scotland and Northern Ireland than say in China or Japan. The main reason for this is that the dietary habits of people living in these countries are very different.

The amount of animal fat plays an important part. Inhabitants living in China and Japan consume very low levels of meat and very high levels of rice and vegetables. Once those living in China or Japan come to live in the UK the story is very different. Within only five years of living on our Western diet they fall prey to all the vascular diseases, in particular heart disease. It seems that because of the drastic change in eating habits, the onset of heart disease is very rapid.

In areas of the North of England where there is high unemployment and therefore children are living on very poor diets, high in fat, sugar and salt and very low in fibrous material where fruit consumption is uncommon, fatty deposits have been found in the arteries of eleven year olds!

The lowering of cholesterol levels slows down the growth of the fatty plaques and even causes shrinkage of the congested areas which allows a better flow of blood through the arteries and in turn causes less stress on the heart.

Obesity which settles around the trunk directly worsens the risk of a heart attack.

The importance of water

When the human body developed from species that were given life in water, the same dependence on the life-giving properties of water was inherited. The role of water in the body of mankind and all living species has not changed since the beginning of time. Our entire bodily fluids comprise a salty watery solution. Every function of the body depends on an adequate flow of water. Our brain tissue is said to consist of 85 per cent water.

It is essential to drink sufficient water every day. Most people are dehydrated. Six, eight ounce glasses of water are the absolute minimum. Cups of tea, coffee, herbal teas and other soft drinks are not included, as many of these beverages contain dehydrating agents, coffee and tea in particular. All 'diet' drinks are dehydrating too as they contain so many additives and sweetening agents.

Drink at least one pint of water first thing in the morning, add a squeeze of lemon juice as this encourages the break down of fat in the liver as lemon is very cleansing. You may prefer to take your water warm, particularly in cold weather.

You can see how absolutely vital it is to work on the liver reflex area when using reflexology to help in cases of heart disease of all types, as this is the major organ for detoxification and also the processing plant for the production of cholesterol.

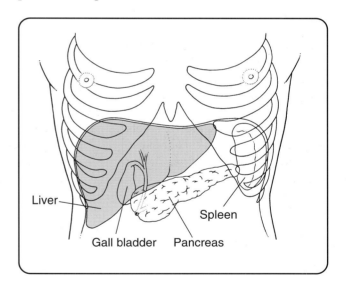

Cholesterol and diet

Most medical authorities agree that the level of cholesterol is largely determined by the intake of cholesterol, saturated fat and polyunsaturated fat. As an example, vegetarians have less incidence of developing heart disease whereas high red meat eaters are more prone.

A high fibre diet is advised as high fibre absorbs the fat and binds it before it reaches the liver. Porridge is an excellent habit to adopt, as oats have a high fibre content and fibre laid down at the beginning of the day ready to absorb any of the fats which would be detrimental to health is recommended.

In a very simple study that was carried out as a way to improving cholesterol levels, patients were requested to eat two medium sized raw carrots each morning. After three weeks the significant results included an 11 per cent reduction in cholesterol levels and a 50 per cent increase in faecal fat and bile excretion and most important, a 25 per cent increase in stool weight.

Foods low in saturated fat and cholesterol are: olive oil, all vegetables, oats, citrus fruit – especially lemons, apples, bananas, fish, chicken and lean meats.

Foods high in saturated fat and cholesterol are: chips, prawns, fatty luncheon meats, beefburgers, hamburgers, kidneys, liver, cream, butter, egg yolks, cheese, particularly full fat cream cheese such as brie, and sausages.

Hypertension

We hear high blood pressure referred to as 'the silent killer' and it certainly can be. Stress encourages it to rise and so do many everyday drugs, in particular Cyclosporine – a powerful immunosuppressant, oral contraceptives, hydrocortisone and antidepressants. Even nasal congestants and cough linctus can induce hypertension if taken in large enough quantities.

Pressure to remove calcium antagonists from the market, which are given to treat hypertension, is likely to grow following new research which links them to causing cancer.

Heavy caffeine consumption can raise your blood pressure. High blood pressure can lead to ballooning of the arteries which can cause 'a stroke'.

Losing weight and cutting down alcohol are the first steps to encourage your blood pressure to become lower.

Anaemia

Anaemia reduces the amount of red blood cells in the body. Red blood cells carry oxygen, a depletion of red blood cells therefore deprives the heart of oxygen and creates even more stress on a weakened organ.

A stroke

Strokes are frightening, devastating and can be totally disabling, with little warning one can be robbed of many physical and mental skills. A stroke is the third most common cause of death in the West. Among those over the age of sixty-five it is the most common cause of death after heart disease.

A stroke can cause paralysis of a limb or limbs: usually loss of power occurs on one side of the body. Speech and visual disturbance are common which are caused by the damage which occurs to brain tissue. A clot occurs in the arteries causing a blockage. Sometimes the artery erupts causing massive haemorrhage to the brain. (Lancet 1992 339; 342-4)

About aspirin

Aspirin has been recommended in cases of high blood pressure and/or heart conditions because aspirin has been shown to thin the blood and slow blood clotting. It also depletes the body of vital minerals and vitamins, especially iron. Many patients who have taken aspirin for a long period suffer from severe anaemia which in turn affects the functioning of the heart.

Aspirin also causes dyspepsia, nausea, stomach upset and acid reflux, and gastrointestinal haemorrhage can occur. Aspirin can have serious consequences on asthmatics, and can induce quite serious life-threatening attacks. Aspirin also causes skin eruptions in some, particularly hives and urticaria.

As a preventative to heart disease and strokes, it is much safer to follow the life changes as recommended in this article and treat the body in a gentle holistic fashion, which involves the body, mind and spirit.

The adverse effects of sugar

Common white sugar increases the concentrations of cholesterol, uric acid and platelet aggregation, all of which are known to be involved in the development of heart disease, in particular atherosclerosis. Just consider the huge increase in the consumption of white sugar since the war!

Coffee and cholesterol levels

There is a strong association between the consumption of more than six cups of coffee per day and a raised cholesterol level. Caffeine stimulates the adrenal glands, putting the body on 'red alert'. Excesses of adrenaline stimulate all bodily functioning, raising the heart beat, stimulating the liver, affecting all our hormonal outputs, and creating excess 'stress' within the body

Problems with alcohol

Any excess of alcohol elevates serum cholesterol levels, as well as raising the blood pressure which greatly increases the risk of atherosclerosis. Spirits in particular should be avoided in any heart condition. Red wine is the first choice, and small amounts of beer are acceptable. Any excess of alcohol stresses the liver which can only deal with one unit of alcohol in any hour. An excess of alcohol causes a malfunction of the liver.

One of the marvels of the liver is dealing with cholesterol and excesses of hormones in the body. When confronted with large quantities of alcohol the other liver functions are placed 'on hold'. Bad news for those suffering from high cholesterol and atherosclerosis.

And what about vitamins?

Evidence reveals that a chronic low intake of vitamin

C can lead to elevated cholesterol levels. Vitamin C is essential in controlling fat metabolism.

A vitamin E deficiency results in higher levels of free radicals. A supplementation of vitamin E has been shown to prevent atherosclerosis through its inhibition of the platelet-releasing action, and its elevation of HDL levels.

Low levels of magnesium, calcium and potassium have been found in those suffering a fatal sudden heart attack.

Calcium and Potassium are necessary in muscle function, too little and muscle spasms occur, not only in the muscles of the heart but in the delicate muscles of the coronary arteries.

Despite the millions of dollars that are thrown at research into coronary heart disease and the development of yet more and more drugs to thin the blood, slow the heart, lower the blood pressure and decrease cholesterol levels, statistics still give a very gloomy picture.

Little importance is placed on the need to check on vitamin and mineral deficiencies, on dietary habits, and the need to make lifestyle changes.

In so many cases atherosclerosis can be prevented by the intake of the vitamins and minerals as discussed above.

Foods for your heart

Onions and **garlic** have been shown to counteract the increased platelet aggregation seen after a high fat meal: garlic, in particular, helps to break down fatty plaques.

Root ginger has been shown to lower cholesterol levels.

Alfalfa leaf decreases cholesterol and has a 'shrinkage effect on atherosclerotic plaque.

Lecithin aids in the removal of cholesterol from the tissues.

Special factors to help the health of your heart

The hormone, **serotonin**, is a compound widely distributed in the tissues, particularly in the blood platelets, intestinal wall and central nervous system. It is thought to play a role in inflammation similar to that of 'histamine' and possibly acts as a neurotransmitter especially concerned with the process of sleep. Serotonin not only plays a major part in the development of depression, but also influences the formation of blood clots. This may well be one of the causes of the risk of blood clots forming, particularly in the legs, when we are flying through different 'time zones' which affects the serotonin levels in the brain.

And what about smoking?

You are encouraging death if you dare to smoke when suffering from atherosclerosis or any other heart condition. The more cigarettes smoked and the length of time you have smoked plays a significant role in damage to the coronary arteries.

The sticky tar-like compound in cigarettes adheres itself to the arterial walls, which in turn attracts any minute clots of blood which could have passed through the circulation with little cause for concern. The clot becomes 'glued' to the artery wall and in an already 'narrowed' artery, complete closure of the artery results in a heart attack, or instant death.

Each time you inhale tobacco the arteries go into spasm, restricting the blood flow to the heart, and placing yet more strain on an already overworked, overstressed organ.

Nicotine is the addiction, the tar and all the other chemicals cause the damage. Every time you take 'yet another puff' there is another 'nail in your coffin'.

When you give up smoking the risk of having a heart attack decreases steeply. For those who have already had a heart attack giving up smoking will halve the chance of a second attack. So while the afflicted heart sufferer puffs and pants his way through life, with very limited mobility, his quality of life reduces yearly.

It is when there are multiple factors involved that are detrimental to the health of the heart that heart attacks occur.

Whilst looking at a very old black and white film recently, the most striking feature of it all was

Alfalfa leaf, root ginger, garlic and onions

how much smaller were all those involved in the film. In one particular scene there must have been about three hundred people in a city centre – men, women and children of all age groups. There were no fat people in the scene at all: most people were, in fact, very slim. Obesity is therefore the cause of so many vascular illnesses.

During the years of the last war, our health was at its best. We were living on a very restricted diet, because we had no choice. Material possessions were of no concern, as everybody was totally involved in 'fighting for survival'. During those difficult war years, people were very neighbourly and everybody helped each other as much as they possibly could. The sparse diet, comradeship, and lack of concern about wealth must have helped considerably.

There is absolutely no doubt that atherosclerosis is a disease directly caused by the western diet and lifestyle. To make lifestyle changes requires major effort on behalf of the sufferer and, unfortunately, the average person prefers to take 'a magical pill' believing that this will solve all his health problems.

Our central heating system

Our circulatory system works in exactly the same way as a central heating system. Energy is created within our body, the boiler, and is distributed by a pump, the heart. Our heart is a muscular pump only the size of its owner's fist, which works constantly from birth to death.

Our pump, the heart, pushes the blood through our pipes and radiators – our arteries. Our arteries need to be supple and have an elastic-like contraction and relaxation, and need to be freed from fatty deposits which constrict the space available for the blood to flow unimpeded.

In order to understand atherosclerosis fully it is necessary to examine closely the structure of an artery. An artery is divided into three major layers.

The intima of the artery consists of a layer of endothelial cells lining the vessel's interior surface. Beneath these surface cells there is a layer of connective tissue which provides support to the endothelial cells as well as separates the intima from the media.

The media consists primarily of smooth muscle cells which provides elasticity of the artery.

The adventita consists primarily of connective tissue providing structural support and elasticity of the artery.

Our heart supplies oxygenated blood to enable all our bodily functions to work efficiently. Every single cell depends on its survival by receiving oxygenated blood.

When arteries become 'narrowed' by corrosion your heart has to pump harder to force the blood around the body.

It is quite a feat of achievement to pump blood up to the brain and down to your toes and back up the legs through the lower abdominal area, on through your diaphragm and then back to your heart.

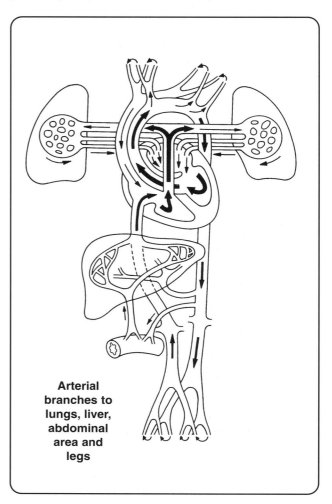

Arterial branches to lungs, liver, abdominal area and legs

Angina

Angina is a symptom of a condition. The word 'angina' simply means 'chest pain'. I prefer to refer to it as a 'crying heart'. The heart muscle, called the myocardium is being starved of sufficient blood and goes into cramp like spasms which are very disturbing. The angina sufferer should stop smoking and take no alcohol or coffee at all.

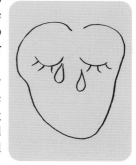

Stress should be decreased by taking up progressive, aerobic exercise. Daily, deep breathing exercises should be encouraged particularly in the fresh air and during brisk walking.

Do consider acupuncture which can alleviate pain. Bromelain, often referred to as the pineapple enzyme can ward off attacks.

Surgical intervention and other medical procedures

Angioplasty is a comparatively simple procedure which involves the threading of a tiny balloon through blocked arteries and expanding them. The balloon is inserted through an artery in the groin. This treatment offers temporary relief but the artery very rapidly becomes restricted again.

Stents A stent is a tiny stainless steel coil used to prop up a collapsed or clogged artery. The stent is shunted into the artery with the use of a catheter. In theory it keeps the artery open, improving blood flow to the heart. There is a risk as blood clots tend to collect around any foreign object in the body .

By-pass surgery This surgical procedure actually uses other channels to replace the clogged or damaged arteries. There are risks with this surgery but generally patients have had an improved ability to walk and perform usual daily functions, and it does improve attacks of angina.

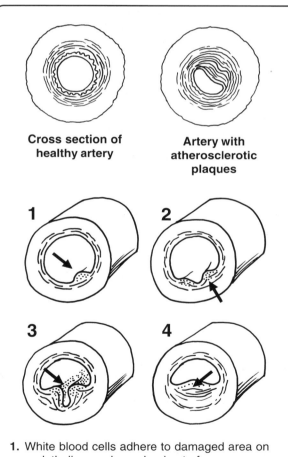

Cross section of healthy artery

Artery with atherosclerotic plaques

1. White blood cells adhere to damaged area on endothelium – plaque begins to form.
2. Smooth muscle cells move into area.
3. Endothelium can be broken. Deposits continue to build up plus surface adherences.
4. OR Endothelium remains complete and plaque continues to build up.

A good diet to help the health of your heart

The most important foods to include in your weekly intake are fruits and vegetables of all description, especially grapefruit, oranges and lemons. Kiwi fruits are also recommended. All citric fruits help break down the cholesterol. You should include at least one from this list daily.

Porridge oats, pulses, whole grains, nuts and seeds, broccoli, oily fish, carrots and garlic should also be included in your diet. You should include at least three from this list daily.

Foods rich in vitamin E are important and include sunflower, corn oil, brazil nuts, hazelnuts and almonds. Those rich in folate are liver, cereals and yeast extract.

Foods rich in selenium are cod, fish roes, walnuts and sardines, and a high concentration of mono-unsaturated fatty acids is to be found in olive oil and rapeseed.

Working to reduce stress levels

We hear it said he 'died of a broken heart'. We meet hardhearted or warm hearted people during our lives. Have we not said 'my heart turned to stone' when.......

We therefore associate our heart as the very dynamic source of our emotional and physical life.

Work at finding ways to reduce your stress levels: transcendental meditation, yoga, getting in 'tune with the infinite'. Have a go at sorting out emotional issues that have been buried 'too deep for too long'. If you find that all attempts to solve the problem with the person involved don't work, then let them go.

Visualise the problem and the person as a feather held on the palm of your hand and blow the problem away. Don't harbour resentments, bad feelings affect the person who is 'feeling bad', not the person to whom the bad feelings are directed.

The power of love certainly affects our emotions, old people living alone but who had a pet and were able to stroke a dog or cat had considerably reduced stress levels than those who lived isolated lives.

In another study it was revealed that people who used words like 'I', 'me' and 'mine' in an ordinary conversation multiplied the risk of dying from heart disease. (Psychosom Med 1986; 48; 187-99)

Again, those suffering a heart attack who had a supportive partner or family had a far higher chance of survival than those who were isolated and lonely.

Close bodily contact is 'very healing' and mentally therapeutic, and anything that promotes a sense of isolation leads to chronic stress and often to illnesses like heart disease.

The heart of the matter

Reflexology and the heart

If you are a Reflexologist and are working on people suffering from heart conditions the areas identified in the chart will give you some guidance of the most important reflexes to work upon.

- Work out the liver. Apart from helping detoxification remember that cholesterol is produced by the liver and also excesses are eliminated from the liver, so this is a valuable organ to target when treating all manner of heart conditions.
- Work on the heart area. The heart is a muscle and needs to be helped – reflexology will improve the nerve and blood supply.
- Work out the thoracic spine. Nerves arising from the thorax serve the chest cavity.
- Work out the kidneys. Any impairment in circulation, as in the case of a heart attack can cause added stresses on kidney function.

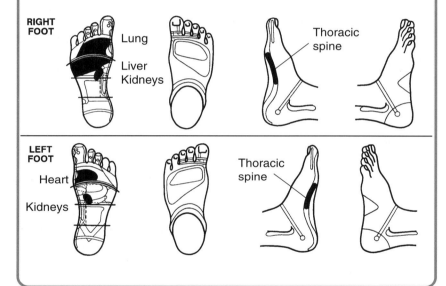

RIGHT FOOT — Lung, Liver, Kidneys, Thoracic spine

LEFT FOOT — Heart, Kidneys, Thoracic spine

Did you know?
Bruising

Bruising occurs when capillaries – small blood vessels – rupture and blood leaks out causing discolouration of underlying tissue. If you are anaemic you are more likely to bruise easily as the 'clotting factor' of your blood will be affected. You will get bruises if you fall or become injured in some way.

Anyone who suffers frequent bruising without no apparent cause should seek medical advice.

Diet and Lifestyle
Consume a well balanced diet with plenty of fresh fruit and vegetables: avoid saturated fats.

Useful supplements
Anthocyanidins such as **grape seed, bilberry** and **pine bark extract** appear to improve the maintenance, strength and resistance of capillary walls and soak up free radicals, and appear to assist the absorption and use of vitamin C.

Vitamin C is an important anti-oxidant and free radical scavenger needed for tissue repair.

Did you know?
Acne

This wellknown disfiguring skin disorder is very common, particularly amongst males, and it occurs during puberty. The recurrence of black heads, white heads and cysts affects primarily the back, face and shoulders. Orthodox medicine usually involves giving long term antibiotics but this can lead to candida and encourages the overgrowth of bacteria in the intestines which encourages toxins.

Diet and Lifestyle
The diet should be low in saturated fats and high in fibre. Avoid refined carbohydrates such as white bread and white sugar, also dairy foods, and fried foods, and keep animal fats to a minimum. Increase soluble fibre, particularly fruit and vegetables. Cleanse the face thoroughly with sulphur based soap and ensure the individual receives plenty of rest and regular exercise.

Useful supplements
To boost the immune system, promote wound healing and reduce inflammation and infection:
High Potency Multi containing selenium, zinc and chromium.
Vitamin A as a boost to the immune system.
Vitamin E to help prevent scarring.
Selenium for pustules.
Echinacea pupurea

CHAPTER 4

Let's learn more about multiple sclerosis

Multiple sclerosis – MS, is a syndrome of progressive nervous system disturbances occurring early in life, recognised since the description by Charcot in 1868.

Despite considerable and very extensive research, medical science has not been able to 'unlock the mystery' of this degenerative disease. Medical researchers have become almost obsessed with finding a viral cause for this condition although there are implications that suggest this could be an auto-immune disease.

The nerve fibres of the brain and spinal cord are enclosed within a white sheath made of a fatty substance called myelin and without the presence of this they are unable to conduct impulses.

MS is a disease causing demyelination of the nerves. As the areas of deterioration heal there is considerable atrophy or wearing away of the nerves worst affected. Areas of demyelination (plaques) vary in size and location within the spinal cord. Symptoms correspond in a general way to the distribution of the plaques.

There are disabilities of varying degrees associated with this illness, from very mild to very severe. Some people have just a weakness, say in one foot, which never gets much worse. Others have quite frightening episodes of loss of sight or visual changes which last from days to weeks.

Others less fortunate have total paralysis within five years or so from the onset of the disease. It does depend on which main functions of the body are affected as to how your lifespan will be affected.

What are the possible connections between MS and geographic location?

The cause is really unknown, however the disease is a condition of temperate countries and is much less common in the tropics. In fact, the incidence of MS increases corresponding to the distance from the equator.

Areas with the highest rates of MS are all located in the higher latitudes in both the northern and southern hemispheres. These high risk areas include the northern United States, Canada, Great Britain, Scandinavia, northern Europe, New Zealand and Tasmania. It is interesting to find that the disease is uncommon in Japan at any latitude.

Considerations such as diet, sun exposure, genetics and other environmental factors do arise.

Victim profile

Young or middle aged adults are the usual victims which number one in two thousand of the population in this country and women are more at risk than men. In about two thirds of cases the onset is between the ages of 20 and 40: the disease rarely occurs after the age of 50.

Vaccinations as a possible cause

There have been associated links with vaccination. Just as some vaccinations have been known to cause brain damage by creating inflammation in the brain, surely it is quite possible that the effect of a vaccination in some people could start an inflammatory condition of the spinal cord, resulting in nerve impairment.

Symptoms of MS

The initial symptoms are variable, but those more commonly experienced are:

Numbness and tingling in an area of the body lasting a few days and then clearing up.

Weakness of a foot or hand causing clumsy movements and frequent falls (in the case of a foot being involved). Unsteadiness of the whole body, blurred or double vision, slurred speech, bladder incontinence. These symptoms often disappear altogether but more often recur months later.

Depression is a symptom of the illness and the painful spasms in the spinal area or legs cause great distress to the sufferer.

Little to offer from the medical profession

The medical profession has little to offer in the way of support. Physiotherapy is usually recommended and drugs to control the painful spasms in the legs which are most common at night.

Massage therapies encourage circulation to weakened spastic limbs and is very comforting to the patient.

Hyperbaric oxygen treatment was once very popular and seemed to offer 'great hope' for sufferers. Patients were actually placed in hyperbaric oxygen chambers, similar to the ones divers use when recovering from dives which take them to very deep levels of the ocean where their oxygen levels are affected.

Progress was noticed for just a few days following the treatment but very quickly the patients reported that the progress was not maintained.

If the disease progresses to a stage when the patient is suffering from a multitude of increasing symptoms, treatment by steroids usually gives a rapid respite from many problems, in particular incontinence and muscle spasms. Those who were still mobile reported that their walking improved and limbs felt stronger.

However, as we all know, steroids especially taken over a long period are not without their serious side effects.

Viruses

There are various demyelinating diseases that affect animals and humans that are similar to MS. Post infectious encephalomyelitis is a disease which starts 10 – 40 days after an acute viral infection or after immunisation and symptoms are similar. It may well be that a virus destroys the myelin producing cells.

Measles antibodies

In 1962 Adams and Imagawa reported that the blood of patients with multiple sclerosis had elevated levels of antibodies against measles, and there is the possibility that the illness could arise following an attack of measles.

Abnormalities in the immune system

A variety of immune system abnormalities have been reported in MS patients that would seem to support an autoimmune defect.

Dietary factors

Much data exists concerning dietary factors and the onset of MS. Diets high in gluten and milk are more common where there is a high rate of MS.

Some first investigations into diet and MS were interesting. It was discovered that the diets of inland farming communities in Norway had a higher incidence than areas nearer the coastline.

It was discovered that the diets of the farmers contained higher levels of animal fat and dairy products than the farmers in coastal areas, the latter eating quantities of cold water fish.

Maybe this is why MS is hardly known in Japan where the staple diet is high in fish, rice and seeds, and very low in dairy products.

Conclusions

The conclusion is that a diet high in fat and dairy products is associated with the onset of MS. Deficiencies of the omega-3 oils are thought to interfere with lipid elongation which impair the formation of normal myelin.

Maybe we should consider the possibility that MS sufferers may have a defect in absorbing essential fatty acids which results in a deficiency state. As these are rich in the beneficial omega-3 oils, these oils are important in maintaining normal nerve cell function and myelin production.

Other recommendations:

- Flaxseed oil.
- A good wholefood diet with attention to the intake of omega oils and flaxseed.
- Cold water fish should be included in the diet three times a week.
- Avoid extremes of temperature, fatigue and stress.

Severe stresses

Most patients reported that, prior to the onset of the disease, they had been through an extremely stressful period, say one or two years previously. The 'stresses' included bereavement, divorce (very high on the list), redundancy and relationship stresses.

The natural approach to Multiple Sclerosis with Reflexology

The main area to concentrate your work is, of course, the spine and brain. The damage occurs in this area, so here we have the root cause.

You need to work with a ***very deep pressure*** between eight and ten times up the medial side of both feet. Work over the brain, and down the sides of each of the first three toes: this will stimulate the nerve and blood supply to the brain.

Everything works better if the body is in a toxin free state, so remember to work out the whole of the intestinal area. When the bowel is cleared of waste, essential vitamins and minerals can be absorbed. When the bowel is laden with waste, absorption is not possible and we can suffer a demineralised state of health.

For those of you who have recently completed my new Advanced Course, **Reflexology and the Intestinal Link**, remember to use the **Central Nervous System Link: Point 1**.

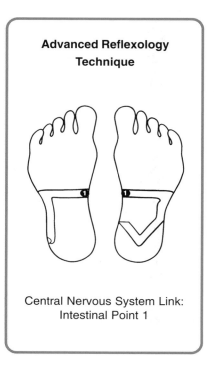

Advanced Reflexology Technique

Central Nervous System Link: Intestinal Point 1

Daily Reflexology

Maximum benefit will be obtained if you can get the partner, friend or carer of the multiple sclerosis sufferer to work on this spinal area daily. It is not difficult to teach somebody to work this vital part and even if they are not able to use the pressure that a trained practitioner has, it is still better to have this daily stimulation than to leave treatment for just once a week which really is not nearly enough.

Reflexology and Multiple Sclerosis

The illustrations show the vital areas to work:
- Work up the spine, brain and neck.
- The entire intestinal area.
- Intestinal Point 1 on both feet (see page 24)

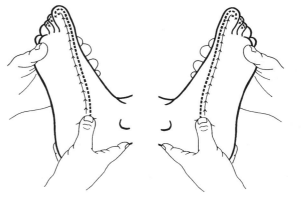

Working the spine, neck and brain areas

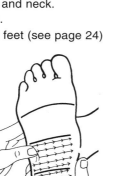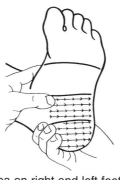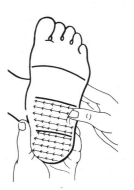

Working the entire intestinal area on right and left feet

Did you know? **Cat's Claw**

A recent discovery – a herb from the Peruvian rainforest – may turn out to be one of the most important discoveries yet. Its particular benefit is in stimulating the immune system.

Made from the inner bark of a vine, it has thorns which resemble a cat's claw. This bark has been used by the Ashaninka tribe for arthritis, gastritis, cancer and many other diseases.

Cat's Claw is beneficial as an anti-inflammatory, antiviral, anti-tumour herbal preparation. It has a healing effect on the digestive system and good results have been achieved in treating chronic fatigue syndrome – M.E.

It was brought back from Germany in the 1970s by a Dr. Klaus Keplinger. Since this time the doctor has obtained two US patents for isolating six alkaloids from the root. The most active one, Isopteridin is a powerful immune stimulant.

Another alkaloid from the Cat's Claw has shown an increase in the ability of the white blood cells to attack and digest bacteria, viruses, cancer cells and other toxins. The remaining alkaloids seem to inhibit platelet aggregation and thrombosis, suggesting that Cat's Claw may help to prevent strokes, lower the blood pressure and improve circulation generally. It is therefore recommended that those suffering from heart conditions and arterial insufficiencies generally try this.

Cat's Claw is traditionally called 'The Opener of the Way' because of its remarkable ability to cleanse the entire intestinal tract and help those suffering from stomach and bowel disorders.

A key concept in naturopathic philosophy can be summed up as 'bad bowels' – bad immunity resulting in cancer. By helping to undo a deterioration of the intestines, many health benefits can follow.

There is also evidence that Cat's Claw may be helpful with numerous stomach and bowel disorders including gastritis, haemorrhoids, ulcers, Crohn's disease, diverticulitis, leaky gut and irritable bowel syndrome.

CHAPTER 5

Diabetes – need it be permanent?

It seems to me that diabetes can be quite a savage disease with quite cruel long-term effects. People can suffer from insulin shock, diabetic coma and, of course, have haemorrhaging from painful kidneys, and many youngsters have already lost their sight from diabetic retinitis. Arteries become congested with fatty deposits which is an inevitable part of this disease making the likelihood of strokes and heart attacks far more likely. People, as you will probably know, develop gangrenous feet and have to have parts of their feet, or sometimes all their toes amputated. Healing of this type of surgery takes an eternity.

Why do we have so much diabetes around today?

Again, diabetes is another disease of affluent living. Persons who are overweight are especially susceptible to diabetes and excess calories from any source increase the vitamin B requirements.

Diabetes has been produced in animals by prolonged feeding of sugar. Sugar increases the need for both insulin and vitamin B. There are certainly links to people who live on a very high calorie diet being more likely to contract diabetes. Such people will be those who ladle three or four teaspoons of sugar into tea or coffee and apply the same amounts to cereals and also take a lot of confectionery in their daily diet.

During the war time when food was limited and food with a particularly high sugar content, such as chocolate and sweets, was in short supply, the level of diabetes dropped markedly.

Persons mildly deficient in vitamin B excrete xanthurenic acid long before any other signs of the dietary insult appears. When diabetics take vitamin B they show a rapid and marked decrease in urinary xanthurenic acid. The fact that diabetics are deficient mainly in vitamin B will clarify many of the mysteries concerning this illness.

The general belief is that diabetes is hereditary so there is nothing much that you can do about it. It may be because of the deficiency in vitamin B which could be of genetic origin. Cholesterol and lecithin, which reduce high blood fat, cannot be produced unless vitamin B and magnesium are adequate therefore any person with a family history of diabetes would be advised to take vitamin B and magnesium daily.

The onset of diabetes is normally known by an intense thirst, drinking excessive amounts of water and the corresponding large urine output. All B vitamins and many other good nutrients are already lost in the urine so the more urine excreted the greater the loss. Even after treating with insulin injections sugar frequently is eliminated into the urine so to dilute the sugar, water is withdrawn from the blood and again an excess of urine is experienced. Diabetics also have the tendency for a sticky layer to form on the arterial surfaces. This is why they are far more prone to coronary heart disease and strokes. With the sticky surface layer in the artery it only takes a very small blood clot to become adhered to the artery wall and then a myocardial infarction could occur or worse still, an eruption of a blood vessel in the brain.

The damaged pancreas can no longer produce sufficient insulin, sugar can neither enter the cells nor be changed into body starch or fats so therefore sugar coming in from digesting foods accumulates in the blood and eventually it spills over into the urine. The quantity of insulin is determined by each individual: a study of their body weight, height, size, etc. is taken into consideration. If too much insulin is given and too little food eaten the symptoms of low blood sugar, weakness, nervousness, wooziness, headaches, trembling hands and blackouts can be brought on with lightening speed. We call this an insulin reaction or insulin shock. To prevent insulin shock the doctor carefully balances the type and amount of food recommended against the insulin dose.

Simultaneously the blood fats, usually excessive in persons with this disease, soar even higher and in diabetics with atherosclerosis the stage is set for a heart attack.

Although diabetic specialists are experts in adjusting insulin levels it is tragic that few have become sufficiently interested in nutrition to make an all out effort to stimulate the maximum insulin production or to prevent devastating complications.

It has been long known that if the nutritional needs of the diabetic can be reduced, the disease sometimes disappears. When diabetic patients with over-active thyroids have been successfully treated or chronic infections cleared up, it is not unusual for insulin to be discontinued.

Sometimes a severe episode of stress can worsen the diabetic patient. The patient will have far less control of the insulin levels when under stress. When the stress has been removed then normally the diabetic patient improves.

Overweight diabetics can reduce their insulin after reducing their weight as in each of these cases the body requirements have decreased and the effect is the same as if the diet were improved.

In the badly damaged pancreas that still has some element of functioning, vitamin C has often produced good results in the diabetic.

A lack of vitamin B$_{12}$ or potassium causes rats to have prolonged high blood sugar. A wide variety of animals developed diabetic symptoms when given 2ml daily but not if allowed to eat frequently.

Concentrate on keeping active cells helathy

As long as there are some pancreatic cells which are able to produce insulin the emphasis should be on keeping these cells healthy and on helping them to increase insulin production. The conclusion that diabetes is permanent is justified only when the insulin producing cells have been largely or completely destroyed.

Doctor Kendal Emerson of the Harvard Medical School, an outstanding authority on diabetes, emphasises that diabetic diets should contain far more protein than they usually do. He points out that when the blood sugar level drops following an insulin injection or when too little food is eaten, the increased secretion of the pituitary and adrenal hormones causes destruction of body proteins

including those of the pancreas thus damaging the organ still more and further decreasing insulin production. Physicians will usually increase the protein allowance if a patient requests it. Despite a seemingly adequate intake, diabetics often show abnormally small amounts of vitamin A in the blood, they frequently lose this vitamin in the urine and have symptoms of vitamin A deficiency.

Similarly when diabetic diets have appeared to be adequate in vitamin B, neuritis has developed which was relieved as soon as the larger amounts of this vitamin were given. Vitamin B is said to be especially valuable in preventing damage to the brain during diabetic acidosis.

Reflexology and diabetes

Reflexology has proved quite successful in treating diabetic patients. Again the abilities to give a good result would definitely rest on the amount of natural pancreatic function that was left in the patient's body. When the pancreas is not working at all it withers away and hardens to form a small 'walnut'. It would, therefore, be very difficult to expect any marked improvement here, but when there is still a moderate function in the pancreas I believe there is a great chance of the pancreas producing more activity, the symptoms lessening and the patient needing far less insulin to control his symptoms. In any case, even in the most severe cases, the greatest benefit we can offer to the diabetic sufferer is an improvement in their circulation, which I am sure makes them less likely to contract the coronary artery and cerebral vascular diseases to which they are so prone.

Did you know?
Depression

There are many 'variations on a theme' when we try to describe 'depression' ranging from just feeling inexplicably low in energy for a few days resulting in poor concentration and a lack of interest in work, relationships or hobbies, to its worst state when 'depression' can become a serious, debilitating disease. Most people suffering from depression are unaware they have a problem and therefore do not seek help, but just go on year after year getting very little out of life. This is sad because much can be done to help depressed individuals. Depressed people often resort to 'comfort eating' large amounts of confectionery, especially chocolate. The less good nutrition for your body, the worse symptoms will become. The cause of depression is not always clear: its roots can lie in a physical cause such as an under-active thyroid gland or food allergy. Depression can also stem from an emotional problem such as marital difficulties, bereavement or unemployment which can all put undue stress on an individual.

Diet and Lifestyle

Sufferers should consult their doctors and have tests, if thought necessary, to rule out any physical causes. Counselling is often of great benefit.

It is important to eat a well balanced diet and have three meals a day. Missing meals out and going for long periods with no food at all play havoc with your blood sugar levels, and avoids over-reliance on stimulants such as caffeine, alcohol and sugar-rich foods.

Useful supplements

DL-Phenylalanine An amino acid which increases the body's own level of natural endorphins, morphine-like substances, which are its brain stimulants, mood regulators and anti-depressants.

Calcium and **Magnesium** are minerals with a calming effect on the tense muscles of stressed individuals.

Vitamin B-50 Complex-B vitamins for healthy nerves and nervous system.

CHAPTER 6

The health of our emotions

There is no hard and fast way of defining mental and emotional health.

Most people would accept a number of common factors which all add up to a state of being well, feeling good about yourself and coping with life and the situations that arise.

For those of us involved in the field of treating the general public we need to maintain a balance between the wellbeing of the person we are treating and the balance of our own health and needs.

We also need to learn to distribute time and energy between working and relaxing, or being alone and relating to others.

A strong mental constitution is when you are able to accept growth and change without feeling unduly threatened; have a sense of humour and be able to laugh at yourself; retain a sense of purpose; be able to keep your balance during times of stress and let go of situations in life that are not creating much pleasure or purpose.

The effect of the mind and emotions on the body

It is now becoming very widely accepted that the mind and emotions have a far greater affect on the human body than was previously recognised and even orthodox medicine is coming to terms with this, finally.

Most of us realise that if we feel worried or unhappy we feel sluggish and weary and that we are far more prone to infections and aches and pains because, as we all know, stress does reduce the power of our immune system.

Diseases were, once upon a time, considered only to have an exclusive external origin and that the sick person had been visited by a demon or negative power. We all know that the body, mind and spirit interact for the wellbeing of the whole person. So if you can maintain a positive, optimistic outlook you should improve your physical health.

Reflexology, relaxation and a sense of wellbeing

Many people find that after having treatment with reflexology the sense of relaxation and wellbeing was such that they have never experienced before.

I am sure that you have all heard it said that 'I always thought I was quite a relaxed person until I had the treatment and now I understand how good my body and mind can feel after a few sessions'. It is a good idea, therefore, to have a monthly treatment just to maintain the level of harmony in your life.

*'My success
and my happiness lie
within myself.
They multiply when
shared with others.'*

CHAPTER 7

Herbalism

Herbalism, which is using plants for healing, is undoubtedly the world's oldest and most comprehensive therapy. Since the dawn of humanity, a knowledge of herbal remedies has been handed down from generation to generation.

The growth of synthetic drug manufacture has been going on exclusively since the war years: prior to the 1940s there was very little medicine available: M&B tablets to control high temperatures, various cough linctuses and emollients, inhalations with camphor and wintergreen to help clear congestive airways, and then attention to the general rest and care to help the sufferer through the illness was also given.

One also had the privilege of a visit from a local GP who, if they had an excellent bedside manner, was very responsible for the recovery of his patient.

The main purpose of herbal remedies is to stimulate the body's own natural healing resources by eliminating toxins, stimulating the immune system, helping respiration and cleansing the bowel. Like the synthetic drugs of orthodox medicine, many herbs also have an antibacterial and antiviral property. But they have the advantage of returning the body back to a state of health without the risk of the damaging side-effects of modern everyday medication.

When correctly prescribed, herbs can be combined to target and activate the body unless the tissue has been completely destroyed by accident, injury or severe disease.

The earliest records of medicinal herbs, circa 3000 BC, reach back to China. Myrrh and frankincense, which are linked to the birth of Christ, were presented as gifts by the three wise kings to the infant child as a luxury healing herb.

Herbal medicine has been continuing to form the major part of traditional medicine in both the East and West for several thousand years. Nicholas Culpepper *'The Complete Herbal'* 1653, reflected an insatiable demand for knowledge about medicinal plants. Herbalism was linked to astrology and folk lore. Since the 1970s, The World Health Organisation – WHO – has been encouraging a revival of traditional herbal medicine in developing countries, but in the United States of America, despite a great interest the professional practise of medical herbalism is considered illegal in many states. In fact, even today in England, a medical herbalist is unable to say he can cure the body of anything, all he can say is that his treatment helps the patient's general state of wellbeing!

For centuries it was accepted that the picking of a plant or herb remedy at a certain specific time of day enhanced the healing properties of the herb. Shortly after the war years this was looked at with absolute ridicule, but today many universities and research establishments have confirmed the value of the traditional use of whole herbs and have also started substantiating claims of the herbalist that by picking plant remedies at a certain time of day will give the prime effectiveness of a remedy.

What is the difference between herbalism and the orthodox medical approach?

The herbalist's approach to illness or allergy is totally different to the orthodox medical approach i.e. the allopathic one. Conventional medicine regards tonsillitis or any other inflammatory state of the body as an invasion of a specific virus or bacteria which will definitely need to be treated by an antibiotic. The infection will subside with this treatment, however, the root cause of the problem has not been dealt with and will leave the patient to continue with more repeat prescriptions for antibiotics and more invasive throat infections. This is like forcing down the lid of a dustbin on to a very full bin and all we are doing is forcing the diseased or dysfunctional state further down into the body where we become, as a result, chronically sick.

Herbs and lifestyle

The herbal approach to medicine is that the illness is a secondary effect to the lifestyle of the patient which the sufferer's body cannot cope with. In children the most usual cause is a diet which is too rich in dairy products, sugar or high processed foods particularly those foods which contain many hidden sugars. In adults it is more likely to be a lack of nutrients or an allergic reaction or some other dietary factor. The herbalist, therefore, would prescribe herbs to help all the functioning of the body, again, the immune system, the respiratory system, the digestive system and the improved functioning of elimination by the kidneys.

There is nothing equal to the value of a fresh plant picked from a garden or wild area. Today, people are getting very involved and interested in growing their own herbal preparations either for culinary or medicinal usage. Gather your remedies on a dry morning before the sun has dried out the plant. The longer the herbs are kept, the weaker their virtues become.

If you grow your own herbal preparations be sure the area in which they are growing has not been sprayed with synthetic chemicals which would make them have an adverse effect upon the body rather than a positive one.

Do make sure that if you consult a medical herbalist that they are members of the National Institute of Medical Herbalists, which is a very well refined discipline requiring vigorous training. There is a full degree course in herbalism at the Middlesex University.

Parsley

CHAPTER 8

The truth about antibiotics

Every time you take antibiotics you are giving the bacteria and viruses around you a new opportunity to develop resistance. In addition, whenever you eat dairy food products including eggs and most meat (unless they are organic) you are being exposed to antibiotics. Livestock are given daily doses virtually from birth because antibiotics are growth promoters and keep milk and eggs fresher for longer which, therefore, increases the farmers' profits.

The consequences are that fewer and fewer antibiotics are effective against deadly infections. The patients who contract serious infections like bronchitis and pneumonia, or pick up a hospital infection often die because the bacteria are so resistant to antibiotics and they just cannot be treated. Tuberculosis is making a comeback because it is increasingly antibiotic resistant.

Clearly we need to find other ways to help infection when we get ill. Antibiotics also suppress the natural ability of the body to fight infection – using these drugs really encourages further infection and every parent knows the nightmare of the child who needs antibiotics every few weeks because the infections occur again and again.

We are now suffering from a condition called 'antibiotic abuse'. Children are brought up to expect a dose of antibiotics when the slightest sore throat, painful ear or cough invades their territory.

In the past decade, deaths from infectious diseases, including HIV, have risen by a stunning 22 per cent worldwide. Most of these deaths are caused by infections in the lungs or the blood that are resistant to antibiotics.

Antibiotics, unfortunately, kill the beneficial gut bacteria: these helpful gut residents are our natural frontline defence system against harmful bacteria, viruses, environmental allergens, irritants, allergens and toxins such as pesticides. Antibiotics also weaken our immune system, encourage the growth of candida bacteria and create an inner environment that attracts parasites. Very frequently infestations of worms in the bowel, which occur frequently in young children are caused simply because the friendly bacteria in the gut have been destroyed and so the invasions of small parasites that are normally carried on the outer coating of fruits, vegetables, etc. have the opportunity of invading the bowel area. Antibiotics can also create an excessive loss of vitamins and minerals through digestive problems and also cause diarrhoea.

Alexander Fleming, who discovered penicillin, warned us nearly a century ago that the overuse of antibiotics would create resistant bacteria.

Clearly, antibiotics should only be used as a final resort when fighting potentially life-threatening infections. We need to find other more simple ways to help general infections that we get from year to year.

It is very important to watch the hygiene in the kitchen. The E coli and salmonella outbreaks should remind us to handle uncooked meat and eggs with care. Did you know that even if you wash your hands in hot soapy water after handling raw meat there can still be live salmonella on them? When you handle food like these, always clean your kitchen utensils, cutting boards and kitchen surfaces with an antibacterial/antiviral substance.

The fundamentals of preventing an infection are to drink at least six to eight glasses of water daily so that the body gets a proper flush through. Take plenty of rest and avoid sugar which is a useless calorie. In fact, it has no benefit to the body whatsoever. Avoid refined carbohydrates which are white flour, and alcohol. Chamomile tea before bed is a good sleep inducer. The grapefruit seed extract kills viruses as well as bacteria including many staphylococci and streptococci and E coli.

As your body fights infections it uses vitamins and minerals in the battle against the bacteria so you will benefit by doubling your multivitamins while fighting an infection or take a special immune stimulant like echinacea or astragalus – also plenty of zinc and vitamin C. Your body's supply of the amino acid glutamine is quickly used up when fighting infections and recently doctors have discovered that certain immune cells cannot multiply or function without glutamine. Fatigue and muscle wasting commonly experienced during a heavy infection, particularly associated after a heavy bout of influenza can be due to the glutamine deficiency.

There is nothing like vitamin C for fighting infection. Vitamin A is an important infection fighting vitamin and also an immune stimulant that boosts the thymus gland, particularly in young children and helps to maintain the health of the cells in your mucous membranes.

Two most important minerals which help to fight infection are zinc and selenium. An American researcher found that the group of people who sucked zinc lozenges got over a cold faster than those who used a commercial cold formula.

A wonderful daily tonic for the immune system is a cup of Cat's Claw mixed with blackcurrant juice. This is a new herbal discovery from South America – it is an exceptional immune booster and energising tonic, good for arthritis and helps to protect from cancer.

A fever is Nature's way of burning up toxic junk in the body and it will eventually kill the bacteria. A fever is good news – it is when your body does not create a feverish state when bacteria and viruses are multiplying that there is a problem. A fever is a furnace and works exactly the same way as we would expect when we set light to a waste mound of junk in our back gardens: it burns out the waste and reduces them to just a black dust or powder. So unless your fever is dangerously high, it is important not to bring it down. It will reduce as soon as the burning process of waste is completed.

The Leaky Gut Connection

One of the most damaging results antibiotics can cause is known as a leaky gut which is responsible, I believe for ME, chronic fatigue and food allergies. Leaky gut

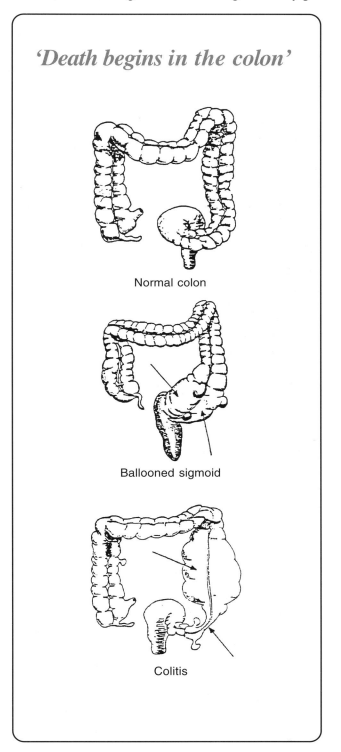

'Death begins in the colon'

Normal colon

Ballooned sigmoid

Colitis

syndrome is where there are small erosions – holes – in the intestinal wall. Antibiotics do this by weakening the lining of the digestive system. A leaky gut literally has holes in it that allow incompletely digested food to escape into the bloodstream. If a food molecule is not properly broken down before it reaches your blood, your immune system thinks it has been invaded by foe not friend and attacks. Therefore you end up with toxic immune complexes which are dumped around the body and tend to attack your weakest point. The results may vary from irritable bowel to brain confusion, excessive weight gain, hyperactivity, depression, various aches and pains in joints which are unexplainable and even skin rashes or ear infections, especially in young children.

Since antibiotic use is one major cause of a leaky gut, and painkillers and alcoholic abuse are other causes, you can see how even one course of antibiotics that is not properly handled can lead to years of a different sort of misery.

Improving a leaky gut

To reverse a leaky gut, start by removing foods causing the reactions. There are several ways of sorting out your food allergies. You need to remove, stage by stage, one or two foods and wait for at least two months to decide whether you are much better without this food in your diet. During this time you need to rebuild your gut's lining and amino acid glutamine is the benefit here. Glutamine helps rebuild digestive cells. Concentrated aloe vera is also helpful. Your intestinal flora is intimately tied in with your immune system. A very good slogan used by a well known medical herbal college stipulates that 'death begins in the colon'.

You can always help the flora balance in the bowel by eating live yoghurt. Make sure that it is a live culture so check the label. A probiotic supplement should be taken if it is absolutely essential that you take an antibiotic course. This will help rebuild your immune system and also the intestinal lining. Yoghurt helps but it is not sufficient to do a good job.

Antibiotics affect childrens' health

It is believed that ear infections treated with antibiotics lie behind the epidemic of hyperactivity and learning disorders.

The doctors routinely give antibiotics to small children who get ear infections simply because they have no idea what else to do. The antibiotics satisfy the parent because the immediate symptoms disappear very rapidly until the next infection comes along which then requires yet another antibiotic to be given.

One of the best ways to prevent ear infection is to breast feed your baby. Only one per cent of breast fed babies get ear infections, while 50 per cent of totally bottle fed babies do.

An ear infection can be serious and must be checked out by your doctor if your child has a fever or is in pain. Studies have repeatedly shown that 70 – 80 per cent of ear infections will get better without antibiotics. On the other hand children who have antibiotics are two to six times more likely than children not given drugs to have another ear infection within six weeks.

The immune system does have to learn how to fight off infection and generally it does a very good job. There is also recent evidence that children with recurrent ear infections have a much higher rate of allergies, especially food sensitivities which in turn are strongly associated with learning disorders and hyperactivity. The most common food allergens are cows milk, wheat, egg white, peanuts, soya, corn, orange, tomato and chicken. If you suspect any or several of these foods try removing one or two of them from your child's diet for a few weeks and just see what happens.

Antibiotics and autism

A study undertaken on children with problems in school showed that those who had had many courses of antibiotics were 50 per cent more likely to have slow development. Hyperactivity has been linked to ear infections over and over again and the rise of children with autism has corresponded with the recent rise in the use of antibiotics.

There was a fascinating interview recently with Dr William Shaw by a chemist who was working with urine testing in a childrens' hospital when he noticed that two autistic brothers had similar unusual abnormalities in their urine.

He checked out the charts of other autistic children in the hospital and discovered the same substances. As he continued to check charts he discovered similar substances in children with hyperactivity, learning difficulties and speech disorders.

As he dug deeper into this research he found that the substances in the urine were by-products of yeast and/or fungi in the bowels. Upon searching the scientific literature he found that nearly all autistic children had frequent infections, usually ear infections early in life, treated by broad spectrum antibiotics.

This is relatively new information brought to us by pioneering scientists – it should be more than enough evidence to inspire greater caution when prescribing antibiotics for ear infections in children or indeed for anyone.

CHAPTER 9

Understanding liver function

The liver is truly an intricate, complex and remarkable organ and, without question, it is the most important organ of metabolism in the body. The health and vitality of an individual is determined by the health and vitality of the liver.

We have frequently heard the grumble that we feel 'liverish' but wonder if we actually know the reason the liver produces such unpleasant symptoms as it well can do.

It is amazing how well the liver survives the constant onslaught of toxic chemicals and is responsible for detoxifying. In fact, the body is working under extreme stress as many of the additives and colourings in our diet were not even meant to have a place on this planet let alone be ingested into our digestive system.

Some of the toxic chemicals known to pass through the liver include the polysyclic hydrocarbons: these are components of various herbicides and pesticides. Although the exact degree of exposure of people to these compounds is not known, it is probably quite high as yearly US production of synthetic organic pesticide alone, exceeds 600,000 tons.

It is well known that cancers of the liver are frequently induced by the ingestion of these chemical compounds. As the liver is responsible for detoxifying chemicals and many others, every effort should be made to promote optimal liver function.

There are many nutritional and herbal compounds which can prevent damage to the liver associated with these harmful chemicals while its lipotropic factors are, by definition, substances that hasten the removal and detoxification of chemicals and help remove the deposits of fat in the liver.

Compounds commonly employed include: choline, methionine, folic acid and vitamin B_{12} along with herbal choleretics – these are agents that stimulate bile secretion by the liver as opposed to the expulsion of bile by the gall bladder.

Formulae containing these agents have been used for a wide variety of conditions by naturopathic physicians particularly in hepatic conditions such as hepatitis, cirrhosis and alcohol-induced, fatty infiltration of the liver, and have also been used in treating premenstrual tension syndrome as they are

believed to aid the liver in its ability to excrete oestrogens.

The role of the liver

The liver has three basic roles:

1. Vascular

The liver's vascular functions include being a major blood reservoir and filtering over a litre of blood per minute. The liver effectively removes bacteria, toxins, antigen/antibody complexes and various other particles from the circulation.

2. Secretory

The liver's secretory functions involve the synthesis and secretion of bile. Each day the liver manufactures about 1 litre of bile. Bile is essential for the absorption of fat soluble substances, including many vitamins. Most of the bile secreted into the intestines is reabsorbed and many toxic substances are effectively and efficiently eliminated from the body by the bile.

3. Metabolic

The metabolic functions of the liver are immense as the liver is intricately involved in carbohydrate, fat and protein metabolism. It stores vitamins and minerals and excretes into the bile various chemical compounds including hormones such as thyroxine, cortisol, oestrogen, histamine, drugs and pesticides.

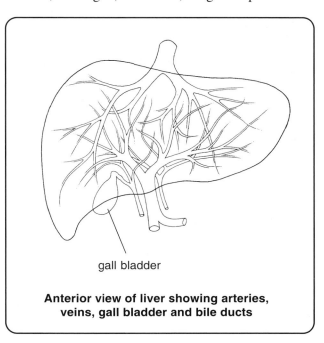

gall bladder

Anterior view of liver showing arteries, veins, gall bladder and bile ducts

Gallstones

One of the leading contributions to impaired liver function is diminished bile flow or cholestasis. This unpleasant conditions can be caused by many factors including obstruction of the bile ducts due to large gall stones impairing the bile flow within the liver. It is estimated that twenty million people in the US have gall stones – nearly 20 per cent of the female and 8 per cent of the male population over the age of forty are found to have gall stones on biopsies, and approximately 500,000 gall bladders are removed because of stones each year. The main cause of this condition is a low fibre/high fat diet.

When we often feel lethargic and sluggish it can quickly be caused by the inadequate excretion of waste from the liver. It really means that our livers have become so congested with toxins that they are not able to effectively do their job. Amongst the symptoms people with this condition may complain of are: fatigue, digestive disturbances, allergies in particular and chemical sensitivities, premenstrual syndrome, migraine and constipation.

Perhaps one of the most common causes of cholestasis and poor liver function is alcohol ingestion. In some individuals, as little as one ounce (25g) of alcohol can produce damage of the liver which results in fat being deposited within the liver (alcohol induced fatty liver).

You can see now how this problem can be very instrumental in exacerbating any form of heart disease.

A decreased liver function increases the risk of arteriosclerosis, poor circulation generally and angina pains, and you will find undoubtedly that when treating any cases of heart related conditions, the liver reflex on the right foot is always extremely sensitive. It also shows up its sensitivity in treating patients with allergies as 80 per cent of allergies stem from liver function and as high as 89 per cent of chronic migraine sufferers have their problems in an allergic situation created by the liver.

Nutritional considerations

A diet high in saturated fats increases the risk of a fatty liver. By contrast a diet rich in dietary fibre, particularly the water soluble fibres has an effect by promoting increased bile secretion.

Vitamin C and E, zinc and selenium are essential in protecting the liver from free radical damage. Optimum tissue concentrations of these compounds should be maintained when treating hepatic disease as well as for the promotion of liver health.

Choline

In a recent research programme, monkeys, several species of poultry, dogs, pigs, rats and guinea pigs were fed a diet proficient in choline and protein. This resulted in the animals acquiring a fatty liver.

Carnitine

Carnitine is a vitamin-like compound that we produce within our own bodies. It facilitates the conversion of fatty acids to energy. You need a high level of this compound in order to handle increased fatty acid loads produced by alcohol consumption, a fatty diet and/or chemical exposure.

Dandelion root

Many of us consider the dandelion to be an unwanted weed, but herbalists from all over the world have respected this valuable herb for many centuries. It is a fine, liver remedy and has been used in folk lore for a variety of ailments.

In Europe, dandelion was used to treat fluid retention, liver congestion, diarrhoea, skin problems, heartburn and fevers. In China it was used to treat problems of the breast: cancer, inflammation, lack of milk flow, etc. In Russia and India and other parts of the world its main use was for its action on the liver.

The dandelion has high nutritional values, far more than many other vegetables, being very high in vitamins, minerals, protein and pectins. It has a vitamin A content higher than that of carrots. (Dandelion has 14,000iu of vitamin A per 100g compared with 11,000iu for carrots.)

Dandelion is regarded as one of the finest liver remedies both as food and medicine. It enhances bile flow, helps inflammation and improves the complete functional capacity of the liver.

Artichoke leaves

Evidence goes back a very long time in the use of artichoke leaves for treating liver complaints. It has been proven to have great regenerating effects and the common spice, turmeric, contains the yellow pigment, curcumin, which has demonstrated liver-protective effects and has also been shown to drastically lower cholesterol levels.

Diet

For optimum liver function a diet rich in dietary fibre and plant foods, very low in fat and sugars and as free from pesticides and pollutants as possible, is preferred and alcohol consumption is not advised in those suffering from any form of high cholesterol or poor liver function.

Remember that the liver has been referred to for many hundreds of years as the 'butler to the brain'. When liver function fails, all functions in the body suffer drastically, particularly the brain.

If you are treating your patients for allergies, migraine or those who just feel generally lethargic and sluggish, do encourage the use of the minerals, vitamins, etc. described in this article.

Reflexology and the liver

Plenty of work on the liver reflex area will help to eliminate waste products more efficiently and give the liver a 'spring clean' on which it can start to heal its overloaded liver cells.

Working the liver area on the right foot

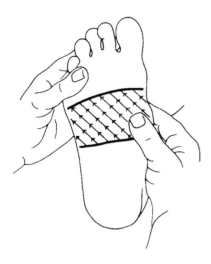

Medial to lateral. Supporting the right foot with your left hand and using the right thumb, work out the entire area in a criss-cross direction from the medial to the lateral edge.

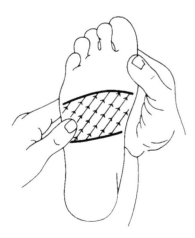

Lateral to medial. Supporting the right foot with your right hand and using the left thumb, work out the entire area in a criss-cross direction from the lateral to the medial edge.

References: *The Encyclopaedia of Natural Medicine*, Michael Murray MD and Joseph Pizzorono.

CHAPTER 10

Cystitis – the female complaint

Bladder infections in women are surprisingly common. 21 per cent of all women have urinary tract discomfort at least once a year: 37.5 per cent of women with no history of urinary tract infection will have one within ten years and two to four per cent of apparently healthy women have elevated levels of bacteria in their urine, indicative of an unrecognised urinary tract infection.

The dangers of untreated infections of the bladder can lead to kidney infections which are far more serious and can cause damage or poor kidney function.

Urine, as it is secreted by the kidneys, is sterile until it reaches the urethra which transports the urine from the bladder to the urethral opening. Bacteria reach the urinary tract through the urethra. Bacteria are introduced into the urethra from faecal contamination or, in women, vaginal secretions.

The body has many defences against bacterial growth in the urinary tract. Urine flow tends to wash away bacteria and the surface of the bladder has antimicrobial properties. The pH (acidity or, in this case, alkalinity) of the urine inhibits the growth of many bacteria.

Many factors increase the risk of bladder infections: pregnancy, sexual intercourse (nuns have one tenth the incidence) homosexual activity (in males), mechanical trauma or irritation and perhaps, most important, structural abnormalities in the urinary tract which block the free flow of urine.

In general, the diagnosis is made according to the signs and symptoms and urinary findings. Microscopic examination of the infected urine will show high levels of white blood cells and bacteria. The presence of fever, headache, chills and low back pain can indicate involvement of the kidneys.

Botanical medicines
Cranberry juice
Many herbal preparations have been used for centuries in the treatment of urinary tract infections, but in particular cranberry juice has been used successfully to treat urinary infections. 16oz of cranberry juice per day were shown to produce beneficial effects in 75 per cent of sufferers.

Recent studies have shown components in

cranberry juice to reduce the ability of the bacteria to adhere, or stick, to the lining of the bladder and urethra. In order for bacteria to multiply they must first adhere to the mucosa. By interfering with adherence cranberry juice reduces the likelihood of infection and helps the body to fight infection. Do not, however, use sweetened cranberry juice; sugar has such a detrimental effect on the immune system.

Garlic

Garlic has been shown to have antimicrobial activity against many disease causing organisms.

Goldenseal

Goldenseal is one of the most effective of the herbal anti-microbial agents. Its long history of use by herbalists and naturo-pathic physicians for the treatment of infections is well documented in scientific literature.

Reflexology and sensitivities in the feet

As well as the main areas shown in the illustrations, you may well find many sensitivities in the intestinal area when treating those sufferers with cystitis, apart from an obvious sensitivity in the entire urinary tract.

Working on the intestinal area will help correct the imbalance and enable the body to heal: the urinary infections will then become less frequent and certainly less severe and if attention is paid to the dietary advice above, cystitis should become a thing of the past.

Maybe you will learn from this article that drugs actually cause diseases and, after all, *we are exactly what we eat!*

Cystitis – the female complaint

The reflexology approach to cystitis

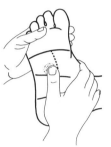
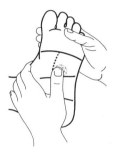

- Working on the bladder, ureter tube and kidney are the first and most important reflex points to work upon.
- Work on and over the bladder area with the thumb. Proceed up the medial side of the ligament line to work out the ureter tube.

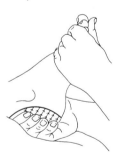

- Supporting the right foot with your left hand and placing the right thumb on the lateral side of the ligament line, work out the kidney area.
- Reverse procedure when working on the left foot.

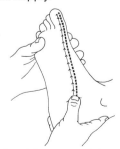
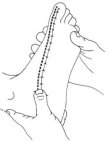

- Work out the area of the pelvis and hip to improve the nerve and blood supply.

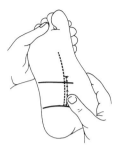
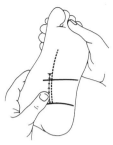

- Work out the area of the vertebral column, zone1, support top.
- Support the right foot with your left hand and use the right thumb to work up the vertebral column.
- Reverse procedure for left foot.

Q&A Cystitis

Gain a better understanding of the causes and relief of cystitis.

Q. Why are bladder irritations such a problem?

A. One reason is the prescribing of antibiotics for things such as a common cold. Antibiotics depress the immune system even though the intent is to fight infection – which they do quite well. Antibiotics cause a rebound effect that particularly affects women – as far as recurrent infections are concerned. In other words one irritation, such as a cold, is treated. The patient returns to the doctor a short time later with complaints of a bladder or yeast infection. These two problems frequently occur as a result of taking antibiotics. Sometimes patients are troubled by bowel irritations as the result of antibiotic treatment.

I think we all should be aware of the fact that antibiotics alter the immune system and that appropriate action is needed to counterbalance this tendency. It is a big help to take acidophilus capsules, or yogurt to replace the good bacteria in the colon. Remember that these nutrients must be separated from the antibiotic dosages by at least four to six hours. This keeps the 'good bacteria' present which will then check viruses and yeast infections. That's the key!

Q. What else can be done to prevent these conditions?

A. Use liberal quantities of acidifying juices to keep the urinary tract as acid as possible. In my opinion a preventative douche using diluted apple-cider vinegar during the course of antibiotic therapy would be logical. Fortunately, most doctors use only short term therapy when it comes to antibiotics but the immune system is being altered because of the repeated, excessive prescribing of these drugs. Much stronger potencies, dosages and formulas must often be used now to get the same effect that a much smaller amount did in the past.

If you must go on antibiotic therapy for a particular reason, take the precaution of saturating your body with material containing 'friendly' bacteria. Besides acidophilus and yogurt mentioned above, buttermilk is also excellent. Chronic cystitis sometimes induced by antibiotics can be a serious problem.

Q. What causes cystitis besides the overuse of antibiotics?

A. The second most common cause is the use of birth control pills. We know, from having numerous patients who are on the Pill, that they have a decreased resistance to many viral infections. They lose their immunity easily. Perhaps this is because the Pill does some damage to the vitamin C stores of the body which in turn lowers the immune system.

B complex deficiencies can also occur, which allows the body to let down its defences against infections. Repeated bladder and kidney infections are expected side effects for females on the birth-control pill. One postulation is that the Pill's hormones cause the tubes connecting the kidney and the bladder ureters to dilate, which provides passageway for these infections.

Most women find that when they go off the Pill, their chronic vaginal and bladder infections cease. Visualise how many millions of women are on this medication and may be you will be able to see why one of the most troublesome annoyances for so many women is cystitis. In my estimation we are dealing with an epidemic!

Q. What can users of the birth control pill do to improve the situation?

A. Women must understand that there is an antagonistic effect of the Pill on vitamin C. Therefore, one to three thousand milligrams of vitamin C per day is recommended to build up the immune system and counter this effect of the birth control pill.

The entire vitamin B-complex should be prescribed, with the emphasis on folic acid and vitamin B_6.

Zinc and vitamin A should also be added to the supplements taken by women on the Pill. It is necessary for building the immune system and mobilising vitamin A from the liver so that vitamin A can be properly utilised by the body. This nutrient's serum levels rise with the use of the Pill, but must have zinc with it to work correctly as an anti-infection agent against viruses.

Since there is an open pathway from the kidney to the bladder, making it easy for bacteria to enter, it is extremely difficult to keep these infections under control.

Q. Are exercises any help for these infections?

A. Tension exercises, leg lifts, sit ups or any other type that offers muscular support to the bladder-vaginal area are important.

A number of women on the Pill report stress incontinence as a side effect. Placing a soft ball or sponge between the knees and doing some isometric strengthening exercises can help the entire pelvic area.

Q. Does childbirth have anything to do with these conditions?

A. Scores of women have weak pelvic muscles as a result of childbirth. In times past women had to work extremely hard to survive, so they usually stayed in better shape.

Exercise programmes and the sessions in health spas are helping more and more women maintain healthy muscle tone.

Q. What about the yeast that causes vaginal bladder irritations?

A. This is a fungus, Candida albicans, that is nasty and difficult to control. Candida has been around for a long time and we can find it on the skin and mucous membranes, particularly the mucous surfaces of the gastrointestinal and genitourinary tracts. Candida contains no chlorophyll and is a scavenger which, since the advent and frequent prolonged over-use of antibiotics, birth-control pills and the use of cortisone type steroids, along with a high carbohydrate intake of junk foods, has multiplied and flourished in humans.

Candida albicans toxins circulate through the bloodstream to all parts of the body and can produce the following symptoms: diarrhoea, constipation, bloating, gastritis, headaches, depression, gas, colitis, acne, hyperactivity, lethargy, cramping, yeast vaginitis, menstrual irregularities, numbness, cold hands and feet, joint pains, loss of libido and chemical sensitivities.

This fungus appears to multiply easier in humans with poor eating habits and diets; who are taking drugs (especially hormone-altering drugs such as the birth control pill and steroid type chemicals); who have depressed the immune system by stress, and who have not replaced the beneficial intestinal flora after taking antibiotics. Take extra amounts of vitamin C, zinc and vitamin A along with a potent multiple vitamin for all over support.

If you have Candida, avoid all yeast products, raw mushrooms, chocolate, mature cheeses, nuts and nut butters, white sugar in all its forms, alcohol, ham, pickled foods, vinegar and soy sauce. Reduce all grains containing gluten, (wheat, oats, rye and barley). Corn and rices can be eaten as they are gluten free.

You can eat most vegetables, all fresh meats, fish, poultry, butter, oil and lemon juice. If the above strict diet is observed, you will usually see good results in several weeks. Give your body time to heal and then introduce favourite foods in small doses, but not sweet, salty, or high fat food unless you feel that you can just not live without it, and avoid foods with colourings and E additives like the plague.

CHAPTER 11

Cancer – the disease of the 20th century

The two major life-threatening conditions of mankind are cancer and coronary heart disease.

We all know of some family member, friend or acquaintance who has just been diagnosed, or worst still, has 'passed away'.

To mainstream doctors, cancer is viewed as a localised disease which must be treated by localised means. It can, we are led to believe, only be tackled by surgery involving cutting out the tumour and irradiating or poisoning the growth thus saving the patient.

In opposition to this aggressive treatment which looks at the tumour as 'the enemy' which must be 'destroyed' as rapidly as possible, the complementary or holistic approach to cancer is to treat the whole person.

Instead of attacking the tumour, alternative therapies aim to rebuild the body's natural immunity which, after all, is a sensible approach. If the immune system were working efficiently, as it should, disease would not manifest in the first place. With a strengthened immune system the cancer cells would be destroyed. It is sad to see that only four per cent of the Health Care Fund is spent on preventing disease.

As you read this article you must be aware that within your blood stream are cancer cells. In most people the white blood cells recognise these invaders, engulf these dangerous cells and destroy them .

Every day all of us absorb small amounts of carcinogens – substances that can cause cancer. Lead from car exhausts, additives in the food chain, even by-products of our own digestion can do us harm. They penetrate our cells and attack the cell nucleus promoting cancer by muddling the genetic code that programmes our health.

We can't stop pollution but we can try to make efforts to protect ourselves in some way or other. There is new evidence that the trace element selenium and vitamin E work together to protect cell membranes and chromosomes from damage.

John A Milner Ph.D. of the University of Illinois speculates that selenium's effect on rapidly dividing cells might explain why laboratory mice did not get cancer when they received selenium supplements. Misconceptions about alternative cancer therapies abound and general opinion throughout the medical profession is that all alternative cancer therapies are worthless. This is the general opinion of the cancer industry – a \$80 billion a year concern.

There are many patients who were brave enough to refuse chemotherapy, surgery and radiation and who sort out their own 'cures', found 'gentle ways of healing their bodies' and are still alive and well today some 10 to 15 years later. How do the medical profession react to these 'cures'? Most of them say, that it was probably due to a wrong diagnosis: how sad! They also add that alternative therapists are untrained, unlicensed and out to make financial gains!

There are many forms of alternative therapies which are ineffective or even fraudulent but many are very successful, in particular herbalism, homeopathy, reflexology, acupuncture, diet reforms and colonic irrigation. Massage and reflexology can make the patient feel relaxed, and encourage the body to detoxify. In turn this relaxation aids the efficient working of the immune system.

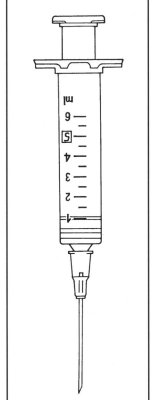

There have been few changes made in the conventional treatment of cancer over the past 30 years. The same approach continues.

Chemotherapy

This treatment uses toxic drugs which may certainly destroy cancer cells. The treatment also attacks normal cells, including those of the bone marrow which is the foundation of the immune system and it destroys the cells of the intestinal walls and as our intestine is also very involved in aiding our immunity, two of the body's most effective protection mechanisms are damaged.

The drugs used throughout the years have changed and one drug has been replaced by another, and cocktails of drugs have also been tried but still the end results and statistics in undertaking this form of treatment are poor, and statistics from *'What Doctor's Don't Tell You'* state that no more than five per cent of cancer patients benefit from chemotherapy.

The late Dr. Hardin Jones, professor at the University of California, stated that the possibility exists that treatment makes the average situation worsen. (WDDY Volume 2 No.7)

During chemotherapy and radiotherapy, particularly for those who have had long term repeated treatments, the organs of detoxification are so overloaded and overworked with toxic chemicals from drugs that they eventually are unable to do the job they were intended to do – in particular the liver and kidneys are affected. Many patients die eventually from pneumonia or kidney failure due to the destruction of their immune systems, not the cancer for which they were being treated in the first place.

Radiation

This is useful in slowing down certain cancers but does not cure. Damage occurs in other organs and tissues. Bone tissue can 'dry out' particularly the hip and pelvic area when radiation is used in the low abdominal areas, causing bone fragility and consequently fractures.

It is always a great confusion to me, and I am sure to many of you, to understand how we are told that radiation can cause cancers and then we are told that it is necessary to use radiation to treat the disease!

Surgery – does this really help?

As the tumour is excised, cancer cells have to be released into the blood stream. If you had an abscess cut, the pus would leak out into the surrounding tissues and would easily cause another eruption to form in the surrounding areas.

If our immune system was working efficiently the cancer cells would be engulfed, but during surgery the shock to the system and the anaesthetic create havoc with our immune systems. So just at a critical time in our life when we need our immune system to protect us, it is depleted by the intervention of surgery and the anaesthetic.

The poor diet in most hospitals leaves much to be desired in helping the body to heal itself in a time of crisis.

It is well known that it takes over a month for our immune systems to return to the state they were in before the surgery, and that was probably very poor. Hence the occurrence of so many postoperative infections following operations.

Breast cancer and the Pill

In the 35 years since the Pill and hormone replacement therapy have been proclaimed as 'the greatest gift to the health of women' we see ever increasing rising statistics of breast, uterine, cervical and ovarian cancer.

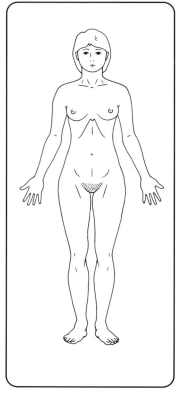

Three major studies prove that the risk of breast cancer doubles after using HRT for more than six years. There has to be a reason why the statistics of cancer are constantly rising. The reasons are drugs, in particularly hormones, chemical additives foods, stress, smoking, and alcohol.

We are living in an age where most of us have good standards of living. Even the poorest have a roof over their heads, food, clothes hot water and some form of heating.

We are not living in rat infested properties, with one lavatory in a communal yard to serve 'the road'. We are not living on bread, lard and some sort of soup and tea, as the poor did in the Victorian times. This was the cause for so much disease and premature death.

Even those of us who rely on the State for our survival do have somewhere to live and money, sparse though it may be, to feed ourselves. Lack of education leads to the money allowed by the State to be spent very unwisely by some – cigarettes and alcohol coming before food.

Fruit and vegetables bought from markets are so very cheap: nutritious soups can be made from these. Rice, pasta and lentils cost very little, and chicken is a nutritious and comparatively cheap food, so even the poor can live on a vitamin and mineral rich diet with a little effort and wise purchases.

As cancer is now almost epidemic, it just has to be what we are putting down our throats in the form of drugs, hormones and food that is causing the destruction of our bodies leaving them unprotected against all the degenerative diseases of our modern times.

If we 'play about with the miracle of the hormonal

system' we do so at our peril. Had nature intended women to have synthetic hormones passing through their veins for ever and a day, so that menstruation could still be occurring in their seventies, she would have provided this service without the drug industry needing to be consulted.

Breast cancer is the commonest female cancer and the main cause of death in women up to the age of 55.

In countries where there is a high dairy fat consumption there are high statistics of breast cancer. Just a note for your interest, up to 1994 the Japanese had an extremely low incident of breast cancer. Japan had never sanctioned the Pill up to that time and they also consumed very little dairy products.

However, the Japanese are becoming westernised. More Japanese women are using the Pill and some are eating a diet high in animal fats. The beefburger and hamburger industries are making their mark. With the increase in this type of food and an increased usage of the birth control pill and hormone replacement therapy, their cancer statistics are now on the rise!.

Another potentially damaging drug which had great links with breast cancer was stilbestrol – this drug was given to new mothers who choose not to breast feed their babies The drug dried up their milk production very rapidly.

Fertility and infertility

Apart from increasing the risk of cancers, hormone replacement therapy and the contraceptive pill lowers

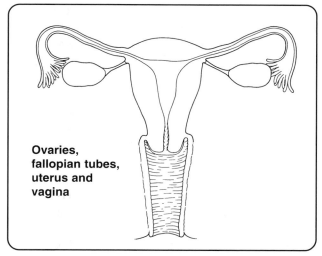

Ovaries, fallopian tubes, uterus and vagina

your zinc levels and zinc is very necessary for the health of our thyroid gland which automatically affects our fertility.

Deficiencies also occur in vitamin B, magnesium and manganese: they also affect our copper levels, which in turn affect our liver function.

Another matter of interest is the rise in boys having undescended testicles, and the connection here too of toxic chemicals in the blood stream!

Could these vitamin deficiencies and chemical overloads not be the reason why one in every six young couples today suffer from infertility? The number of visits to US doctors for infertility services rose from 600,000 in 1968 to about 1.6 million in 1984. Approximately two million women had taken fertility drugs in 1998. (N. Engl J Med Sept 22 1994)

Infertility is treated by strong hormonal drugs which stimulate the ovaries to bursting point: Clomiphene is one. Ovarian and breast cancer are the latest risks to be associated with fertility drugs.

Yet another serious risk in the taking of fertility drugs is a serious condition caused by over-stimulation of the ovaries. There is a build up of fluid in the abdomen, and often the sac around the heart. Thrombosis, heart attacks and strokes are other risk factors.

One would think of the womb as a safe haven for the unborn child but there are warnings to suggest that even before birth the child can suffer quite serious consequences from the polluted environment in which its mother lives. The level of pollutants in our lives today could well be the reason for a variety of birth defects.

Hormone replacement therapy

Why the menopause is today treated as an illness is quite mind-boggling. The medical profession believe that the symptoms of the menopause, which are quite disturbing, such as hot flushes, depression, brittle bones, thinning and dryness of the vagina, are dysfunctions which need to be treated as an illness by replacing the reduction of oestrogen and progesterone in the form of a tablet, patch on the skin or a cream to be 'rubbed in'.

HRT has been marketed as a 'cure all' for the maladies of old age. And it seems to be 'inviting' to remove all the problems that are encountered with the menopause. That it triples the risk of breast cancer and quadruples the risk of endometrial cancer are not brought to the attention of the general public in the alarming way it should be.

It is obviously a very lucrative proposition to the drug industry to have millions of women taking synthetic hormones, which is what HRT is, on a long term basis.

However, there are other ways of encouraging the body to produce oestrogen. The ovaries cease most of their production but the adrenal glands produce some small amounts too. We do not need large quantities of oestrogen pulsating around our blood stream in our more mature years.

Large quantities of hormones are needed to stimulate the brain to activate the secretion of hormones during our reproductive years to stimulate the ovaries to produce ova, build the lining of the uterus, the endometrium, and then shed the lining if conception does not occur – quite a feat of achievement for the endocrine system.

When using hormone replacement therapy, we take the same quantity each day. When the hormone is naturally produced by the endocrine system, it only produces the amount we need. When produced synthetically we have an excess of hormones building in the body and many cancers are oestrogen dependent.

The 'youth hormone' oestrogen as it was heralded does not suit all women. In fact many women suffer from bloating, weight gain, breast tenderness and headaches and have to cease taking it.

There is a great connection between migraine and HRT, as the artificial hormonal preparation interferes with the blood supply through the arteries and can affect the brain, hence the migraine.

There is substantial evidence to prove that breast and endometrial cancer risks are increased and so is the likelihood of thrombosis when taking HRT.

It is supposed to help bone density, but only when you have taken it for nine or ten years. If you take oestrogen alone for 15 years or more the likelihood of breast cancer rises by 30 per cent. If oestrogen and progesterone are taken together the risk almost doubles.

Regular weight bearing exercise encourages bone density. Cigarette smoking accelerates the destruction of oestrogen and hastens the onset of the menopause and osteoporosis.

There is a wealth of other measures that you can take to protect your bones, besides interfering with the delicate balance of the hormonal system.

Calcium and vitamin D supplementation, also magnesium and zinc.

Reduce the amount of protein you take in your diet. A high protein diet means that calcium is removed from the bones. Osteoporosis is not known in Africa, where protein consumption is less: it is very common in the West where protein intake is excessive.

You can take natural oestrogen by eating rhubarb, soya beans and soya products like tofu and miso. Other sources of phytoestrols include celery, fennel, ginseng alfalfa, red clover and liquorice. Japanese women with their high soya diet suffer far less menopausal symptoms than women in the West.

In one trial it was found that Japanese women on a traditional low fat diet had phyto-oestrogen levels in their urine up to one thousand times higher than American women. (WDDY Volume 4 No. 9. Page 2)

Smear tests

Having a smear test, to look for possible cancer cells in the cervix is not a particularly pleasant experience, and it is quite alarming when you are recalled for a further test because some abnormalities were found in the first one.

There are many irritants that we use that can cause an abnormal smear test such as spermicidal gels or lubricants which can cause infections.

Sometimes a tampon can start an infection in the cervix. Those suffering from Candida can also experience changes in the cervix.

Smoking, the contraceptive pill and hormone replacement therapy can also be responsible.

If you have been called for a repeat test in three or six months time, take folic acid. This seems to maintain the health of the mucous membrane. You will need to take 5mg of folic acid daily for several months and perhaps permanently.

Sometimes, unfortunately, cancer cells are detected and treatments in the form of colposcopy and laser treatment are recommended. Early detection and treatment are extremely successful.

Prostate cancer

The cases of prostate cancer are rising: it is the third most common cancer in men and 14,000 new cases each year are being treated in Britain.

A tendency to prostate cancer may be hereditary: if a father or brother suffered the disease the likelihood of contracting it increases the risk.

Studies in the USA reported that vasectomized men had a 60 per cent

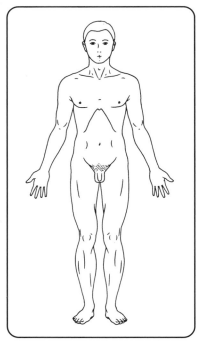

increased risk of developing the disease. At the present time diagnosis for the disease is by a rectal examination and a blood test.

Treatment varies according to the age of the patient concerned. Sometimes surgery is carried out, otherwise treatment with chemotherapy or radiotherapy or hormone therapy is sometimes used to slow down the development of the disease. Even with the latest forms of surgery, half of all males become impotent.

As the statistics of prostate cancer are rapidly rising and this disease, it is believed, will be the number one killer in males within the next twenty years, the way forward should be to educate the public in natural ways to prevent prostate cancer.

A low fat high complex carbohydrate diet, with a high fibre content can do much. Avoiding alcohol as far as possible and stopping smoking are other ways.

Again, soya products which are a rich source of isoflavonoids are known to restrict the growth of prostate cancer (Lancet 1993; 342; 1209-10)

Peas, beans, lentils, dried fruits, especially apricots, figs, and garlic are recommended, and make sure you take an adequate supply of zinc in your diet. You can buy zinc granules to sprinkle on your food. A healthy prostate contains high levels of zinc – zinc is needed for producing male hormones. Zinc also protects from the toxic metal cadmium which has been shown to stimulate the growth of cancer in the prostate. (Am J Epidemiol 1989:129 (1) 112.24).

Men with the most malignant form of prostate cancer were found to have high levels of cadmium and very low levels of zinc!

Power Lines

We have read about the dangers of living near exposure from low levels of magnetic fields generated from mains electricity or power lines and the links with childhood leukaemia. In fact it can raise the chances of your child contracting this blood disease by as much as three or four times.

The National Grid can no longer dismiss these links and are being forced to look into the seriousness of this claim as the public are demanding

investigations into the causes of leukaemia and this exposure. Many parents have suffered the loss of a child due, they are sure, to EMFs and legal actions are being undertaken.

Electric and magnetic fields surround all electrical conductors including power lines, appliances and even the wiring in your house can be the cause. Every piece of electrical equipment in your home generates a magnetic field, your microwave, television, your mobile telephone, your computer.

If you sleep with a radio-clock alarm right next to your face, you are encouraging a risk. Just think of the hours of exposure you could be subjecting yourself to, and don't leave a computer plugged on in your bedroom.

No generation has been exposed to so many contaminants before, both inside and outside the home, so the best course of action is avoidance as far as possible.

Increase your intake of antioxidants because exposure to electromagnetic fields increases free radicals in the body. They also reduce the production of melatonin which is produced from the pineal gland, another powerful antioxidant, thus helping cancers to develop.

Green vegetables and fruit help the body to fight the harmful increase in free radicals caused by EMFs. A daily intake of necessary vitamins and minerals are also to be recommended.

Do move all electrical equipment away from your bed and never sleep with your electric blanket turned on.

Flouride – another poison

Would you feel angry if you discovered that the Government are planning to contaminate the public through the water supply, upon which they depend, with a substance that has been associated with genetic disorders, brittle bones and cancer? Flouride is the culprit and it is being added routinely to the water supply in some areas because it is said to prevent dental cavities.

We are also encouraged to use flouride toothpastes and flouride mouthwashes to stop dental decay. If there were a choice, I am sure false teeth would be more acceptable than brittle bones or cancer!

Why do we suddenly need fluoride to help prevent decay in our teeth? Could it be that we are consuming such high quantities of sugar in our diets today from birth to the grave that our teeth are suffering. Children are absorbing high sugar contents in their diets even before they have teeth – squashes, chocolate, ice cream, and lollies. It is quite horrific. Sugar is white, deadly and a poison when taken in excess: it has absolutely no food value whatsoever. Apart from the visible sugar we take in daily, it is also present in most tinned, packaged and frozen foods.

Surely the way forward is to reduce sugar, we would not then need fluoride.

An overload of fluoride can cause headaches, chronic fatigue, dizziness, visual disturbances, constipation or diarrhoea and sleep disturbances. Heavy tea drinkers also consume large quantities of fluoride.

You can help yourself counteract the adversities of fluoride by taking daily supplements of magnesium, zinc and iron and stick to bottled water or spoil yourself and have a water filter fitted in your kitchen. You really are worth it!

Cancer and the benefits of vitamin C

Since 1960 some ten billion dollars has been spent on cancer research in an effort to get some control of the disease. If trends continue one in four of us will eventually have cancer. This is approximately 36 million people, and the annual global figures point towards four million sufferers in the not too distant future.

There have been many papers written on the benefits of vitamin C, could it be of positive value in the prevention of the illness, and controlling the disease once one has it?

A Doctor Pauling has been interested in the benefits of vitamin C for well over 10 years, and has proven that large doses of vitamin C equivalent to 10g daily both orally or intravenously if necessary gave cancer patients a better quality of life, so that their remaining years were comfortable, productive and useful.

Vitamin C is safe, cheap and easy to take: it has no damaging side effects. It has also proved very effective in controlling pain levels. Patients have been able to remove themselves from strong pain killing drugs when using the vitamin C treatment.

Drug therapies are expensive, very destructive to the body, wipe out the protection of the immune system and make the patient feel very sick.

The immune system

There can be few of us today unaware of just how vital is the efficient functioning of the immune system. We only have to think of AIDS and consider the consequences when the immune system goes into total collapse.

To a less severe degree we can see a weakened immune function in action in conditions such as Chronic Fatigue Syndrome and the considerable increase in allergies, particularly allergic conditions in children, such as asthma and eczema.

An allergy is an overreaction on the immune system against a foreign particle, pollen or house dust for example.

Our immune systems are already in a state of overdrive due to the increases in chemicals which we inhale and consume daily, these stressors on the body have been elaborated throughout this article.

Too much overload and the immune system seems to go berserk and it starts to attack the body it is supposed to be protecting.

The body's defence

Your immune system is not just your spleen, it comprises a combination of many different processes, scattered throughout your body which act as a 'defence force'. The immune system is in your cells, your liver, digestive system, particularly the intestines, lungs, and skin.

An unhealthy bowel can result in some serious health problems, often involving immune suppression. Chronic candidiasis where this yeast has spread into regions previously denied it by friendly bacteria, is a condition caused by damage to the bowel flora by antibiotic or steroid drugs (the Pill) and a high sugar diet.

Many conditions such as rheumatoid arthritis and ankylosing spondylitis have their origins in a toxic bowel. Unfortunately as both these conditions are treated with pain killing drugs and often steroids, the condition becomes chronic because of mismanagement. The cause of the condition was never investigated, never recognised.

The central overall command still lies in the brain, dominated by the hormonal system which excretes vital information for survival of the whole human organism, including the immune system.

The need to use substances to stimulate the body's defence to fight disease is being considered but immunotherapy is a comparatively new idea. It should be high on the list of priorities in any 'research funding'.

Let's accept that the immune system protects us against foreign and mutant invaders, including cancer: vitamin C is essential for its mechanisms to work properly.

In a further trial, a Dr. Jorgen Schlegal a Urologist at Tulane University Medical School was involved in research into bladder cancer. Dr. Jorgen implanted a proven bladder carcinogen into mice and then added vitamin C to their drinking water. The mice did not develop cancer.

It was also reported that those who drink high quantities of coffee, alcohol or cola increase the risk of bladder cancer.

Sugar seriously affects our immune system, if 100g of sugar is taken into the body the efficiency of the white blood cells to scavenge and destroy invading bacteria is reduced in efficiency within 30 minutes.

Artificial sweeteners are again harmful to the immune system and when broken down in the body methanol is formed, which is a highly toxic immune suppressing substance. A little would do you no harm, but sweeteners are used in so many foods today, particularly in cola drinks, squashes, ice cream, all 'diet' low calorie foods and in confectionery, lots of little amounts of sweeteners become large amounts when consumed daily.

On a more positive note, we can help our immune systems by taking daily amounts of zinc. A deficiency of zinc affects the efficiency of the thymus gland which lies behind the breast bone. This gland is very large in young children and is the gland which gives them maximum protection against severe infection in their early years.

A decrease in zinc leads to the thymus reducing in size, the child would then become prone to increased infection and poor wound healing. You can get zinc in a natural form by eating pumpkin or sunflower seeds, soya beans too are a rich source of supply.

Eat your sunflower and pumpkin seeds as 'snacks' during the day: a teaspoonful of each is very beneficial. Alternatively, add them to your breakfast cereal.

Personality and the patient

Although it is difficult to demonstrate a clear link between personality factors and disease, many practitioners have observed that when a prolonged stress response affects a particular personality, a specific disorder will result. Personality clearly influences the way a patient copes with stressful circumstances.

Certain personality types are associated with heart disease, arthritis, cancer as well as migraine, diverticulitis, and bowel diseases generally.

Cancer victims are generally described as exceptionally fine, thoughtful people, too good to be true. They are often referred to as 'martyrs'. Underneath this mask are feelings of unworthiness and self-dislike. There is usually much bottled up hostility and aggression, and an ability not to express or share feelings with others, whether of a positive or negative nature.

The uncomplaining victim suffers from a degree of depression, which often arises through 'suppressed anger'.

Had they been able to 'explode', insist on their rights, and expect more of their partners, husbands, or families and not accepted 'the crumbs that fell from the table',

they would probably never have suffered from cancer or any of the other degenerative diseases in the first place.

Our body undoubtedly 'mirrors' our minds, and we must be aware that many of the signs and symptoms of the sick person are expressions of emotional conflicts, causing an anatomy of despair.

The relationship between patient and practitioner whether in the conventional medical field or in the complementary approach is rather like 'a marriage'. The two people concerned need to form a commitment: they need to form a 'safe haven'.

It is very difficult for the average doctor to offer this support, time is restrictive with too many patients to see in too short a time.

The complementary therapist therefore is able to offer this indulgence to his or her patient. Most practitioners offer their patients an hour's appointment which is such a luxury in today's rush and tear. They have time to listen to the individual and to understand that the underlying cause of their illness has many factors involved. The practitioner really has time to get to know her patient and time for the patient to build confidence in the practitioner.

Many doctors question the benefits offered by the complementary practitioner and suggest that the relief the patient obtained was because there was time to listen, and that the rapport between the patient and practitioner brought about the improvement in the condition they were being treated for.

It really is not so simple as that. There is far more to healing than autosuggestion. But what if the rapport between the patient and practitioner – a good listening ear – was a contributing factor? As long as the patient benefited that should be the main concern.

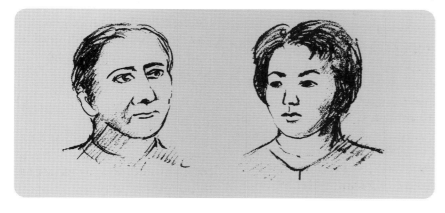

Why also is it deemed necessary to 'ask the doctor's advice' before even contemplating a form of complementary treatment, despite the fact that the orthodox treatment has failed to offer little benefit, and rather than accept when the doctor says that 'there is really little else I can do for you' the patient desperately looks elsewhere for help.

Do any of us contact our doctor to ask his advice when we decide to start smoking, imbibe heavy intakes of alcohol, take cannabis, or put on four stones in weight? None of us dream about taking the advice of a doctor as to the adversities of our choices.

We each choose the path we take and take our chance on the outcome, why then do we consider it necessary to ask our doctor's advice when we decide to have reflexology, acupuncture, massage, Chinese herbal medicine, or some other dietary reform in order to seek a healthier body?

Your body is your own responsibility and has nothing to do with the doctor. The decisions on how you wish to treat yourself in times of illness must be **yours and yours alone**.

Reflexology and cancer

If you are a Reflexologist and are working on people suffering from cancer, the areas identified below in the chart will give you some guidance of the most important reflexes to work upon.

- Work out the liver to help detoxification.
- Work out the entire intestinal area, remembering that 85 per cent of our immunity stems from the intestine which is rich in lymphatic tissue.
  Reflexology will help to rid the body of unwanted waste material and balance the ecological flora of the bowel.
- Work out the spleen.
- Work out the entire central nervous system, spine and brain.

Do not use reflexology on a patient who is having chemotherapy or radiotherapy: always wait for at least one week after the treatment. There is no 'danger' attached to this, but working on the feet after these treatments could cause 'side effects'. (Reflexology detoxifies, particularly when we work on the organs of elimination such as the liver and the intestines.) The patient would then suffer the effects of chemotherapy or radiotherapy, plus the effects of reflexology treatment and the combined reactions could make the patient feel extremely unwell.

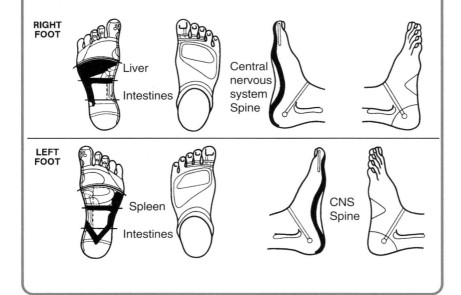

RIGHT FOOT — Liver, Intestines, Central nervous system Spine

LEFT FOOT — Spleen, Intestines, CNS Spine

Did you know?
Herbs that help cancer

A herbal formula that is useful for cancer patients is Essiac, which was put together by a nurse called Rene Caisse in Canada in the 1930s. ESSIAC is her name, CAISSE, spelt backwards.

I understand that she obtained the original formula, a traditional treatment, from the local native Indians.

The Essiac herbs have been shown to be effective in controlling the rapidity of the reproduction of cancer cells and hence are useful in controlling the primary site of cancers and also secondary growths.

There is no doubt that Essiac has prolonged life in people using this formula and prolongs it in a form that is of value.

It is not a protection of life at all costs. Essiac has great abilities as a herbal preparation in relieving pain. Unfortunately, in many cases, patients who have already been treated with morphine to relieve pain are addicted to it.

Cat's Claw and Essiac are good for well people too. They both strengthen the immune system, help prevent cancer developing and increase resistance to other infections.

Both help detoxify the liver and blood. You have to remember to drink a lot of water at the same time: this is something that is often forgotten. Even if you have a very good detoxifying herb, you can end up feeling poorly if your body does not have the means of removing the waste products. So it is important to increase your water intake generally, and certainly when you are going through a detoxification process.

CHAPTER 12

A better understanding of the brain

As we need to increase our knowledge all the time to keep up with an insight into the types of diseases and conditions we are treating, thus giving us more confidence as a practitioner and more ability to communicate with our patients on the illnesses they present with, I hope this article on the brain will be of good support to you when treating all conditions from strokes to epilepsy and migraine, to name but a few.

Strokes

The term describes a condition of the brain which has quite widespread effects. Often referred to as a cerebro-vascular accident or CVA, years back a stroke was described as 'brain fevers' or apoplexy, indicating that the cause of this condition was indeed vascular.

Our brain demands more oxygen at any given time than any other part of the body, indeed our brain can never rest during either our waking or sleeping hours, as all functioning depends on its instructions. Whether it be the beating of our hearts, our respiration, the amazing balance of our hormonal secretions, our digestion or renal functions, our brain needs a rich supply of oxygen which is carried in our blood stream by our red blood cells.

If at any time our brain is starved of oxygen for more than six minutes, all is lost for ever. That is why when respiration ceases say in the case of a road accident, or a heart attack, mouth to mouth respiration keeps some oxygenated blood flowing through our brain.

Because the brain is especially vulnerable to oxygen lack it is well supplied by four major arteries which link together at the base to form the Circle of Willis, enabling blood flow to be restored in the event of one artery failing.

From this circle a number of branches penetrate the brain and these are particularly liable to atherosclerosis and attendant complications of haemorrhage, embolism and thrombosis. Depending on the site chosen, symptoms may vary from visual disturbance and dizziness to paralysis and anaesthesia.

Who then is at most risk from strokes?

Men are more prone than women, particularly those suffering from, (a) a heart condition, (b) hypertension, (c) diabetes, (d) smokers, (e) those with a family history of high cholesterol levels. The incidence in the over sixty-fives is relatively high – about one in 450 and this makes it the most common cause of death apart from heart disease and cancer.

In some cases a spasm in one or other of the arteries in the brain leaves the sufferer unable to speak, and probably a paralysis will occur in one side of the body. If it is just a spasm in the artery, then normal functioning will return very rapidly. However, when the brain has suffered from an actual haemorrhage from a blood vessel, the prognosis is very poor, particularly in the elderly.

Symptoms usually come on over a few days, with an underlying head pain, which gets worse, confusion and a general feeling of extreme weakness.

Frequently the cause of the CVA is from a clot which has probably formed elsewhere in the body, i.e. thrombosis, and will therefore be quite a distance from the brain, often in the wall of the heart. Instead of being broken up by the flow of blood, in the case of the elderly or those with hardening of the arteries, the ability for small clots to flow through the arteries without causing any undue damage is restricted, because the formation of calcium or fatty deposits in the artery walls, restricts the space. Just as the furring up of our pipes in our homes would cause a restriction in the flow of water in our taps, exactly the same effect is created in our circulatory systems.

Occasionally elderly people develop a more generalised form of cerebro-vascular atherosclerosis which leads to senile dementia, loss of memory, interest and severe intellectual deterioration.

Subarachnoid haemorrhage

A haemorrhage of this type is caused by a leakage of blood into the space beneath the arachnoid layer. The famous composer Mendelssohn died at the age of 38 from just such a cause, as did his sister, father and grandfather and it was noted that he suffered from severe headaches for months, when the aneurysm was slowly leaking, often accompanied by stiffness in the neck, nausea, and dizziness.

A true diagnosis of this condition will be confirmed by giving the patient a lumbar puncture which will reveal a bloodstained cerebro-spinal fluid, and if necessary an X-ray of the vessels, called an angiogram, which will show the exact position of the leak.

Subdural haemorrhage

Develops beneath the dura and is liable to occur in babies born prematurely, and this is one of the reasons for using forceps to protect the head from compression when a normal entry into the world is for one or other reasons not possible.

The cause of this type of haemorrhage will arise from a head injury which ruptures the outer vessels, and symptoms will vary according to the severity of the accident. At the worst they could result in loss of consciousness and deep coma or mild symptoms of headache and nausea.

Infections
Meningitis

The meninges which are the protective linings in the brain act as a barrier. The only route for infection to arise is via the bloodstream. Many infections in the brain result in the virus or bacteria arising from an acute ear infection. The gap from the workings of the ear, which lie just behind the eye, and the brain are very short. That is the reason why ear infections are treated rapidly.

As most of you know, meningitis is life threatening and needs to be treated rapidly: stiffness in the neck, severe headache and extreme drowsiness plus the inability to be able to stand bright lights are symptoms. The condition causes severe swelling in the brain tissue.

Encephalitis

This viral infection can accompany many of the more common childhood illnesses, mumps, measles and glandular fever.

An unusual and somewhat strange type of encephalitis is thought to arise as the result of the Coxsackie virus and takes the form of extreme muscular fatigue, lethargy and often depression. We probably see this type of condition in our practices today which is often called ME. This virus can remain dormant in our systems for years and then resurfaces when our immune systems are not so competent in performing their duties and give rise to these unexplainable symptoms.

Epilepsy

What is epilepsy? It is a symptom rather than a disease. Normally neurones transmit their nerve impulses in a calm, efficient manner but in epileptics they discharge their energy chaotically, leading to a behaviour known as a fit. About one person in 200 suffers from some form of epilepsy, being more common in children because of their easily stimulated nervous system. Especially likely in the event of a high fever. There are three types of epilepsy: grand mal, petit mal and temporal lobe epilepsy.

Grand mal epilepsy

This is a form of generalised but temporary convulsion which can however be repeated sometimes several times in a day. The epileptic attack will follow a certain set of symptoms. Usually the sufferer has a premonition that an attack is about to occur and a change in mood several days before is not uncommon.

The **tonic** phase is when un-consciousness suddenly occurs, with the person falling suddenly to the ground and sometimes injuring themselves. Rigidity of the body is a further symptom.

The **clonic phase** which follows consists of jerking of the limbs and incontinence, with frothing of the mouth.

The **relaxation phase** is the final phase when a sleepy state develops and then a return to full consciousness. Sometimes the epileptic sufferer will be unaware of a fit having occurred.

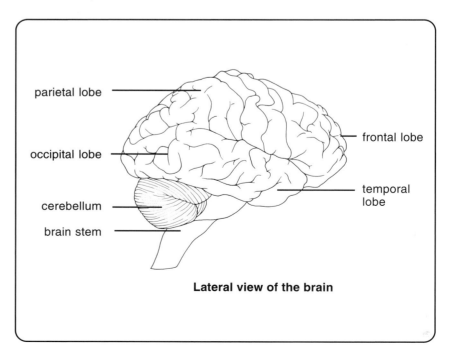

parietal lobe

occipital lobe

cerebellum

brain stem

frontal lobe

temporal lobe

Lateral view of the brain

Petit mal is rather like a 'day dream' and is far milder. It is seen mostly in young children who suddenly drift away in their thoughts and do not respond to the stimulation of communication. This state only lasts for a few seconds.

Temporal lobe epilepsy

This is localised in the temporal lobe of the brain where memory and some sensations are coordinated. There is often a disturbance in consciousness, such as hallucinations, dream states and behaviour which is totally out of character.

Headache

Most headaches are caused by tension in the muscles around our neck and eyes. They tend to increase as the day goes on and then are alleviated by sleep. Too many hours working with a word processor, lack of oxygen, or being involved with very close work which cause a strain on our eyes such as fine sewing are some causes.

Migraine

This very specific form of headache will make it impossible for you to function. If your friend or relative is able to perform their everyday duties with a migraine, then it really is not a classical case of a real migraine attack.

Migraine can be triggered by hormonal changes around period time, from the contraceptive pill or following the consumption of certain foods: chocolate, oranges, cheese, alcohol and some additives such as tartrazine are most common.

Symptoms of migraine are flashing lights, tunnel vision, a difficulty in focusing, and sickness. They are caused by the initial contraction of vessels in the visual cortex which later expand to cause the throbbing sensation which can last for many hours, and in some poor sufferers, it can cause them to have to resort to bed, in a darkened room for several days.

In extreme cases the sufferer may complain of a numb sensation around the mouth which extends to tingling and weakness in an arm or leg, often both. Head pain usually starts on one side of the head (hemicrania).

Orthodox treatment for migraine uses drugs containing ergotamine, a drug which constricts the vessels and thus counteracts the dilation which causes the headache. These drugs are sometimes given in the form of a suppository which will speed the action.

Reflexology and migraine

Reflexology has proven to be very helpful in treating migraine cases, the liver being one of the most beneficial areas to treat, particularly when the cause is of an allergic nature and is related to foods or substances in foods which affect efficient elimination by the liver.

Working on the liver reflex will put this matter right, and helping the head and cervical spine, I am sure, will give some relief to the constriction in the blood vessels.

As most migraine cases are food related, reflexology can offer relief to most sufferers.

I have not found the treatment so successful when the cause was hormonal in character, although I would like to hear from anyone who has had good results in the treatment of migraine, whatever the cause.

Did you know?
Anaemia
An iron deficiency
Anaemia refers to a condition in which the blood lacks sufficient red blood cells to carry oxygen to all parts of the body. Symptoms of the condition are pallor, generalised weakness and a tendency to tire.

Iron deficiency is often caused by excessive blood loss such as excessive menstrual bleeding, stomach ulceration, or haemorrhoids. The most common cause of a deficiency of red blood cells is nutritional: deficiencies of iron, vitamin B_{12} and folic acid are most common. The groups at highest risk are teenage girls, pregnant women and the elderly. Decreased absorption of iron is often caused by poor digestive enzymes, in particular hydrochloric acid which is produced in the stomach. As we age our digestive secretions become less effective.

Diet and Lifestyle
Include leafy vegetables, offal, black strap molasses – which is excellent and dried fruits such as apricots. Foods that inhibit the absorption of iron are tea, coffee and wheat bran.
Vegetarians have a higher incidence of anaemia.

Useful supplements
Iron – preferably in chelated form for maximum absorption without gastro-intestinal upset.
Vitamin C encourages absorption.
L-lysine increases iron absorption.

CHAPTER 13

Kidney Stones

It is not unusual to have little or no symptoms of kidney stones until one tries to leave the kidney, then excruciating pain will be felt in the low back: back pain can often be confused with kidney stones.

Stones, or more usually, gravel in the urinary tract have been recognised for thousands of years. In the past, stones were almost exclusively in the bladder whilst today most stones form in the kidney, which is far more serious, as large stones can actually damage kidney function.

Over 10 per cent of males and 5 per cent of females experience a kidney stone in their lifetime. In the US one out of every 1000 hospital admissions is for kidney stones. The rate of the formation of these stones has been steadily increasing paralleling the rise in other diseases associated with so-called western diet, i.e. heart disease, gallstones, high blood pressure and diabetes.

In the western hemisphere kidney stones are usually composed of calcium salts (75 – 80 per cent), uric acid (5 – 8 per cent), or struvite (10 – 15 per cent). The incidence varies geographically, reflecting differences in environmental factors, diet and components of drinking water. It normally occurs in those over thirty years of age, and is more common in males than females.

Causes

Human urine is usually saturated to the limit with calcium oxalate, uric acid and phosphates. These compounds normally remain in solution due to pH control and the secretion of various protective compounds. If these protective compounds are overwhelmed, crystallisation will occur.

In general, the majority of kidney stones are preventable. Occasionally a number of metabolic diseases cause kidney stones, but these are rare, hyperparathyroidism (where the parathyroids produce excesses of calcium), vitamin D excess, destructive bone disease, Cushing's syndrome and sarcoidosis.

As calcium containing stones are the most common type, this is the condition we will deal with in this article.

The high rate of calcium forming stones in affluent societies is directly associated with dietary patterns of low fibre, highly refined carbohydrates, high alcohol consumption, large amounts of animal protein, high fat and salt containing foods. Although each one of the above factors can encourage the formation of stones, it is usually the cumulative effect that is responsible for most of them and our western diet is undoubtedly the reason for the rising incidence of kidney stones.

Vegetarians have a decreased risk of developing stones, and even meat eaters who have a high consumption of fresh fruit and vegetables are less likely to develop them.

Bran supplementation as well as the simple change from white to brown bread results in lowering calcium levels.

Magnesium and vitamin B$_6$ A deficiency of both of these is of critical importance, particularly magnesium which has been shown to inhibit the solid formation of the stones.

Glutomic acid Depressed levels of glutomic acid (due to Vitamin B deficiency) also encourages stones.

Vitamin K The urinary glycoprotein that is a powerful inhibitor of calcium oxalate crystalline growth requires Vitamin K for its synthesis.

Milk and antacids The long term over consumption of milk or antacids often results in the development of kidney stones.

Heavy metals Hair mineral analysis may be of value in patients with recurrent kidney stones since many heavy metals (mercury, aluminium, gold, uranium and cadmium) are toxic to the kidney. Cadmium in particular has been shown to increase the incidence of kidney stones.

Treatment

Reflexology, we know, is invaluable, and many patients have passed a further stone after treatment, but what can we do to prevent further episodes?

1. Increase liquid intake.

2. Increase intake of dietary fibre, complex carbohydrated green leafy vegetables.

3. Decrease meat and fish intake and try to avoid yeast products.

4. Increase barley, bran, corn, rye, soy, oats, brown rice, avocado, banana, Lima beans, potato.

5. Reduce coffee, tea, cocoa, spinach, cranberry, and nuts.

Reflexology and kidney stones

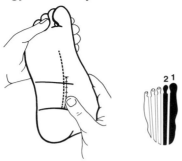

Right Foot: Bladder/ureter tube – medial top support. ZONES 1 & 2
- Supporting the right foot at the top with your left hand, work on and over the bladder area with the right thumb.
- Proceed up the medial side of the ligament line to work out the ureter tube.

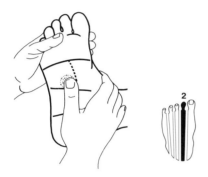

Right Foot: Kidney – top support. ZONE 2
- Supporting the right foot with your left hand and placing the right thumb on the lateral side of the ligament line, work out the area shown.
- When working on the left foot, reverse the above procedures.

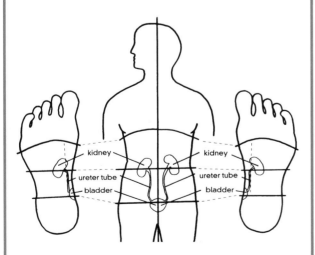

Areas relating to the Urinary System

6. Limit your intake of dairy products.

7. Aloe vera juice at levels below that which can cause a laxative effect may be useful as a preventative measure and to reduce the size of the stone during an attack.

An Interesting Case History

A patient of mine came to try to find some relief from his recurring problem of producing kidney stones.

The patient concerned was a man in his fifties who had had episodes of kidney stones for many years which caused him excruciating pain as they were released from the kidney.

The usual treatment was Pethidine to relieve the pain and just wait for the stone to pass. His kidneys were badly scarred after so many episodes.

After the first reflexology treatment he telephoned the next day to report that just six hours after his treatment he had passed a kidney stone, but the remarkable thing was that there was no severe pain, only discomfort in his low back.

Every time the patient had a treatment, exactly the same procedure occurred, a kidney stone was passed between six to eight hours following treatment. The stones were collected in a jar and taken to the hospital where the incident was reported and the consultant did actually listen and agreed that this had happened on every occasion after a reflexology treatment. That was proof enough that this 'peculiar treatment' as he called it, must have some effect.

Unfortunately, although reflexology got rid of the stones and the patient was saved the painful episodes, the stones still kept forming.

Maybe if I had known that the causes of the stones could be dietary or mineral deficiency, I would have been able to put my patient on the right path to a freedom from the problem altogether.

However, that was a long time ago, twenty years in fact, and a *'lot of water has passed under the bridge since then'*.

CHAPTER 14

Caesarian operations

When is an operation not an operation? When it is a section!

It is only recently that Caesarean operations have become commonplace. Earlier this century Caesarean operations were used as a last resort in an attempt to save the baby, usually after the mother had died.

Fifty years ago mothers were likely to die as the result of wound infections, haemorrhage or thrombosis. Today, with improved surgical techniques and better anaesthesia, a wide range of antibiotics and blood transfusions, this operation does not carry the risk factor of the past.

When is this surgery necessary?

1. If the placenta is lying in a low position in the uterus, frequently at the exit of the birth canal. In this case the pressure of the baby on the placenta once labour has got under way would cause a massive haemorrhage.

2. When the baby's head is too large to fit in the pelvic cavity. This often happens when a woman is 5ft in height and has a shoe size of four or smaller. There is an even greater risk of a Caesarean if the baby's father is a tall man, when the likelihood of a large baby would be great.

3. If the baby is in a transverse position.

4. If the woman has pre-eclampsia.

5. If the cord is prolapsed.

6. If there is kidney disease present in the woman.

7. If there are twins lying in an awkward position

8. Breech presentation.

Many Consultants still have a 'once a Caesarean delivery always a Caesarean' policy, which is unfortunate, for many women could go on to deliver a baby normally.

Resulting distress

A Caesarean operation is a major surgical intervention which ever way you look at it. Many women are left with an increased number of physical and emotional problems to deal with, as well as dealing with a new baby and maybe other children in the family as well.

The distress ranges from insomnia, constipation, backache, depression and haemorrhoids to trouble-some flatulence. Some mothers feel deprived at not being able to have experienced a natural delivery.

There may be wound infection and damage to internal organs resulting in adhesions and fistulas which can compromise health and subsequent pregnancies.

Apart from the disadvantages to the mother, the baby is also affected. Stress hormones known as catecholamines released during the hours of labour, trigger the baby's lungs to begin drying out in readiness for life in an airy environment. Not only do these hormones affect the respiratory system, they also stimulate the liver, kidneys and digestive system to function independently. A Caesarean section deprives the baby of this important preparation for life out of the womb.

It is thought that far too many Caesareans are being performed all over the world without any real benefit to mother and baby. There are many areas of concern regarding the rising statistics of Caesarean sections being performed. Chief among these is doctors' fears of litigation, should they not intervene soon enough in a difficult labour.

Exercises in pregnancy

Many of the problems of birthing today are due to the fact that women are not so physical as they were, say forty years ago. A marvellous exercise for the pregnant woman is scrubbing a floor on hands and knees; a perfect way to encourage the baby into the correct position in the pelvis.

Women walked many miles most days fifty years ago; walking is considered the best exercise for the pregnant woman and should be encouraged right into the end of the first stage of labour.

Statistics tell us that women who walk, stand or sit upright during labour have shorter labours, use less pain relief and feel far more in control than those who are encouraged to deliver in a lying position.

Midwife relationship

The relationship a woman has with her midwife is of supreme importance. Studies show that one-to-one midwifery care from the beginning to the end of your pregnancy cuts the average length of labour by half. The more confident and familiar a woman is with her midwife, the greater confidence a woman will have with herself.

CHAPTER 15

Positive answers to depression & addiction

What is Depression?

It is a feeling of gloom and doom that permeates the mind and affects bodily functions.

Most of us have our 'off days'. We may suddenly awaken feeling tired and 'out of sorts'. Everything and anything annoys us. We are near to tears and find it difficult to concentrate. Life is full of difficulties and sometimes suffering: the result, understandably, can be depression.

Addictions

Like animals, human beings learn that they can relieve their suffering by eating, drinking and inhaling or ingesting substances, or behaving in other pleasure inducing ways. Some of these pleasurable addictions have been around for a long time and are socially acceptable, like alcohol and tobacco. All these substances can easily become addictive and make demands on the body. Some are relatively harmless: some addictions can kill you. The alternative to sinking into a depression is just as dangerous for your wellbeing.

Positive effects of nutrition

In the last few decades the science of nutrition has discovered that many nutrients can not only replace what is lost, but can be a positive influence on our state, reducing depression and the desire for dangerous addictive substances.

The hormonal system, the brain and its chemical messengers or neuro-transmitters are the main sites of action. Three related hormone/neurotransmitters are known to be important in the response to stress and mood: adrenaline, noradrenaline and dopamine.

It is dopamine that is considered most closely allied with the brain's response to pleasure. For example when rats eat, become sexually aroused or learn an action that rewards them with cocaine, their dopamine levels increase.

If dopamine is important in depression and addiction then what is the precursor in the brain?

It turns out to be a normal fraction of dietary protein, an amino acid called tyrosine, found in animal and vegetable protein foods.

In experiments in the sixties, tyrosine levels in rats were found to be depleted during stress. But rats receiving extra tyrosine showed neither stress-induced depletion of noradrenaline, nor depressed behaviour.

Laying up stores of these neurotransmitters could help us to cope with stress, suffering and depression.

Tyrosine is also a precursor of thyroid hormones and by normalising the thyroid, energy levels, appetite and mood can be stabilised.

In 1980, Dr. A. K. Gelenberg at Harvard Medical School treated depressed and drug resistant patients with large doses of tyrosine and noted significant improvement. Later, similar results were found with lower doses.

Since sex drive is also affected by dopamine Dr. Carl Pfeiffer concluded, on the basis of clinical and experimental experience that L-tyrosine may decrease adrenal hyperactivity to stress, decrease appetite and stimulate sex drive.

Reports of problems with large amounts of extra tyrosine include some schizophrenics, patients on 'monomine oxidase inhibitors' and those suffering headaches after taking it. According to Dr. Pfeiffer toxicity is rare or almost nonexistent in tyrosine therapy.

Other amino acids can be very useful in balancing out depression and addiction. For example L-glutamine is normally highly concentrated in the brain where it can affect the amount of other neuro-transmitters produced but perhaps even more important, it serves as an alternative fuel.

Lack of energy in the brain

Lack of energy in the brain could be a central feature of the depression/addiction cycle because the brain is so sensitive to blood sugar levels, and experiments since the sixties have found glutamine to be effective at reducing alcoholism and other addictions.

Nutrition is certainly not the whole answer to depression and addiction but it can provide a very sound basis for a natural state of wellbeing that encourages recovery from these universal problems.

CHAPTER 16

What do you know about homeopathy?

The principle of homeopathy was known to Hippocrates the 5th century Greek physician and to the Swiss Alchemist Paracelsus in the 16th century, both of whom recognised the role of nature as the curer of diseases.

'Let like be treated with like'

In the 16th and 17th centuries the principle Simila Sililibus Curentor – 'let like be treated with like' – was often mentioned by physicians, but homeopathy as it is practised today owes its establishment to one person, Dr. Samuel Hahnemann, the great German physician, scholar and chemist who, in the late 18th and early 19th centuries, was appalled by the existing medical practices which he believed often did more harm than good.

Hahnemann sought a method which would be safe, gentle and effective. He believed that human beings have a capacity for healing themselves and that the symptoms of disease reflect the individual's struggle to overcome the illness.

Thus the homeopath's task must be to discover and, if possible, remove the cause of the trouble and to stimulate the body's natural healing power.

In his experiments, Hahnemann found that remedies obtained from animal, vegetable, mineral and, more rarely, biological materials were effective in extreme dilutions. This was especially apparent in the case of poisons which often produced symptoms similar to those of certain illnesses and which, in very dilute doses, suggested themselves as remedies on the 'like cure like' principle.

Over a long period Hahnemann and his followers took small doses of various reputedly poisonous substances, carefully noting the symptoms they produced. These were called 'provings'.

Subsequently patients suffering from similar symptoms were treated with these substances. The results were usually encouraging and often remarkable.

Hahnemann then worked to establish the smallest effective dose for he realized that this was the best way to avoid side effects. In so doing he also found that the more the remedy was diluted, the more effective it became. By close observation and careful experiment he established the three principles of homeopathy:

1. A medicine which in large doses produces the symptoms of a disease will in small doses cure that disease.
2. By extreme dilution, the medicine's curative properties are enhanced and all the poisonous or undesirable side effects are lost.
3. Homeopathic medicines are prescribed individually by the study of the whole person, according to basic temperament and responses.

The homeopathic practitioner will take a detailed case history, and this will not just be based on medical information. He will need to know all about you, how you react to situations; do you feel better in the spring or winter? Would you consider yourself as a 'chilly individual'?

Do you prefer sweet foods to salty tastes? Do you sleep well before midnight? Do you rise early? Therefore, would you consider yourself to be a 'morning person'? Maybe you prefer to go to bed well after midnight and do not really get going until after lunch! Do you suffer from headaches? Do you get depressed easily, and so on.

All these individual reactions plus your medical history must be considered before the homeopath prescribes a suitable potency. Therefore it is the skill of the homeopath in selecting the correct homeopathic potency that is vital in getting a good result.

> *'A smile costs nothing at all but gives much. It creates happiness in the home and fosters goodwill in business. It is Nature's best antidote for trouble.'*

CHAPTER 17

Rheumatism and arthritis

Rheumatic aches and pains in our joints and inflammatory conditions in our knees, hips, spines and ankles are very common situations which most doctors treat in their surgeries day in and day out. In fact, about 20 million people in the UK suffer from a rheumatic complaint.

What is the difference?

Rheumatism affects the ligaments and muscles but does not affect bony joints. Arthritis on the other hand is severe inflammation of one or several joints, causing pain, heat in the area, and swelling of the joint which severely affects mobility.

Eventually the joint deteriorates and becomes stiff and is difficult to use – there may be nobbly swellings on fingers and toes resulting in quite severe deformities.

Sometimes arthritis occurs in a joint that has been subjected to damage by a fall or, worse still, a road accident where there has been a break or fracture of a limb which causes crystals to be deposited in the joint lining.

Doctors usually prescribe pain killing and anti-inflammatory drugs which do give some relief but can play havoc with the digestive system. Many people complain of quite severe stomach ache and an unpleasant feeling of sickness, and sometimes the bowel becomes affected either by episodes of diarrhoea or constipation.

Spondylosis – slipped disc

The spinal column extends from the base of the skull to the bottom of the buttocks and consists of more than 30 separate bones called vertebrae, which really resemble 'cotton reels on a rope'. The spine is extremely flexible and allows us to bend forwards, backwards, and from side to side. The vertebrae in the lumbar spine are large and strong, which is very necessary as they support the pelvis and hip, and must also be strong enough to support the pelvis when it contains a nine or ten pound baby.

There are spongy discs that separate each vertebrae, called intervertebral discs. They have a fibrous outer covering and a jellylike inner. As we age the discs become thinner, that is why old people tend to

'shrink'! Each disc creates a separation from the bony vertebrae: they stop the discs having contact with each other. The spinal cord runs through a channel made up of the vertebrae.

The spine is very susceptible to mechanical problems such as a prolapsed or slipped disc. As the fibrous discs narrow as we get older, the spine automatically loses its elasticity and sometimes bony spurs develop on the vertebrae or along the edge of the degenerating discs which can press on various sensitive nerves and cause pain.

When pressure on the disc becomes just 'too much' because of strain on the spine, sometimes caused by excessive obesity particularly in males who may have a very large bulging abdominal area which places extreme strain on the lumbar spine, or because of the ageing process generally, pressure may cause some of the jelly-like substance in the disc to squeeze out through a weakened spot in the outer fibrous layer of the disc. This is known as a prolapsed or slipped disc.

Why some people suffer from arthritic and rheumatic diseases quite early in life and others go on to old age without even a stiffened joint is puzzling.

We do know that a certain type of arthritis is due to excessive uric acid in the blood. Arthritis of a single joint can raise a suspicion of tuberculosis, or a reaction to a severe throat or ear infection.

When there is infection in the blood stream, whether affecting the ear, nose or throat, the overload of toxicity in the body can settle in the joints.

Many chronic sufferers say that their aches and pains are worse in cold damp weather.

It is vital to keep the body moving, some form of exercise is really a must if you want to retain some sort of mobility. Swimming is ideal as the body is well supported and it will be easy to move the limbs about in water. Massage to the stiffened areas can be relieving.

There is no doubt that a stressful situation in your life can bring on an episode of arthritis. Bereavement, redundancy, a crisis in the family, destructive angry feelings about a situation or an individual that have not been dealt with are 'poisonous to the body'.

Some sufferers have found that removing all citric fruits from their diet has proved beneficial.

What you should avoid in particular is sugar. Sugar is deadly, white and poisonous: it has no food value whatsoever and has a very acidic effect on our blood. Most brown sugar is just white sugar, coloured, unless you get a rich dark brown sugar with added molasses. If you really can't do without some extra sweetening, then choose molasses which also has a good iron content and brown sugar with molasses, obtainable from your health food shop, will also help the iron content in your blood, which ultimately will make you feel more energised.

Those suffering from arthritis or rheumatism who have taken anti-inflammatory and pain relieving drugs for many years usually have some inflammation in the stomach, or, worse still, ulceration from which there is quite likely to have been some bleeding. Anaemia is therefore very common in arthritic and rheumatic sufferers.

Salt is another product to be avoided like the plague. Salt creates a stiffness in the joints.

Make sure that your bowel actions are regular, again pain killing and anti-inflammatory drugs can cause constipation. The longer toxins are retained in the bowel, the more toxic your body will become. When there is an overload of toxins in the body, the 'junk' has to go somewhere. If it cannot be eliminated through the bowel, or skin, Nature will use the joints as a 'safety valve' and deposit her wastes in the joints.

A Case History The reflexology approach

Malcolm was 40 years of age when he came to my surgery. He looked like an old man, hunched over, with obvious severe swellings in his hands, knees and feet. He said he suffered from arthritis which also affected his spine.

He had been taking paracetamol and anti-inflammatory drugs for the last five years. On three occasions, when he had been confined to bed because of such severe pain in his limbs, he had taken a short course of steroids.

His life was very restricted, his mental attitude generally was gloomy, which was to be expected. He worked in an office and was just able to cope with his job but, as he said, he could not see himself being able to work to retirement age.

Malcolm was married with two sons, one was 10 and the other 12. He did not mention much about his relationship with his wife, and apart from his job and seeing relatives from time to time, he did not seem to have any recreational activities. He said that he was so exhausted by the time he got home from work that he usually went to bed about 9.30.

His feet told a very sad story. The reactions in the reflexes in his big toe, the pituitary and hypothalamus were severe, a sign I thought of a total imbalance in his body.

There really were very few areas in his feet that did not reveal a sensitivity. The cervical and lumbar spine in particular were acutely reactive, his stomach and intestinal reflexes were so sensitive to even the slightest pressure. The spleen, liver, solar plexus, the knees on both feet, in fact the only areas that did not react were his lungs and heart. Where did one start here! I was concerned that he was likely to have quite a strong reaction after the reflexology treatment.

Malcolm was not very convinced about the benefits of reflexology, as he said, "a colleague at work has been trying to encourage me to try some reflexology treatments". Evidently his colleague had been to me for his migraine attacks and had responded very well. He found it hard to accept that there could be a link in the feet that could help his body!

Malcolm's diet was poor: lots of coffee with white sugar, cornflakes with sugar for breakfast, white bread sandwiches for his lunch, normally filled with cheese, sometimes an apple, and mostly meat with potatoes and vegetables and always 'a pudding with custard or ice cream'. He had never taken a vitamin in his life, and did not drink water. He drank alcohol occasionally.

I really thought that he would only have the one treatment and that would be that, there were so many changes that he would have to make in his life in order to receive some relief.

Malcolm found the treatment very 'uncomfortable' although I used the lightest of pressure. I gave him some 'life changes' to consider, in particular a better diet to stop the white sugar and salt. To start drinking water to try and encourage the body to flush out the toxins, cod liver oil tablets and garlic as an aid to help detoxify and break down the inflammatory state he was in – more fruit and vegetables.

Malcolm rang me the next day, which I was pleased about, although surprised. He said he felt very ill, had a raised angry rash all over his body, had been sick, definitely had a temperature and was unable to go to work because of his frequent bowel actions. I explained that this was a 'healing crisis.' And although it was unpleasant for him, it was good news, as firstly it reassured him that reflexology really did work and secondly the body was detoxifying.

As Malcolm was in bed, I encouraged him to use this opportunity to fast on 'grapes and spring water' for a couple of days. Grapes are a healing fruit, the pips must be eaten as they are a great stimulation to the bowel, and then I advised that he drink just as much water as he could.

The reaction continued for three days, it lessened in severity by the third day, but on the fourth day Malcolm telephoned asking if he could come back for another appointment earlier than had been planned.

A different person walked in this time, far more upright, he had lost his grey pallor, and said that he had been able to bend down and tie up his shoes for the first time in years, and there was generally a lessening of pain and more mobility in all his joints. He was amazed that this improvement could be obtained by just working on his feet.

To cut a very long story short, Malcolm became a very committed patient, attended for regular reflexology treatments for three months, and made great efforts to change his lifestyle.

He regained most of his mobility apart from occasional pains in his lumbar spine, came off all his drugs and started going to the gym. He had a smile on his face and his tension had reduced.

After the three months of consistent treatment he decided to come monthly and it was not until I had been treating him for six months that the 'real story behind the face was revealed'.

He had been in a frustrating unhappy marriage for years, his wife was a cold, very house-proud woman, and they had grown apart years ago, in fact had agreed to stay together for the sake of their sons. He said that the tensions in the house were 'inflammatory' and he felt sure that this situation was the trigger factor in the commencement of his arthritis.

All this happened a long time ago, ten years in fact. Malcolm eventually divorced his wife and remarried and as he told me 'I have found my soul-mate'.

And his arthritis? Oh, that's a thing of the past! He is 50 now and walks with a spring in his step and a smile on his face. Reflexology and love can conquer everything!

Reflexology: areas of sensitivity

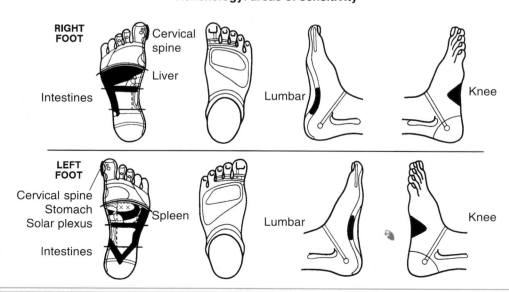

CHAPTER 18

Holistic care during pregnancy

Pregnancy is a very special time in a woman's life. It is a maturation of a very basic female instinct to house, give birth to and nurture a child. Every woman wants to have a baby with optimum health, intelligence and immunity to disease. We want our baby to reach its full potential in life.

Whether we like it or not, we do tend to pass on our genetic strengths and weaknesses to our children (allergies in particular): we need therefore to get our bodies in tip top condition before conception to give the baby the best possible start.

Cleansing the body

As both parents are involved in creating a baby it is necessary to eliminate all old toxins and drug deposits that can be stored in the tissues for many years.

Getting rid of all your aluminium cookware and stopping smoking and drinking alcohol for at least three months before you conceive will help your body to start eliminating aluminium and cadmium.

The chemical residue produced by cigarette smoking is extremely harmful and poses many risks whichever parent is involved. Smoking can damage and mutate sperm and babies have lower birth weights and increased risk of cot deaths than the children of nonsmokers and tea-totallers. The children of smokers also have a high rate of respiratory illness. A hair mineral analysis will show mineral imbalances and levels of toxic metals which should be corrected before conception.

It is in this preconception phase that vitamin and mineral supplementation for both men and women should start.

Detoxification

There are various ways to detoxify but a fruit fast is a great way to start. It is an ideal way to cleanse your whole body. You can fast for one day each week, or three days in a row, eating only one type of fruit per day. Fasting on water alone is too severe for those who have not fasted before and it would be best to consult an experienced practitioner if you intend to do this for more than a day or two.

Take vitamin C when fasting, as it helps to speed up the cleansing process.

Do not fast if you are pregnant or a diabetic.

When you have been on a fast do not suddenly return to a normal way of eating. This acts as rather a 'shock' to the body and can undo all the good work that has already been done.

Apples purify the blood and grapes are a good detoxifier. If you buy grapes that contain pips, eat the pips as well as they are excellent in stimulating the functioning of the bowel.

Eat your way back to a normal diet by reintroducing vegetables, nuts and seeds at a rate of one new food each day, include sunflower, sesame, pumpkin and almonds which are especially good. You do not need to eat large quantities of meat or fish in order to have a nutritious diet.

Other useful ideas are to use fresh vegetables rather than frozen and

steam rather than boil: grill, microwave or roast – forget the frying pan: eat as much raw salad, vegetables and fruit as possible and if you get the chance to buy organic fruit and vegetables or can spare a space in the garden to grow your own, then do so.

Vitamin C, zinc and vitamin E, are all essential ingredients needed for a healthy mother and a healthy baby.

Everything you eat and drink is constructing your baby's body and mind through the placenta, which works in a very similar way to the liver. A foetus is very sensitive to toxic substances and this includes toxins in foods, so therefore avoid refined food including pre-packaged, tinned and prepared foods. Don't fill up on junk foods. Eat dried apricots or sun-dried banana if you constantly crave something sweet.

It is proteins and calories generally that are crucial in the development of the baby. White flour and white sugar products have no nutritional value what-soever, in fact sugar is a white poison. I always say it is 'deadly, white and addictive'.

Pregnant mothers need iron, and silicon. Good sources are straw-berries, celery, carrots, pineapples and spinach. Silicon is found in whole grains, oats, barley, sprouted seeds, especially alfalfa and seaweed.

Pregnancy requires large quantities of iron which the foetus demands, particularly in the later stages of pregnancy. Coffee, tea and chocolate all inhibit iron absorption and so many young women who consume vast quantities of coffee, tea and chocolate, and who are then maybe suffering from heavy menstrual periods, are very deficient in iron content before they become pregnant. You do not need to take iron tablets, or eat quantities of liver. Seaweed and chlorella, plus pumpkin seeds, millet, sunflower seeds, black beans and molasses are very high in iron content. Molasses in particular is a wonderful source of iron, take a tablespoonful of it in hot water as a drink if you find the strong flavour unacceptable.

Do pregnant women need lots of milk?

We are told that it is the best form of calcium, this information is not actually true. When milk is heated to about 150 degrees Fahrenheit one third of its calcium is destroyed along with all the natural enzymes. Milk is also very mucus-forming in the gut, which prevents absorption of other beneficial nutrients.

As we reach puberty we generally become less tolerant to dairy products as we gradually stop producing the enzyme rennin which coagulates the milk for digestion. Lactase, an enzyme which digests the milk sugar lactose, also declines from childhood. Goats milk and goats yogurt are generally more easily digested. Calcium can be obtained from low fat live yogurt, almonds, hazelnuts, brazil nuts, sesame and sunflower seeds.

Most of us have heard of the need for folic acid during pregnancy approximately 0.8mg (800mcg) daily. Low levels have been related to neural tube defects such as spina bifida. Lambs liver contains large quantities of folic acid together with wheatgerm, avocado and asparagus.

It is as important to have a nutritious diet before you conceive as it is when you are actually pregnant. The most vital time in the life of the foetus is from the moment of conception until the first six weeks. At this time few women even know that they are pregnant.

Avoid chemicals and drugs

If you are anticipating conception it is really much safer not to use the contraceptive pill for at least six months before you plan to conceive, so another form of contraception will be necessary.

It does take your body several months to rebalance the side effects and remove the drug deposits from your body. The Pill also affects mineral and vitamin balances. Copper levels are raised whilst on the pill whilst zinc levels become very low. A deficiency of zinc is often the cause for postnatal blues, not the hormones adjusting, as is commonly believed. In fact, daily doses of zinc for just a three week period have resulted in

---

Complementary therapies and pregnancy

There is no doubt that reflexology offers some good support to the pregnant mother, helps digestion, and if backache becomes a problem in the later stages of pregnancy some reflexology treatments will take away the discomfort.

Aromatherapy using certain very specific oils will aid relaxation, raise energy levels and balance the body. However do be sure to consult a well qualified aromatherapist as there are certain oils that are not recommended to be used during pregnancy. Yoga, swimming and walking are all to be recommended as a good form of exercise.

If you are concerned about stretch marks on your abdomen and thighs, use some vitamin E cream; also massage some into the perineum daily which will soften and make the whole area more elastic.

Where you choose to give birth will determine whether or not you can have the comfort of some aromatherapy or reflexology during the early part of labour.

If you can, ask your practitioner to work on the low spinal reflexes. This can be achieved if you are sitting or even lying on your side. If reflexology is your chosen therapy, ask your practitioner to concentrate on working on the endocrine system, the uterus and the whole of the spinal area. This will encourage good nerve impulse to all the hard-working muscles that are involved when giving birth.

Remember, pregnancy is a very natural event, and so is childbirth. Women have been giving birth since the world began. Unfortunately, today, the whole event, if the birth takes place in a hospital, is so clinical and technical that many women have reported that they felt as if they were 'robots' wired up to a series of machines.

A home birth is a far more enjoyable experience, but, of course, there are situations that make a hospital birth best and safest for the mother and the baby too.

almost miraculous results in the treatment of postnatal depression.

Try not to take any drugs: aspirin, antacids and cough mixtures are believed to have caused birth defects.

We hear much about the hazards of mercury fillings for pregnant women: amalgam fillings (silver) contain approximately 50 per cent mercury which is a very poisonous mineral. Mercury is capable of passing through the placenta to the baby and has been linked to miscarriages and birth defects.

Such fillings are already banned for pregnant women in many parts of the world, so if you need a filling have a white one.

Exercise

Start doing some regular exercise now, it aids detoxification and your physical fitness is going to be very important over the next nine months.

Yoga, walking and swimming are all very good.

Did you know?
Fatigue

There are many causes for fatigue, and high on the list are emotional worries which 'burn out' one's energy levels. Other causes of fatigue are lack of sleep, inadequate diet, long term dieting, anaemia and ME.

Any one or more of these factors can deplete the body of nutrients at a time when the body's requirements for certain nutrients is high.

Diet and Lifestyle

Eat plenty of fresh vegetables and fruit, protein including fish or vegetarian alternatives, and carbohydrates such as pasta, potatoes and rice to provide a steady energy supply.

It is also important to eat small regular meals which can help to maintain constant blood sugar levels.

CHAPTER 19

Stories the feet do tell – Migraine

What is migraine?

Not, as is commonly thought, a severe headache, but a severe throbbing pain always beginning and often remaining on one side of the head, and usually clustering around the eye.

Nausea often accompanies migraine with severe attacks of vomiting which although disturbing often reduces the head pain.

Many people suffer auras before the onset of pain, these last a few minutes and include bright spots or flashing lights which disturb vision.

Numbness and tingling on one side of the body are not uncommon and in severe cases sufferers have been known to temporarily lose the use of a limb or limbs, again usually on one side of the body, with symptoms similar to a stroke.

Attacks normally commence upon waking and can continue from four hours to three days and can occur several times a month.

Migraine is surprisingly common, affecting approximately 30 per cent of women and 20 per cent of men.

Those with a predisposition to the condition usually manifest symptoms, not necessarily head pain, but a tendency to suffer from colic, periodic abdominal pains and vomiting, dizziness, and be inclined to motion sickness.

More than half of the sufferers have a family history of the illness, reaching its peak in the thirty-five to forty age group and then gradually declining in severity.

Arterial constriction causing inadequate blood supply to the brain is said to be a contributing factor. Research into the subject has found that there is a restriction in the blood supply to the brain during the warning stage, with a change to an increase in the blood supply during the attack.

Some migraine sufferers have a tendency to faint easily when standing for too long, and thoughts as to the possibility of a defect in the vascular system still arises.

A further consideration is that the nervous system plays a role changing the constriction and relaxation of the arteries, so stress is a major contributing factor.

Migraine and the menopause

You may have found that your migraine abated when you reached your forties only to return again during the menopause.

The reason for this return is the fluctuations in oestrogen at this time of life, when the ovaries are still being encouraged to produce ovum, the rush of oestrogen which gives us a 'hot flush' not only affects our hormonal system but it also increases the fluid levels in the brain. These combined effects can trigger more attacks of migraine.

Food allergy and food intolerance

There is little doubt that food allergy is the major cause of migraine headaches, in fact it has been estimated that 85 per cent of migraine is food related. By the removal and, even more importantly, the detection of intolerant foods many sufferers have found that their migraine has either disappeared or reduced in its severity.

The liver in particular plays a vital role in allergy, being totally involved in detoxification. Sometimes it becomes heavily burden by toxic substances.

In particular, alcohol, caffeine, chocolate and cheese are to be regarded as suspicious when deciding which foods to eliminate. These particular foods contain vasoactive amines which cause vaso-constriction, apart from the work needed by the liver in detoxifying.

Some people have a weakness in the liver and this is frequently an hereditary factor. Other causes could be hepatitis which has caused some residual liver damage. Therefore, if the weakness is in the liver, this is the main area to concentrate upon when using reflexology as a support therapy. If we can encourage detoxification of the liver as the first port of call, the results may well be very gratifying.

Healing of any part of the body needs a clean start: it is not possible to heal over a toxic condition without frequent eruptions such as another migraine attack. The drugs used to control migraine, the most common of which is ergotamine, all have their final resting place in the liver, and are not without many unpleasant side effects, causing yet more toxins to accumulate and more stress on an already weakened organ.

The role of the liver

The liver has so many amazing functions, the Chinese refer to it as the organ of 'heat' and it does have such a vital blood supply, producing bodily heat, storage and production of vitamins, destruction of worn red blood cells, production of bile. As the liver produces the glycogen which fuels the brain, it is often referred to as 'the butler to the brain' – without its efficient function, death rapidly occurs.

Vitamins and minerals can help

Other than considering dietary influences when treating migraine there are many vitamin, mineral, and herbal preparations that can help.

Feverfew Many patients who had been unresponsive to orthodox medicines tried Feverfew which is now available in tablet form and found that their migraine had decreased in frequency and intensity.

Cayenne pepper Capsicum is the major pungent ingredient of hot peppers, it is thought that it benefits migraine sufferers as it does create a long lasting local anaesthetic effect to the trigeminal nerve, rather like the effect clove oil has in helping toothache.

Magnesium Migraine sufferers have been found to be deficient in the mineral magnesium, which helps the relaxation and vascularity of the arteries.

Other precipitating factors

- Food additives, especially monosodium glutamate, which is found in most Chinese and Indian dishes.
- Emotional changes, particularly intense bottled-up anger.
- Hormonal changes, e.g. menstruation, ovulation, birth control pills, exhaustion.
- Thundery weather, excessive exposure to sun.
- In the early stages of withdrawing from caffeine, drugs, etc. a migraine attack may be experienced.

Massage

Massage, particularly applied to the back and neck and high up into the scalp can be beneficial in relaxing and improving blood supply.

Did you know? Eczema

This painful and disfiguring condition of the skin is characterised by dry, thickened skin which flakes and forms blisters, and is intensely itchy.

Atopic eczema is the most common form which is largely confined to childhood.

Seborrhoeic eczema affects the scalp and face and can develop at any age.

Irritant contact dermatitis is a skin reaction caused by irritant substances such as acids, disinfectants or reaction to substances such as rubber, glue or preservatives.

Diet and Lifestyle

Sufferers are advised to avoid common external sources of irritation such as wool and synthetic fibres, rubber, nickel and the house dust mite.

Food allergy is an important factor and many eczema sufferers have received a marked improvement when they removed milk, wheat, red meat, tea, coffee, alcohol and sugar from their diet.

Useful Supplements

Evening Primrose Oil The seeds are rich in gamma-linoleic acid (GLA). Studies have shown that it possesses anti-inflammatory properties which are highly effective in reducing the irritation.

Fish oils

Again, these have anti-inflammatory and anti-allergy properties.

Multivitamin formula
– broad spectrum –
which includes zinc.

A Case History

The reflexology approach to Migraine

Terry: a sufferer of long term migraine, high cholesterol levels and chronic low back pain.

Terry was 45 when he decided to turn his life around, as he described it, and try something new and, strange as it seemed, he felt that reflexology was certainly worth a try.

His health had always been problematic. The migraine attacks he described as a 'curse' that had been with him since puberty certainly had increased during the last 20 years, and despite a variety of drugs from the doctors, which helped the attacks but did nothing to prevent them occurring, he just suffered the debilitating attacks, which occurred on average twice a month, lasting between three and four days.

They usually occurred on Friday evenings and lasted over the weekend. By the time Monday came he was usually able to go back to work, which, as he said was just as well, otherwise he would have lost his job many years ago.

His job involved hours of driving: 250 to 300 miles most days was not unusual and this obviously did not help his back condition. However, I was mystified as to why he had such a high cholesterol level. He was of slight build, a non-smoker and non-drinker with no family history of heart trouble. In fact, his older brother had a low cholesterol reading.

I am convinced that in many cases, high fat levels in the blood are due to the liver being unable to eliminate its fat levels efficiently. In cases of chronic constipation, the toxic congested bowel puts undue stress on all the other organs of elimination, the liver being the main one.

The congested bowel, I am sure, prevents the liver dumping its waste products for evacuation through the bowel so fats and toxins are retained, hence the high cholesterol level. Therefore the most important area for me to work on was the intestinal area. If we could get this area working efficiently this would leave more opportunity for the liver to release its fats and toxins.

Reflexology Treatments

The first treatment was spent explaining my findings and identifying the area that I would concentrate working upon. I anticipated that Terry would have a reaction and he did: frequent bowel actions over the next three days, a slight feeling of nausea particularly in the morning, but no associated headache.

The second treatment – More intense work on the intestine. There was no point in tackling the liver sensitivity yet, the bowel was the main cause of the trouble here.

The third treatment – Terry said that he felt quite energetic during the last week, still was having frequent bowel actions which he was amazed about, and his low back pain had been much improved.

The fourth treatment – Terry had a migraine headache which lasted just one day: the pain was less severe than usual. No sickness with this attack.

The fifth treatment – A symptom free week.

The sixth treatment – No migraine, no back pain at all, bowels still working overtime, felt much 'lighter' and energy levels were still high.

The seventh treatment We had a two week gap this time: still no migraine and no back pain.

The eighth treatment Another two week gap. Patient reported that he was symptom free.

The ninth treatment This time Terry had a one month gap. Still well and due to see the doctor for a further blood test to determine the cholesterol levels.

Analysis Terry had the result of his blood test and much to the amazement of the doctor and himself his cholesterol level had dropped dramatically. Back pain had disappeared and constipation was now a thing of the past.

My conclusion I feel that Terry's condition originated from chronic constipation which caused the liver to retain fatty lipids and toxic waste – hence the raised cholesterol level. His low back pain too was caused by constipation. A congested bowel causes extreme pressure on the lumbar spinal nerves.

Reflexology and migraine

Reflexology treatments should be given weekly until there is a change in the pattern of the migraine. There may be less severity of attacks, or a lengthening of the gaps between them. Then suggest a fortnightly treatment.

When the migraine has been absent for a month it may be time to suggest that treatment is administered approximately once in six weeks.

Many people prefer to continue with this maintenance treatment to ensure that their migraine keeps at bay.

* Apart from working on the reflex areas to the liver and intestines include the cervical spine and brain to help the vascular constriction which is very likely in most cases.

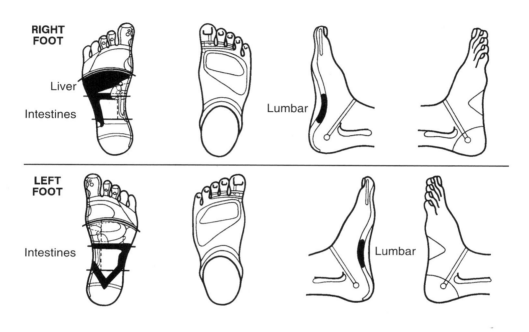

RIGHT FOOT
Liver
Intestines
Lumbar

LEFT FOOT
Intestines
Lumbar

Did you know? Asthma

Asthma is almost epidemic in proportion, particularly in children, and the more 'Westernised' we become the more asthma has increased.

Most people blame 'pollution' as the cause, but as Tokyo is the most polluted city in the world and has a very low incidence of asthma, we can hardly blame that. What we take into our stomachs is one of the main causes.

Asthma is a chronic condition affecting the lungs. It causes difficulty in breathing, tightness in the chest and a wheezy sound is usually heard.

The main cause is inflammation in the delicate mucous membrane lining of the bronchial tubes and lungs which causes constriction. The release of histamine is one of the chemicals that causes this constriction.

Allergic reaction can be the cause, in particular animal fur, dust mites or pollen, but diet is very responsible.

Diet and Lifestyle

A low salt diet is essential as this reduces the sensitivity to histamine. The allergens in cow's milk and dairy products are also often the cause. All artifical additives should be avoided like the plague, in particular aspartamine which is the artifical sweetener used in drinks, such as orange squash and cola.

Light exercise such as swimming is good, but any type of sport which is played on grass should be avoided.

Useful Supplements To help the immune system:
Multivitamin with vitamins B_6 and B_{12}
Magnesium, selenium, zinc and **vitamin C** are recommended.
Ginkgo biloba Helps to expand the small blood vessels which in turn improves oxygen supply. It is well known for its benefits in senility and other disorders where the blood supply to the brain has been reduced.

CHAPTER 20

Cravings – they can be controlled

If you have problems with being unable to survive for more than three hours without a cigarette, cup of coffee, chocolate bar or a snack, you are hooked and, like any other addiction, satisfying the craving can harm your system. Sometimes the very food which we crave has quite a severe allergic reaction on our systems.

Maybe you have known a friend or acquaintance who had very strange desires for certain foods during pregnancy.

Common cravings are coal, fizzy drinks, peanut butter and jam sandwiches, pickled onions and peanuts. These are just a few of the common everyday addictive foods that most of us succumb to at some time during our life.

We all do have cravings, but some, though less flamboyant than others, are equally as strong. Maybe cigarettes helped you during a tricky patch in your twenties; or constant coffee breaks give us an adrenaline boost which maybe allows us to work those extra hours in top gear. Many of us cannot survive a day without a bar of chocolate or a packet of crisps, so therefore we have the craving for sugar and salt.

Putting sugar in your mouth is like putting your head in the mouth of a tiger – it is a great shock to your system! It stimulates your adrenal glands to be on red alert, increases the activity of all the other hormones and makes your body believe that you are just about to 'run for your life'.

Too much sugar in your blood is a great risk to your health as your pancreas is being stimulated excessively to release the insulin to bring the level down.

A very great rise in diabetes, which, after all, is a disease that affects the pancreas, is thought to be due to the excesses of sugar intake that we eat today from the cradle to the grave.

Any organ that is stimulated to work overtime is going to eventually fail from 'exhaustion' and this is what happens to your pancreas. Faced with an ever-increasing level of sugar (on average a person consumes 100 pounds per year) your pancreas learns to respond too fast. Therefore, it does not just bring your level back to normal, it takes it way below.

How do you know if you have a low blood sugar level?

Well you are likely to feel awful, dizzy, probably anxious or sometimes depressed and hungry. So you reach for something to increase your sugar levels to make you feel less stressed, less agitated and to give you more energy – you choose a drink, a bar of chocolate, a sticky bun, or a handful of

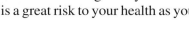

biscuits. So does that help? It does for a very short period of time, three or four minutes, but sugar calls insulin back into action so you end up with a low level again and desperate for more. You feel high as each time you hit that full blood sugar level and it is a great feeling but, unfortunately, only a very temporary one.

People who suffer frequently from low blood sugar levels suffer highs and lows of emotions. Many of the behavioural problems around in today's society, particularly those which affect the younger generation, are due to an excess of sugar in the blood stream.

Children consume high levels of sugar and several times during a day consume a chocolate bar, a cola drink or some ice cream.

Cola drinks are even more disastrous for the digestive system and, again, affect our blood sugar levels. Not only does Cola contain huge quantities of sugar, it also contains huge quantities of artificial sweeteners which again can play havoc with your mood and stress levels. Sugar is very addictive, that is why it is almost impossible to just take one chocolate from a box, most of us 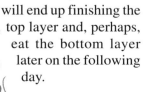 will end up finishing the top layer and, perhaps, eat the bottom layer later on the following day.

Pre-menstrual cravings

A difficult period for women when cravings are sometimes 'quite desperate' is during the menstrual cycle, i.e. pre-menstrually. I have often heard it said, 'I felt so anxious and depressed that I could have 'almost killed' for a bar of chocolate'.

During the pre-menstrual phase, when oestrogen levels soar and symptoms such as painful breasts, dragging pains in the pelvic region, swollen fingers and ankles, and a drastic change in mood occurs, the body retains fluid. High levels of oestrogen cause fluid not only to increase in the body, but also to increase in the brain.

Apart from the physical symptoms, 'Mother Nature' is also busily preparing the body for the onset of pregnancy, and stimulates the appestat centre in the brain, within the hypothalamus to increase the desire to eat and build extra fat in the body to nurture the foetus.

The same oestrogen excesses occur during the early stages of pregnancy when the fluid retained affects the inner ear and stomach, so we suffer similar feelings to 'motion sickness', and this is why we experience 'early morning sickness'.

The adrenals and blood sugar levels

We have two tiny glands in the back called the adrenals: each sits on top of a kidney, and they are responsible for raising blood sugar levels. Drink a cup of coffee, smoke a cigarette, have a packet of salty nuts, and immediately these glands are activated: blood sugar levels soar, confidence rises, pain levels decrease and we feel great for about 15 minutes. Then down we go again in the same old vicious circle. We become high then the level drops, and when the levels drop we crave even more of the substance that we have just eaten.

But you need not be in this trap forever if you understand what you are doing and can adjust your eating patterns to help you to ease your way out of your cravings.

What is the cure for low blood sugar?

The cure is to change your nutrition to foods that will nourish the level of sugar in your blood, that means finding a way to eat that keeps blood sugar levels steady and even.

If the above information is familiar, then read on further and learn the technique of eating before you are really hungry.

You should take a small meal or snack at least six times a day if you suffer from rises and falls in your blood sugar levels that make you feel unwell, uneasy and often anxious. If you have a little snack here and there and it is the *right type* of snack, it does not give your sugar levels the ability to drop to the low levels that give rise to the symptoms. Also, you need to eat good proteins and slow-releasing whole foods. This means your pancreas does not suffer the swings of levels and keeps that small gland satisfied for hours.

If we wish to keep our nervous system calm, we need vitamin C and high B-complex. These are very important; so is a good source of calcium, which is calming to the nervous system.

One interesting and helpful supplement to drinkers and those who are chocoholics or sweetaholics is L.glutamine. It is a protein food first derived from cabbage, and so far it is the only known brain fuel apart from sugar. We get the urge to drink or nibble when the brain feels it is being starved of sugar and L.glutamine can step in here when sugar levels are dropping and help to prevent the craving.

Low blood sugar levels are considered to be a 'disease'. In no way is this a disease, but it is a way of life for the western world and it is considered that at least three out of four of us suffer from this to some degree.

Starvation diets are very dangerous because they encourage us to suffer from hypoglycaemia. If you want to lose weight, reduce the size of the portions and cut out all junk, high sugar and high salt content foods; grill instead of fry, avoid sugars (white or brown, it is all the same) and all foods containing sugar. Try also to avoid foods containing chemical additives, as they are very stimulating once again to the adrenal glands. The same goes for packet soups, instant desserts and fruit squash drinks. Always eat a little before you are really hungry instead of waiting until you are desperate for food, when you will undoubtedly eat far more than is good for you.

With constant stimulation of the adrenal glands they eventually reach an inflammatory state and in order for these glands to heal themselves and consequently stop the repetition of over-reacting, we need to respect what we put into our systems.

What should we choose to eat when we crave sweet or salty food?

When you are desperate for something to eat, choose a little dried fruit or dried apricots, or unsalted nuts such as hazelnuts, almonds, sunflower or pumpkin seeds are excellent, a piece of fresh fruit such as pineapple or melon, an apple or a pear. As well as taking the 'snack', also take a glass of filtered water. Sometimes we get irritated and irrational when our fluid intake is insufficient and we are suffering, unconsciously, from a degree of dehydration which in turn increases the toxic levels in our blood. Think how you feel when you have been on a long-haul flight. Most of the symptoms you suffer are caused by dehydration, which causes a rise in the toxic levels of your blood. You will lose your sweet tooth if you stop feeding it with sugar.

Dietary plan to ease cravings

Here are some examples of a good dietary reform pattern to increase your energy levels and decrease your desire for sweet and salty food. This is a satisfactory and nourishing daily diet to help ease food cravings.

Breakfast

- Choose muesli without sugar or honey and use plain yoghurt or unsweetened apple juice to mix.
- Use raisins to satisfy a sweet taste rather than honey which, after all, is produced from sugar.
- If you make fresh fruit salad, use unsweetened apple juice to mix with the fresh fruit.
- Try to use 100 per cent wholemeal bread: it is far more nourishing and filling than white sliced bread which has little nutritional value.
- Eat fish, but do not choose smoked fish.
- Porridge cooked with raisins or dates and low fat skimmed milk is excellent, but again do not use sugar.

Mid-Morning

- If you want a snack try rye bread, banana or apple.

Lunchtime

- Eat up to 3 oz of any meat, fish or cheese. Do not eat smoked fish or smoked cheese.

Dinner

- Eat meat, fish or cheese with brown rice, jacket potato and steam, rather than boil, your vegetables.

Drinks

- Try to drink decaffeinated coffee and herb teas, and make sure your fruit juices are diluted and unsweetened.

Read your packages for additives in foodstuffs and be sure to avoid monosodium glutamate, found in many Indian and Chinese dishes, particularly the takeaway range. It is very addictive and can have quite disastrous effects on those who suffer from asthma, eczema or similar allergies.

Healthy eating begins in the high chair

We say that our children will not eat this-and-that and that they have great desires to eat large quantities of sugar and salty foods: that they will not eat vegetables, do not like rice, and choose very high fat content snacks. It is not the children who are a problem or who become addictive and have food cravings, it is the parents who instil the guidelines for a healthy eating pattern, which starts 'in the high-chair'.

CHAPTER 21

What is Reflexology?

Reflexology is a science which deals with the principle that there are reflexes in the feet that relate to all organs, functions and parts of the human body.

How does this incredible therapy work?

We hear about the energy fields, crystalline deposits in the feet, the nervous system and so on.

I have thought deeply about this and feel strongly that the reaction we get from the patient when we apply pressure to these tiny reflex points is a reaction through the nervous system – this must be true as the patient would not 'feel' if it were not associated with nerves. But continuing from there, I am sure that the reaction our patients experience is from 'memory' – 'cell memory'.

Memory in the cells

The human body is a huge cellular structure, the first division of cells which form at conception is evidence of the memory bank that cells have – they know what to do – they remember to divide and subdivide to create a human form.

I believe that the cell holds in its memory any disorder, dysfunction or damage to an organ or structure which reflects in the nerve pathway, via our feet, as a sensitivity.

It is rather like 'phantom pain'. When somebody loses a leg or foot, he often suffers extreme pain in the limb that has been amputated.

The pain can be so extreme that the patient has to be given morphine. This phantom pain can be troublesome for months and months after the amputation which causes the patient such distress.

I believe that the pain comes from the memory bank of the cell – cells rely on nerve energy to reproduce themselves, and the feet reflect the sensitivity in the reflexes via the nervous system, when there is inflammation, congestion or tension in an organ function or part.

We not only hold 'memory in the cells' of an organic nature, we also hold memory in the brain cells relating to situations of an emotional nature.

A child can be subjected to a horrifying event in his or her life which eventually he seems to have recovered from. However, years and years later, a similar situation occurs and the adult this time is subjected to a distressing situation which triggers the memory cells to react.

The adult may revert back to a psychotic state and suffer behavioural childish distresses very similar to the reaction he experienced so many years back.

This is a comparatively simple explanation to the reactions a patient experiences in his feet when pressure is applied.

About 'negative energies'

I hear so many practitioners complain of 'picking up' negative energies from patients. Why do the energies that we pick up need to be negative? Why can they not be 'positive' energies?

How do consultants and surgeons manage to work in practices and operating theatres day in and day out if they consider 'picking up' negative energies from their patients?

They have a job to do and they do it without any consideration of 'picking up' anything. They do the job which they have been trained to do.

We should do the same and, just as our local osteopath who sees probably 20 patients a day, we should treat the patient in the professional way that we have been trained. Wash our hands, and go on to do the next one, without considering whether the patient that we have before us is emitting negative reactions which are affecting us.

I personally feel more tired when I treat patients who constantly talk throughout the treatment, but I do not consider that I am picking up 'negative energies from them' – just the confusion that this creates and the need for deeper concentration from the practitioner.

Did you know? Herbal tonics

Most of us have heard about 'Yang' and 'Yin' and the following herbs are used as herbal tonics to restore balance, but are particularly valuable for men and women as restoratives for the reproductive system. These herbs are also energising and strengthening.

Astragalus strengthens and tonifies the body restoring appetite. Improves the functioning of the adrenal glands, kidneys and liver.

The Chinese have used it when treating those suffering from impotence and premature ejaculation.

Panax Ginseng has been a major Chinese remedy for centuries. The best roots come from Korea and Northern China.

One of its great benefits is as a 'stress reliever'. Increased sperm production and better immune function have been reported.

Rubi Fructus, more commonly known as the Chinese Raspberry, is said to help a 'deficiency of Yang in the kidneys' – roughly translated as a deficiency of the adrenal hormones.

The fruit is used when it is full, but green and sour with vitamin C. The raspberry has been used by herbalists to restrain urination, impotence and low back pain. As strange as it may seem, it also helps eye conditions through its action on the kidneys.

Siberian Ginseng is said to considerably increase the powers of endurance. In trials it has been demonstrated to help thousands of Russian troops to survive gruelling physical challenges, taken to the limits during the deepest days of the cold war.

It contains immuno-stimulating poly-saccharides, helps normalise appetite and stabilises blood sugar even under stress.

Damania Aphrodisiac comes from Central America and is usually taken as a pleasant 'tea'. Its main benefit is in strengthening testosterone in men. It is recommended for debilitating illnesses of the nervous system, including depression. It has a slight laxative effect.

Saw Palmetto is a low scrubby palm that grows in the south of the USA. The use of its berries comes to us from a long tradition in American Indian herbology. It was used for chronic congestion of the lungs and catarrhal states.

PROSTATE HERBS

Juniper Berries

This attractive small shrub has bright berries. Juniper is common in Britain and the whole Northern Hemisphere.

Therapeutically they have been used for the kidneys and urinary system, being diuretic and locally stimulant. The antiseptic oils are useful in prostate inflammation and infection.

Small Flowered Willow Herb

A traditional Central European remedy and widely drunk as a refreshing tea, the Willow Herb is recognisable as a common coloniser of waste ground, where its flowers turn whole areas pink.

It was particularly recommended by Maria Treben the famous Austrian herbalist. She has numerous clinical accounts of recovery from a wide range of severe infections and inflammations. This can be taken as a tea and has given relief in prostate cancer.

CHAPTER 22

All about psoriasis

Psoriasis is very common, affecting millions all around the world, and modern medicine, although sometimes able to clear the condition is unable to offer any cure. In America and the United Kingdom between two and four per cent of the population suffer from this skin disorder which affects men and women equally.

Neither is psoriasis confined to a particular race, with sufferers being found worldwide amongst all, from Caucasians to Japanese.

There is, however, a strong genetic influence on susceptibility to psoriasis with a family history in 50 per cent of all cases. 36 per cent of people suffering from the condition have at least one living family member who also suffers. The onset of the condition is also likely to occur from the late teens onwards but some two per cent of cases are affected before they reach two years of age.

The sharply bordered bright red patches, covered with overlapping silvery scales, in some cases are painful or at least itchy, but for many sufferers the main problem psoriasis lesions cause is cosmetic though nonetheless a significant problem to those with the condition.

The body areas most likely to be affected are the scalp, knees and elbows but the condition often appears on the backs of arms and legs, chest, abdomen, the soles of the feet and the palms of the hands. It can however occur anywhere on the body and is often observed on a part of the body subject to repeated trauma or injury.

What causes psoriasis?

The basic problem lies in abnormalities of the skin cells themselves but the condition is often triggered during infection, injury and times of stress.

Some drugs prescribed for hypertension (beta-blockers), manic depression (lithium) and arthritis (when treated with non-steroidal anti-inflammatory drugs) can also lead to aggravation of the condition.

Psoriasis is considered to be a classic example of a hyperproliferative condition, the outer skin layer being reproduced at a rate almost a thousand times greater than that found in normal skin. When skin condition is normal, new cells, which are constantly being formed deep in the epidermis, take up to 28 days to reach the surface. In the skin of the psoriasis sufferer

this process is completed in only a few days. This abnormal rate of production is so fast that the cells cannot be shed like normal skin. The characteristic silvery scales are the result of this rapid build up.

Research has shown that even in the apparently unaffected skin areas of sufferers, the proliferation of the cells can be up to two and a half times that of those with normal skin.

Treatment

Orthodox medicine uses steroid cortisone creams and lotions; coal tar preparations and ointments to remove and soften the scales are widely used. Practitioners of natural medicine would reject steroids used both orally or topically to treat psoriasis due to the effects their long term use has on the immune system and strength of the skin. The skin can also become dependent on the use of such drugs. Instead they would attempt to treat holistically in addition to identifying as many contributory factors as possible and trying to eliminate them.

There are a number of factors that appear to be responsible for psoriasis including poor protein digestion, excessive consumption of animal fats, impaired liver function and bowel toxaemia.

Practitioners would also wish to check stress levels and any psychological or emotional aspects and their patients' exposure to environmental pollution.

Protein digestion

When protein digestion is poor and amino acids (the building blocks of protein) are improperly absorbed in the intestines, the bacteria of the gut convert the amino acids into a toxic form known as polyamines. These toxic compounds, shown to be increased in psoriasis sufferers, slow the formation of cyclic AMP which naturally decreases cell proliferation.

The use of vitamin A and the herb goldenseal are helpful in the treatment of psoriasis as both inhibit polyamine formation. The most helpful way to ensure that polyamines are not formed is to ensure adequate protein digestion. This can be aided by taking a supplement of hydrochloric acid, essential to digestion, or pancreatic enzymes with meals.

Bowel toxaemia

This is the presence in the intestines of unfriendly

bacteria which can penetrate the gut wall and lead to increased cyclical GMP (which increases cell proliferation) in the skin cells.

It is suspected that those suffering from candida may be more prone to psoriasis. A healthy colon populated by 'friendly' bacteria is an important factor in maintaining good health generally and psoriasis sufferers, in particular, should ensure that their diet is high in fibre to maintain intestinal health.

It may be necessary to first cleanse a colon that has become toxic through a build up of impacted material and to repopulate with 'friendly' flora thus ensuring that 'unfriendly' bacteria cannot hold sway. Many people have found their health and condition greatly improved following a simple but effective colon cleansing programme.

The liver

Improving liver function can be of benefit to those suffering psoriasis. When the liver is not functioning properly it is unable to undertake one of its most basic jobs – filtering and detoxifying the blood. If toxins are allowed to build in the bloodstream the psoriasis condition will worsen.

Alcohol can impair liver function by increasing the uptake of toxins from the intestines and must be excluded from the diet of all with psoriasis. Silymarin from the milk thistle herb is a wonderful liver tonic helping to repair liver cells and reduce inflammation.

Nutrition – food and supplements

A wholefood diet low in or free from animal fat, dairy produce, salt, sugar, gluten and the avoidance of all junk food will be a useful aid in overcoming psoriasis. The ideal diet to help improve psoriasis contains:

- adequate quality protein, preferably from organic sources,
- plenty of fresh fruit, vegetables and wholegrains.
- fish, from cold waters, is doubly useful. It is an excellent source of easily digested protein and rich in the essential fatty acids. In addition it provides oils, also available as supplements, which have been shown in clinical studies to significantly improve psoriasis conditions. Psoriasis sufferers typically have abnormal essential fatty acid levels.

Useful supplements

- zinc, which is anti-inflammatory and would help to balance the serum copper /zinc ratio as sufferers are often high in copper and low in zinc,
- chromium to balance glucose and insulin sensitivity
- selenium and vitamin E to maintain glutathione peroxidase levels.

Sarsaparilla, the herb, has been shown to be effective in treating psoriasis. It mainly seems to act by binding bacterial toxins that enter through the colon into the bloodstream. It is very soothing and reduces excessive mucus.

Fasting

A number of studies have been carried out on the benefits of fasting in inflammatory conditions. The improvement shown in psoriasis patients is likely to be due to the decrease of intestinal toxins which are 'burned off' during a fast. A day's fast is always useful for general health but three days would be necessary to show an improvement in a serious case of psoriasis and should only be done under the advice and supervision of a qualified practitioner.

Stress

Stress is often a trigger for the onset of psoriasis and it can often appear around a minor injury. A high percentage (over 36 per cent of sufferers) show the initial onset of psoriasis following a particularly stressful or highly emotional period in their lives.

Often such patients find that when the stress is reduced, the psoriasis condition equally improves.

There are a small number of case histories that have been reported of patients' conditions improving when they have undergone hypnotherapy and biofeedback alone to help relieve stressful situations.

Sunshine

Many sufferers from psoriasis find their condition improves in the sunshine and indeed some make a point of taking holidays in sunny climes for this reason. There are however some types of psoriasis that worsen on exposure to sunshine.

Topical applications

It is important to keep the affected areas of skin clean and moisturised. A blend of herbs and mineral salts have helped to improve the condition, and a unique combination of natural plant oils soothes and comforts.

A shampoo combining both formulas is helpful when psoriasis appears on the scalp and there is a bath formula which lubricates the skin and protects from the harsher elements of soap and water.

Many patients have found the salts from the Dead Sea which are rich in magnesium, potassium and bromine to be very effective and sufferers from all over the world come to this lake to seek help for their condition.

Reflexology – areas to treat

The liver in particular, and the entire intestinal area, are *THE* most vital areas. Reflexology will assist in detoxifying the body which, after all, is the root cause of the disease.

Whilst not totally curable many sufferers find they remain symptom free for many years after following some of the guidelines above.

CHAPTER 23

Men, stress & hormones

Men are coming under enormous pressures. The changes that have come about in the last generation have been extreme and confusing.

They are still expected to be 'the hunter-gatherers'. They must be physically and mentally strong, emotionally grounded and sensitive. They are expected to join in with the physical caring of young children, be good sons, excellent fathers, passionate lovers and devoted husbands.

Living in today's fast track world they are now having to take more responsibility for their health which is coming under extra-ordinary attack.

Oestrogen overload

We are all being exposed to an increasing amount of pollutant oestrogenic substances in our environment, often referred to as 'xenoestrogens'. Oestrogen opposes the male hormone testosterone.

Oestrogens produced in the human body stimulate the onset of puberty which stimulates the breasts and female body shape in young women.

It is now being found that changes are taking place in young male animals and children when mothers have been exposed to toxic environmental oestrogens. The problems of undescended testicles, deformed genitals and failure for menstruation to commence are becoming increasingly common.

Male children in Puerto Rico, exposed to oestrogenic growth promoters in chickens, have also been found to be feminised.

When these oestrogenic growth promoters were given to men who wished to undergo a sex change the oestrogens induced the growth of breasts and female characteristics.

Oestrogen encourages the risk of cancers in both men and women, including prostate, testicular and ovarian cancer, both of which have tripled in the U.S. and Britain in the last thirty years.

Excess oestrogen also increases circulatory diseases particularly thrombosis, atherosclerosis and heart attacks. 55 men recently tested for artery disease were found to have a low testosterone level. Interestingly they suffered a higher degree of atherosclerosis and greater chest pain.

The reduction in male infertility may even threaten the continuation of the human race. Danish endo-crinologist Niles E. Skakkebaek analysed data from 21 countries and found in 1992 that the sperm count in normal men is half what it was in 1938.

There have been various 'scares' that the very powerful synthetic oestrogen in the Pill was likely to get into our systems via our drinking water. However, thoughts are changing and oestrogenic culprits seem to be coming from other sources – some plastics include them, also spermicides, industrial pollutants and pesticides like DDT.

We must also remember that farm animals are dosed with oestrogen to boost their body weight, so we seem to have hormones bombarding us from all directions.

Besides the hormonal link with the life of the male today, there are ever-increasing stresses in our modern lifestyles.

The body produces hormones in times of stress (e.g. cortisol corticosterone). If the body is forced to make too many stress hormones it will reach a point of exhaustion and its ability to produce male sex hormones will be reduced.

The role of good nutrition

Vitamins, minerals and enzymes are necessary for hormone balance and production. Whenever there is a nutritional lack the production of both stress and sex hormones will be affected. Stress also affects our ability to digest adequately, again a depletion of nutrients will occur.

An excess of stress hormones leads the fat levels in the blood to become raised, plus the very unfriendly LDL cholesterol. They also affect blood sugar levels and interfere with immunity.

A man under constant stress, and who eats a refined diet with a high sugar intake is likely to have high blood fats and cholesterol, exhausted adrenal glands, poor immunity and low sex hormones.

It is frightening to know that the British Isles are among the worst areas of the world for stress and diet related death in men!

Coping with stress

By reducing stress men should be able to make more of their own sex hormones.

Stress and how to cope with it is a very personal affair. Some people absolutely thrive on stress, it seems to encourage them to make the best of themselves with greater performance, but these types of people are unlikely to be stressed 'all the time'.

For others, stressful situations create either depression or chronic diseases.

However hard we try to 'duck away from stressful situations' we cannot avoid them all. We do need to take a break, take plenty of exercise, eat good organic, nutrient-high food, and find enjoyable ways to relax and enjoy life generally.

I am a great believer in vitamin C. It is the one vitamin that cannot be stored in the body and it has so many valuable properties. However, we do need to take a good dose for it to be effective.

It is excellent for healing the body, increases the body's ability to fight infection and if you suffer from broken split nails, just see what one month on vitamin C will do for you. Your nails will become so hard that it will be difficult to file them!

Vitamin C was found to encourage continuous increases in the percentage of normal sperm, sperm viability and sperm motility, suggesting that vitamin C is important for the health of the testes as an antioxidant protecting the delicate glandular tissue.

Heavy metals like lead and cadmium have adverse effects on semen and in general the entire hormonal system. The most important nutrients to clear these are vitamin C, calcium and zinc.

Zinc is thirty times more concentrated in sperm than in blood. Semen is high in both zinc and lecithin and zinc is needed in large amounts in adolescent boys. Zinc and selenium correlate with sperm density.

Prostate problems

A condition very common in older men, excellent results have been achieved with taking vitamin C and zinc. Surgery has actually been prevented as the combination of the two has reduced the swelling of the prostate in 80 per cent of older males.

Cancer of the prostate has increased dramatically in recent years, as has cancer of the ovaries. This is probably due in the main to oestrogen dominance.

How will we survive through this millennium?

There is absolutely no doubt that we will have to take more responsibility for our own health if we are to survive at all.

We shall all be living in an increasingly polluted, hostile world. Our skies and seas will be burdened with pollution, even more of our ozone layer will disappear as man produces more and more toxic chemicals, drugs and sophisticated communication systems. Robots will perform most of our household tasks.

We shall all be taking more and more drugs for the diseases which 'man has created' plus another selection of preventative drugs and vaccines as more and more 'new and even more destructive diseases' appear.

Rather than being discontented at not being able to afford the extravagances of life, simple past-times, organic foods, relaxation techniques, meditation, should become the 'luxuries'.

Maybe we will see children 'with skipping ropes' playing ball, flying a kite, tramping through the autumn leaves and throwing stones into a pond again.

Maybe children will sit and read, play the piano, paint and draw, without having to be entertained with loud music, video players, and fast track living.

Maybe these children will choose to eat natural foods, not 'chips with everything' as the general menu is today.

Maybe these children will be able to get back in touch with their own feelings and develop their intuitive powers which have been lost in the fight for more and more progress, more gain, more possessions.

These children will be 'the people of the future' and mankind will eventually 'fight to join them'.

Statistical information taken from Beyond Nutrition Press.

Did you know?
Gout

Gout is characterised by an excess of uric acid in the blood stream. People who eat a lot of red meat create excesses of this acid, so do those who consume regular 'over the top' quantities of alcohol. The uric acid crystals deposit themselves in the fingers and toes, elbows and knees and these are popular sites for the inflammation to reside.

Factors such as increasing age, obesity and poor diet increase a person's susceptibility to gout.

Diet and Lifestyle

Eliminate alcohol and refined carbohydrates since these increase uric acid production. Instead, opt for complex carbohydrates.

Include plenty of fluid in the diet to prevent the build up of crystals in the kidneys.

Follow a weight reduction programme aimed at reducing uric acid levels and preventing gout attacks.

Adopt a low purine diet by avoiding foods rich in purine such as organ meats, shellfish, meat, herrings and sardines.

Useful Supplements

To reduce inflammation:

Fish oils containing high levels of EPA and DHA.

Vitamin E and **Bromelain**

CHAPTER **24**

Lots of little tips to help you take care of yourself

Try to limit your caffeine intake

If you have around four cups of coffee or six cups of black tea per day you may be caffeine dependent. Limit your caffeine intake and avoid it completely if you suffer from insomnia or high blood pressure

Check those iron levels

If you constantly feel tired even after a good night's sleep have a check up and see if your iron levels are within acceptable limits. Maybe your liver is rather sluggish so perhaps you need to detox yourself one way or another.

Food for your hair

If your hair is lank and brittle include mineral and silicon rich foods in your diet. Such foods include oats, whole grains, yogurt, almonds, alfalfa, onions, kelp, avocado, corn and sardines.

Cleanse the alcohol away

If you have been socialising too heavily and have had too much to drink have two or three glasses of water or herbal tea when you get home. Take a vitamin C supplement that contains bioflavonoids and have a hot shower. This will help you to flush out the overload of toxins in your body.

Improve your skin's moisture level

If your skin lacks moisture, include unsaturated fats such as cold pressed olive oil, flaxseed oil sunflower oil and fish oils in your diet. Or you may prefer to take one or two capsules of salmon oil a day.

Strengthen those nails

If you have cracked and damaged nails, don't paint them with the various treatments that are around, always treat the inside to deal with 'outside' complaints. Try grains such as brown rice, more fresh vegetables and yogurt in your diet. Rub some almond oil into your cuticles each night and take a calcium-magnesium supplement daily until the problem is resolved.

Drink enough water each day

Water nourishes our blood and cells and prevents the build up of toxic waste in our bodies. We can't survive without it. Make a conscious effort to drink water or herbal tea daily, around six to eight glasses. Record your habits for a week, as sometimes we can forget to drink at all!

For every cup of coffee, tea or alcohol you drink, have a glass of water. Water helps guard against dehydration and will flush out the toxins remaining in your system.

Foods to help with the menopause

During the menopause the level of oestrogen in a woman's body begins to decrease. To help alleviate the unpleasant symptoms of menopause, it's important to eat foods containing plant oestrogen such as soy products. Alfalfa, parsley and basil are also good. Sage tablets are excellent in controlling hot flushes.

Apple cider vinegar

If your joints grate or crack try mixing one teaspoon of apple cider vinegar in a glass of warm water. It is also helpful to relieve gout, rheumatic and arthritic pains and take it if you suffer from gravel or stones in the kidneys.

Soothe those colds and sore throats

To soothe a sore throat or cough pour one tablespoon of honey over a raw onion cut into quarters. Place in a small dish and bake in an oven for twenty minutes. While still warm, sip the honey syrup from the onion. It will either kill or cure!!

Peppermint tea

Peppermint tea with a pinch of fresh powdered or grated fresh ginger can work wonders for your digestive system, or if you suffer from nausea.

The key to longevity?

Li Chung Yun lived to be 156 years old and when asked to what he attributed his long life he answered, 'inward calm, unprocessed foods, moderate eating and plenty of exercise.

CHAPTER 25

Interesting information about steroids

Steroids are fast catching up with antibiotics as the most abused class of drugs. The discovery of steroids half a century ago was a major advance in medicine – a life-saver for President Kennedy who suffered from Addison's disease, a disease of the adrenal glands which causes insufficient hormone production.

Steroids stimulate the adrenal glands to work to their potential and a dose of steroids to those crippled with arthritis or the disabling symptoms of a severe attack of asthma, can seem like a 'miracle cure' in a short space of time. Steroids can be life-saving and have anti-inflammatory as well as anti-allergic effects.

The types of medical conditions for which they are now used are quite extensive: asthma, arthritis, back problems, eczema, ulcerative colitis and indeed all allergic reactions. Steroids do not 'cure'. They suppress your body's ability to express a normal response. The effect is immediate but, unfortunately, we are beginning to realise that there are many damaging effects after years of using them. There is no such thing as a safe dose.

Steroids and bone mineral density

As steroids are being used so readily in doctor's surgeries today, and as there is now accepted evidence that eight per cent of bone loss can occur after taking steroids for just four months, could this not be the reason for the increase in osteoporosis?

Bone mineral density has also been found to be lower in children the longer they stay on steroids and even inhaled drugs for such diseases as asthma have been found to have adverse effects on bone metabolism and adrenal function.

Steroids and the immune system

Steroids depress the immune system, leaving the patient wide open to contract all manner of diseases – the most worrying aspect of steroids is the possibility that your pituitary gland will stop producing ACTH – a hormone which regulates the adrenal glands, and is necessary to assist the body during stressful states and imperative in fighting infections.

It is essential that patients are weaned off them slowly and patients are usually guided in reducing their daily doses, this gives the adrenal glands the chance to commence making cortisone on their own again.

Steroids, juvenile arthritis and sterility

Many studies of children with juvenile arthritis who have been treated with steroids show that they suffer from growth retardation and delayed puberty and many cases of sterility in boys and girls have been caused by taking steroids.

An old doctor friend of mine says that every steroid is yet another 'nail in your coffin'. I would not go quite so far as to accept that – they are life-saving in many instances – but are we not on the treadmill of one drug which causes a problem in yet another part of the body?

Maybe the fact that we are taking steroids so regularly today for so many problems is the cause of many immune deficient diseases: osteoporosis, infertility, adrenal exhaustion and definitely hyperactivity in children.

It's the same old thing. What came first, the chicken or the egg?

Did you know?
Garlic

The potential of 'Nature's Natural Antibiotic' to help diseases of all manner has been known for centuries. Garlic should be crushed and allowed to stand for ten minutes to allow one of the powerful enzymes – allinase – to begin producing the sulphur compounds which have cancer fighting properties. Heating garlic either by frying or microwaving destroys the allinase.
Garlic has been found to be toxic to mosquitoes, aphids, cabbage butterflies, Colorado beetle larvae and houseflies.
So powerful are the effects of garlic, it is said that if you rub raw garlic on your feet you will taste it in your mouth the next morning.

**Cautionary Advice
from Ann Gillanders**

If symptoms of ill health persist, medical advice should be sought from your healthcare provider, nutritionist or dietary adviser. Regrettably the author is unable to respond to individual queries, and assess individuals' requirements.

CHAPTER 26

Evening Primrose Oil

The rapid rise in fame of Evening Primrose seems to be linked to a family of substances with a hormonal base called prostaglandins. These hold great promise to sufferers of a variety of chronic and acute diseases such as ulcers, migraine, arthritis, glaucoma, menstrual cramps, and hypertension, to name but a few.

Prostaglandins (or PGs) first aroused interest in 1930 when unexplainable effects of an unknown source were found within uterine smooth muscle. The active material in prostaglandins was found to reduce the blood pressure in some laboratory animals.

Many years passed before research revealed that prostaglandin was actually a family of compounds related to essential fatty acids. Prostaglandins are found in virtually every cell of the human body. Prostaglandins somehow seem to be involved with pain and inflammatory states of the body: they also relieve and reduce fevers. At this point the discovery of Evening Primrose Oil gained some respect and recognition.

Essential fatty acids

Prostaglandins are made from vitamin-like substances called essential fatty acids (EFAs). They are not able to be processed in the body so need to be constantly provided in the diet.

One of the most important components in making prostaglandins is linoleic acid. Because of the excessive consumption of junk foods in the 21st century way of living, an excess of the totally wrong types of fats, too much alcohol intake and the general ageing process itself, we are very deficient in the ability to convert linoleic acid into GLA.

Disorders of the immune system and inflammatory states of the body

Most diseases are the result of inflammation of one or other organ or functions of the human body, examples of which are: inflammatory bowel disease, rheumatoid arthritis and eczema. These diseases share two common features: failure of the improper function of certain lymph cells (T-suppressor lymphocytes) and an excessive production of Class 2 prostaglandins. In order to keep our immune systems under constant control we need T-suppressor lymphocyte cells. They ensure that the immune system attacks only foreign bodies and not the body's own tissues.

If these cells are defective, damage by the immune system attacking body cells frequently occurs. It is one of the major components in the case of rheumatoid arthritis, ulcerated colitis, inflammatory bowel disease and multiple sclerosis. An elevated level of Class 2 prostaglandins is also believed to be a contributory factor in local inflammations of the body.

Rheumatoid Arthritis

Beneficial effects have been achieved in taking Evening Primrose Oil for sufferers of rheumatoid arthritis. It is necessary to take the oil for at least twelve weeks before an effect is noticed. Some sufferers have found that the disease became arrested and in other patients who had a very moderate form of the condition, the oil seemed to stop the disease process completely.

Eczema and psoriasis

Eczema is one of the most common skin diseases, particularly prevalent in children under five. It causes inflammation, redness, itching and is often linked to an inability to digest cow's milk and all cow's milk related products, such as yoghurt, ice-cream, and cheeses. Evening Primrose Oil can also be rubbed on the erupted areas of eczema and psoriasis, apart from taking the doses as recommended on most packets, which can be obtained from health food shops.

Hyperactivity in young children

The Hyperactive Children's Support Group in Britain, which is an organisation with many branches, has conducted surveys of the characteristics of hyperactive children. The results of their findings strongly suggest that hyperactive children have deficiencies of EFAs, especially GLA. Experiments with Evening Primrose Oil have witnessed dramatic improvements in behaviour and function.

I can personally relate to a particular case of a young boy I was treating for hyperactivity who was so disruptive in the class that he was being threatened with expulsion and at the age of ten this was rather a bizarre action to take.

He had been under the care of the psychotherapy department in the local hospital and Social Services were very involved in the drastic effect that his behaviour was having on the whole family.

His diet left much to be desired. It consisted of a very high fat content junk-food diet, as this child evidently did not seem to like any everyday foods. Vegetables and fruit were a 'no-no', whereas pizza, chips, baked beans, sausages and large quantities of cola seemed to be the general way that the family lived!

His mother brought him to me for treatments of reflexology and although he did seem to be improved in behaviour for two or three days following his treatment, the result was generally pretty poor.

Having read-up some research papers and articles on the effects of Evening Primrose Oil and hyperactivity, I suggested to the parents that they commenced doses of Evening Primrose Oil on a daily basis combined with Reflexology treatments.

Attempts at improving the diet of the child were not very readily accepted. However, he was removed from cola, which I believe was quite a contributing factor to his overall behaviour pattern. After just two weeks on Evening Primrose Oil, reflexology and a cessation of the large quantities of cola, his behaviour pattern improved so dramatically that the parents were then called to the school, not this time with a threat of the boy's expulsion, but to say that the teacher had never seen such a dramatic and abrupt change for the better in a child's behaviour.

The young boy attended for nearly three months, with reflexology treatments being conducted on a weekly basis, and had a marked general improvement in his disturbing condition. I am sure that he would have had an even better result had he co-operated in a better eating pattern.

Most of the GLA formed in the body is rapidly converted into another substance called dihomagamma linolenic acid (DGLA, for short). DGLA can be converted into a number of compounds the most important of which is PGEI, which has

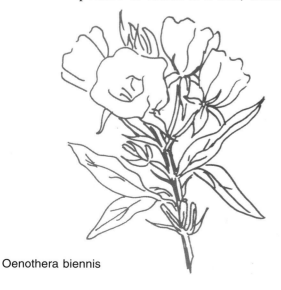

Oenothera biennis

proved itself to be a miracle molecule. It stops thrombosis, helps to open up blood vessels, relieves the constriction of pains in the chest due to angina and, most important of all, it has a slowing down effect on the speed at which cholesterol is made. It has many actions on the brain and is known to produce a sense of relaxation and well being. It should now become clear why GLA and linolenic acid are so critical.

One of the richest forms of taking in this acid is in breast milk. So breast-fed infants in their first year consume large quantities of GLA every day. Cow's milk contains only a quarter of the amount compared to human milk. This is one of the most vital differences between these two foods.

The most substantial source of GLA is in the seeds of the Evening Primrose. The benefits of the seeds were recognised by the early inhabitants of North America. American Indians used this for many years for medicinal purposes and extracts of the plants were found to have healing properties when applied to wounds and inflammations of the skin.

The Evening Primrose grows in abundance on open woody hills and fallow fields. It was one of the first plants to be exported back to Europe and was then referred to as the "king's cure all". Evening Primrose Oil is widely available and recommended in the United States and has been taken by thousands of people for all manner of inflammatory and degenerative conditions of the human body.

It has also been found to reduce the risk of thrombosis in heart disease patients and, as it also helps to lower cholesterol levels, it plays a contributory factor in arresting the production of atherosclerotic plaques. It appears, therefore, that a deficit of this oil could be related to the increase in coronary artery disease.

Hypertension and thrombosis were found to have considerably reduced as well as blood pressure and also the clotting factor of the blood, in as short a time as twelve weeks after the introduction of Evening Primrose Oil. As a preventative measure, therefore, anyone supplementing his diet with Evening Primrose Oil drastically reduces the chance of getting heart disease, and those patients who have already suffered heart attack should consider supplementing their diets with Evening Primrose Oil on a permanent daily basis.

Another factor that could block the absorption of GLA is insufficient magnesium, vitamin B_6 and zinc. We also know that radiation and viral infections have a drastic effect on the absorption of these important minerals.

If you suffer from brittle nails and dry skin, this is usually a signal that you are very deficient in Evening Primrose Oil.

Evening Primrose Oil, childbirth and pre-menstrual syndrome

One of the most advanced discoveries in the action of prostaglandins, is the ability of them to induce natural labour in women at full term. Large amounts of PGs are found during normal childbirth. Some prostaglandins are used in the form of a pessary to induce labour at the end of a normal pregnancy.

Women who suffer from a variety of pre-menstrual syndrome symptoms, such as weight gain, breast pain, irritability, depression and food binges have reported relief of both their physical and mental symptoms when taking Evening Primrose Oil. It has also been particularly beneficial in treating cystitis and inflammatory conditions of the breast.

Evening Primrose Oil is not going to be one of those 'new wonders' that will be here today and gone tomorrow. Its popularity is still rising and top research laboratories in Canada, United Kingdom, Argentina, United States and South Africa are still producing dramatic reports of the therapeutic effects of Evening Primrose Oil.

The ancient laws

So as we start this new millennium with an even further advancement into new and even more toxic drugs to control the growing list of chronic and acute diseases, maybe we should look back to the ancient laws of healing and realise that the answers to many of our 'prayers' are growing for us in the open fields.

This lowly little yellow flower is not some 'new-fangled' synthetic drug, it comes from a plant, the benevolent Evening Primrose.

CHAPTER 27

Spring clean your blood

We have millions, in fact, trillions of cells in our body that are dependent on a healthy blood stream to provide the source for all they are.

These cells divide, creating a whole new body every eleven months and the quality of their reproduction depends on a healthy daily routine, organic food and plants rich in blood purifying mineral salts and other health-giving properties.

An impure blood stream is always as a result of an imbalance and is usually accompanied with symptoms of the imbalance elsewhere in the body. Indeed, there are many conditions such as eczema, headaches, arthritis, vascular diseases and fatigue which are considered by herbalists to have their origins in the blood stream.

Elimination of waste

The organs of elimination – the liver, kidneys, bowel, lymph, skin and lungs – all share functions of blood purification which involve filtering out metabolic wastes and other poisons such as pesticides, sprays, preservatives, colouring agents, bacterial wastes, and more. Even a good diet can create toxic by-products in the body if it is eaten under stress or if it is poorly combined.

A healthy blood stream gives nourishment

A blood purifying programme is one which supports the function of the eliminative organs but it is also much more than that. A healthy blood stream is also a more efficient one. Cells are able to receive the nourishment they need to function at their best.

At its basic expression, disease begins in the cell. By providing the cells with high quality nutrient levels and facilitating efficient drainage of waste, the cell is able to work to the efficiency for which it was intended. It can then produce healthy tissue.

Herbs will help cleanse your blood

Blood purifying tonics consist of herbs that contain nutrient rich mineral salts and active principles which have a cleansing effect on the blood stream. These herbs are often bitter and contain high levels of organic minerals and trace elements essential to the cell and the environment.

Herbal remedies concentrate these elements and to some degree compensate when the diet and daily routine are not up to scratch or living conditions make it impossible. Herbs have been foods and medicines for over a million years of human existence.

Blood purifying tonics are those herbs which enhance the body's ability to cleanse itself of toxic metabolic waste. Their effect is cleansing to all body tissues.

The principle of blood purification is the single most important herbal principle in herbal medicine and its use is universal within all herbal healing systems.

CHAPTER 28

A greater understanding of the functioning of our bowels

The large intestine

The large intestine consists of the colon, rectum and anal canal. The intestinal tract is quite extensive: we have five feet of large intestine and nearly twenty-one feet of small. The large intestine acts as a waste disposal unit: the small intestine absorbs all the nutrients, vitamins, and minerals in our diet and distributes them back into our blood stream for the body to use.

The colon begins just above the right groin where it is known as the caecum and from which springs the appendix. It continues to ascend on the right side, so is known as the ascending colon, climbs to just below the ribs on the right side, then loops across to the opposite side as the transverse colon.

There is then a second sharp bend as it turns downwards as the descending colon, and makes another loop known as the sigmoid colon before joining on to the rectum. The anal canal does the last part of this job but as the canal is only 3cm or so long, this is actually the control part of the bowel that is necessary to open in order that we can pass a motion.

The gut and the throat have the same muscular fibres that create an action called peristalsis, slow-moving rhythmic muscular actions that convey foodstuffs from the point at which we swallow until the exit at the rectum.

The lining of the bowel is muscular and the hole inside the bowel called the lumen has an important lining called mucous membrane or mucosa. This lining has the difficult task of being a barrier to dangerous viruses and bacteria, and letting the good things like salts and water be transported back into the blood stream.

If there is too much water absorbed constipation is the result: too little, and you will be prone to diarrhoea.

The peristaltic action of the bowels becomes extremely active after we have eaten a meal: that is why most people feel the urge to open their bowels after a meal, usually after breakfast.

The large intestine hosts a huge amount of bacteria, normally harmless bacteria which act as scavengers, living off the undigested remnants of our food, mucus and dead cells. They are also responsible for the gas which we pass from the rectum. If you do not have sufficient bacteria in the bowel, you will be more prone to disease.

The colon is acidic, the main acid being acetic acid. It is believed that this acidity may be one of the body's defences against bacteria. Antibiotics, all pain killing drugs and steroids have quite a disastrous effect on the bowel, killing off all the active bacteria, which leaves more waste in the bowel which should have been dealt with by the active bacteria.

Death begins in the colon. All naturopaths, herbalists and the like believe that if you leave waste products in the bowel for long periods of times in a warm environment, this is an ideal putrid condition in which other types of viruses and bacteria can breed and create disease in all parts of the body.

Yes, all parts, not just diseases of the bowel, but diseases in the form of arthritis, skin conditions, bowel cancer, sinus conditions, migraine and so on.

Your bowels should open at least every day. The longer the passage of food resides in the colon the more repercussions on general health.

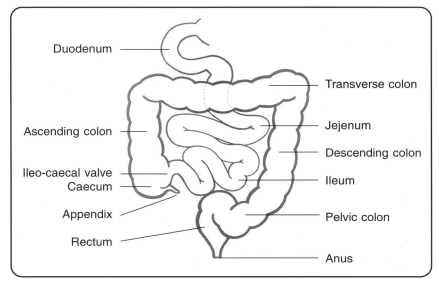

The 'feeling' intestine

The colon is probably more sensitive to emotional and psychological states than any other part of the body. Acute anxiety often creates loose stools, whilst periods away from home when your routine is changed, or travel in any form, particularly air flight, can cause constipation.

Irritable bowel syndrome is a very popular modern day condition – the stresses and strains of daily life, the hustle and bustle of clock-watching all take their toll. Constipation, excessive wind, diarrhoea, quite severe bouts of pain in the colon, all these symptoms are related to irritable bowel.

Lack of exercise causes constipation, so those who suffer from this should take steps to increase their activity if at all possible.

The intestine likes dietary fibre, its enemy is the white flour, pappy foods that we eat so much of to-day in the form of bread, cakes, biscuits, pastry, and so on. Fibre absorbs water, thus bulking out the intestine and encouraging easy evacuation of waste from our bowels.

Primitive man spent many of his waking hours actively engaged in hunting, moving his body during most of the day light hours and had little trouble with his bowels. In fact it is believed that primitive man used to squat and pass a motion after each meal. Primitive man would express his feelings readily and frequently, probably making a lot of noise as he confronted the wild boar or dug energetically for roots and shrubs.

Civilised living to-day requires us to hide our feelings, at least in public. We do give vent to how we feel at football matches, or watching our favourite horse win or lose, or maybe watching our favourite pop star perform at a special performance. Here we cry, laugh, stamp, moan, scream, or faint as the emotional experience is just too much to cope with.

Our bowels react to pent up emotional feelings and angry sensations. They object to being expected to perform in a hurry and dislike being 'delayed' when they call in urgency.

The small intestine

The small bowel is a long convoluted winding tube leading to the large intestine. The first part, known as the duodenum, is a c-shaped tube 20 – 25cm long. It encircles the pancreas, passes behind the liver in front of the right kidney and across the aorta, the body's largest artery.

The second part of the small intestine is called the jejenum. It is about 2.4m long and lies in the region just under the navel.

The reflexology approach

Now that you perhaps have a better understanding of the working of your bowels whose functions are commonly regarded as embarrassing, distasteful and often a mystery, perhaps we can understand how, by working correctly on the feet we can help most of the everyday conditions affecting the colon.

Firstly, it is essential to start working on the right foot to stimulate the caecum (the first part of the colon), treat the reflex points to the colon in the way they are situated, ascending, transverse, descending, sigmoid and then rectum.

Work out the lumbar spine (nerves arising from the spine affect the muscular contractions of the colon, the nerve centre at the base of the brain also gives signals to the colon, so the cervical spine can also play an important part.

Use your relaxation techniques freely and generously. Encourage your patient to take peppermint oil capsules, and charcoal tablets are excellent for settling the digestive system – especially beneficial in attacks of diarrhoea.

Some schools treat from left to right but this is of no advantage to the intestine. We need to work in the order that the intestine flows.

The relaxation that reflexology offers in any case will have a beneficial effect on the working of the intestines, and treating the physical part should improve the function.

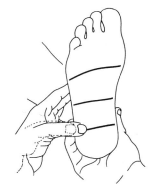

The ileo-caecal valve (right foot), zone 5, lateral - hooking out technique.

Supporting the right foot at the base of the heel with your right hand, place the left thumb on the heel line and use a 'hooking-out' procedure.

Area to sigmoid or pelvic colon, the bend (left foot) zone 3.

Supporting the left foot at the base with your left hand, place the right thumb on the mid point and work towards the medial edge.

Change direction and support the foot at the base with your right hand and work with the left thumb towards the lateral.

The third part of the small intestine, the ileum, is 3.6m long and winds down to the caecum, the first part of the colon or large bowel.

The small intestine is therefore about 6.4m long and is a good example of compact accurate design.

The inner surface of the small intestine is an even better example of good design. It has an inner surface area of about 20m² in the average adult and is therefore some ten times bigger than the total surface area of the skin. The area is enlarged by millions of tiny finger-like projections called villi – from the Latin word villus meaning 'a tuft of hair'– which protrude from the intestinal lining. Resembling a fine, velvet-like carpet these countless microscopic structures separate valuable particles such as protein, fat and sugar from waste material such as cellulose which is an indigestible ingredient, a very rough fibre found in all fruits and vegetables.

Before this happens however the partly digested food, or chyme, runs the gauntlet of the duodenum where it is bombarded by bile from the liver and digestive juices from the pancreas.

Chyme entering the duodenum from the stomach contains a large proportion of hydrochloric acid which is neutralised by bicarbonate, an alkaline substance, in pancreatic juice. This fluid contains three enzymes, lipase, trypsin and amylase which break down fats, proteins and starch into respectively small molecules ready for absorption.

Coeliac disease

People with the unpleasant condition called coeliac disease, do not have this carpet of villi. Their intestine has an unusually smooth, small surface area. Because food cannot be efficiently absorbed they show all the signs of malnutrition. Some 26,000 people are thought to have the disease in the United Kingdom alone.

This disease is often recognised in early childhood: many sufferers cannot tolerate gluten, a protein found in wheat. Gluten actually stunts the growth of villi in the intestine. Sufferers are often sickly looking, can have stunted growth, periods of diarrhoea and very poor immunity.

The Role of Reflexology

Reflexology has given very positive results in treating this condition over a long term basis – say at least three months.

Our bowels react to pent up emotional feelings, and angry sensations. They object to being expected to perform in a hurry and dislike being 'delayed' when they call in urgency. Those personalities who display high anxiety states are

Intestinal area (right foot), zones 1,2,3,4 & 5, working out the whole of the intestinal area (ascending, transverse and small intestines, buttock and base of pelvis.

Supporting the right foot at the base with your left hand, use the right thumb and work in straight lines across the foot from medial to lateral.

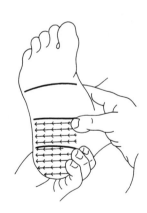

Intestinal area (right foot) zones 1,2,3,4 & 5, lateral to medial.

Supporting the right foot at the base with your right hand and using the left thumb, work in straight lines from lateral to medial.

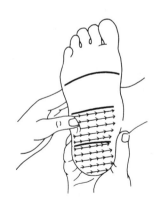

Intestinal area (left foot), zones 1,2,3,4 & 5, transverse, descending and small intestines.

Supporting the left foot in your right hand at the base and using the left thumb, work out in straight lines from medial to lateral.

Intestinal area (left foot) zones 1,2,3,4 & 5, transverse, descending and small intestines, including the buttock and back of the pelvis which are situated below the heel line.

Supporting the left foot at the base with your left hand and using the right thumb, work across in straight lines from lateral to medial.

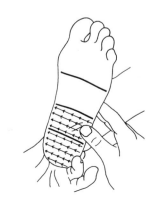

very prone to diarrhoea, whilst those who bottle up their feelings are very prone to constipation.

'Death begins in the colon'
So say all the naturopaths, herbalists and those intent on treating the body as a whole and realising that a condition in the body can be caused by problems in the intestine.

On reading many medical papers there is now evidence that it is not just inflammation or congestion in the colon generally that affects our entire body, but that certain areas of the colon affect specific parts of the body.

Civilized life means an artificial life, and civilized people living in a civilized manner and eating civilized foods cannot have a truly healthy colon.

Health and disease have their roots in the bowel and my book and chart – *Reflexology and the Intestinal Link* – will enable you to concentrate your work on specific areas of the intestine.

As an example there is a very definite link between the pituitary gland and the hypothalamus at the very base of the ascending colon, almost in line with our region for the ileo-caecal valve; a helper area for the liver is on the bend of the hepatic flexure and so on.

This is pretty advanced stuff, but it just means that you would need to incorporate into your treatment extra work on these areas to help an existing condition.

Colonic irrigation has been used for centuries. We are just beginning to find that this treatment is becoming extremely popular and has been found extremely beneficial in relieving all manner of diseases from arthritis to asthma.

It really is quite amazing to find how 'detached the world has become' in the real understanding of healing: there is just beginning to be some 'light at the end of the tunnel'.

CHAPTER 29

The facts about melatonin

Melatonin is known as the body's anti-ageing hormone but research shows it also controls disease, combats jet lag and treats sleep disorder.

Melatonin is a hormone produced in the pineal gland that is located in the centre of the brain, very near to the pituitary. It is produced mainly at night, which is why those who are shift workers can, after three or four nights at work, feel depressed, disorientated and generally unwell – the effects of melatonin deprivation.

Melatonin is used to help the effects of jet lag and to achieve a deep, restful sleep in those who suffer from insomnia.

However, there is more to melatonin than that. It shows exciting promise in the treatment of many life-threatening ailments. It slows the ageing process by fighting free radical damage and rejuvenates the immune system.

Those who are unfortunate enough to be involved in night work – doctors, nurses, engineers, the police and fire brigade to name but a few – are known to have far more time away from work with stress related illnesses. There are higher incidents of depressive illness in those who are night workers and it is an accepted fact that we reduce our lifespan by as much as seven years!

As we age we produce less and less melatonin, consequently there seems to be a link between the reduced production of melatonin and the natural ageing process.

Since melatonin is such a valuable supplement as it is involved in so many important roles, then it is recommended to be taken regularly if you are involved in shift work, or lots of long haul flights and is vital for the older population.

Research is showing that it is helpful in treating many diseases, among them hypertension, high cholesterol, AIDS, Alzheimer's disease, arthritis to name but a few. Taking melatonin in a small dose every night may actually extend your life expectancy and give you a better quality of life.

Sleep disorders
Sleep onset insomnia
Experienced by those who find it difficult to fall asleep and are fighting with their pillow until the early hours of the morning.

Sleep maintenance
Experienced by those who get to sleep and then wake a couple of hours later and have great difficulty in getting back to sleep. They usually get back to sleep at about 4 a.m. and are sound to the world at 7 a.m. In both cases the lack of sleep can cause poor memory and concentration, poor health, irritability and clumsiness.

Sleeping pills do not work long term, they lose their effectiveness after 3 – 14 days continuous use.

Melatonin is a natural and totally safe sleep inducer which occurs in our body as a hormone secreted by the pineal gland.

Tryptophan, an essential amino acid is the raw material for the material which becomes serotonin, the soothing neurotransmitter which, through enzymatic action, becomes melatonin.

Jet-lag

This is a condition caused by desynchronization of the biological clock. Man was certainly not meant to fly through the air at 550 miles per hour, crossing various time zones. Our body clock then becomes confused as to whether we are in the sleeping or waking mode.

Jet-lag can make you feel terrible and is characterised by fatigue, early waking, insomnia, headache, constipation and reduced immunity. The symptoms are worse when flying in an easterly direction and it may take as long as one day for each time zone crossed in order to fully recover. Melatonin taken in the evening (in the new time zone) will rapidly reset your biological clock and almost totally alleviate (or prevent) symptoms.

In all cases and for whatever condition you are taking melatonin make sure that you take it **before mid-night**, which is the time that melatonin is naturally released from the brain. If you are a shift worker take it before you try to sleep in the day.

Melatonin is in its experimental stage for the treatment of SAD and depression. The results so far are gratifying.

Alzheimer's disease

Very recent studies have found reduced levels of melatonin in the cerebrospinal fluid of patients with Alzheimer's disease. Since circadian rhythms are disrupted in Alzheimer's disease, it is interesting to speculate whether restoration of melatonin to normal levels in these patients would alleviate other symptoms as well.

Melatonin remains one of the least toxic substances known to mankind. Dosage can vary from person to person but Dr. Pierpaoli, a leading researcher, has successfully used dosages ranging from 0.1mg to 200mg.

CHAPTER 30

The benefits of reflexology during pregnancy

Reflexology is a science that deals with the principle that there are reflexes in the feet relative to all organs, structures and functions of the human body.

By applying pressure to minute areas of the feet we are able to stimulate an energy through the body from the bases, which are our feet, to the brain.

Reflexology relaxes the body mind and spirit, improves circulation and normalises bodily functioning.

In the early stages of pregnancy, morning sickness can be very distressing and is due to the big changes in hormone levels. Fortunately the symptoms usually subside within the first three months, thereafter, most mothers feel extremely well until much later in pregnancy when there are often stresses and strains due to the enlargement of the womb which presses on all the organs and causes various discomfort from indigestion to constipation, frequency of urination during the latter stages, and an extreme stress on the skeleton.

Regular treatments of reflexology throughout pregnancy have a beneficial effect on all disorders relating to the digestive system, in particular constipation which can be such an uncomfortable and distressing condition to experience particularly during the later months.

Reflexology will help the muscle tone of the bowel, with quite dramatic effects on constipation. Many patients feel the need to have a bowel action just half an hour after the treatment.

We must now consider the stress on the skeletal structures during pregnancy. The lumbar spine in particular has to bear the weight of the increasing uterus which at term has grown to reach the bottom rib, and descends to the low pelvic area.

The lumbar spine bears the brunt of this weight increase, the ligaments and muscles running alongside the spine stretch to support the load: the big changes in the hormonal system give elasticity to the ligaments to allow this to happen.

With regular visits to a reflexologist, the discomfort of backache can be a thing of the past.

Babies seem to love reflexology even when they are still in the womb. Most mothers say that as they have the treatment they can feel their baby kicking frantically.

It is recommended that you continue having reflexology right up to, and including, the early stages of labour.

Practitioners have found that by stimulating the reflexology points to the pituitary in the brain which release oxytocin to stimulate the uterus to start contractions and work on the lumbar spine which helps the pelvic and hip area, good positive results have been achieved in enabling mothers to have better labours.

CHAPTER 31

Stress in the western world

Stress. We hear about it all the time, and the effects that prolonged stress can have on the body are quite extensive.

We do, however, need stress in order to be able to perform our everyday duties. We need to be stressed to achieve anything. A good adrenaline rush can stimulate our abilities whether they are 'achieving at sports', decorating a room, or studying for an examination, indeed without stress we would resemble a rather limp lettuce leaf!

Stress has been the subject of both psychological and physiological speculation. In fact, the word itself is ill-defined and overused for it means entirely different things to a variety of people.

We can suffer emotional stress as the result of a family argument or through the death of a loved one, whereas stresses in our environment are totally different: we could either be exposed to extreme cold, or excessive heat and in both cases we would stress the body.

Physiological stress on the other hand has been described as the outpouring of hormones from the adrenal glands which quicken our heartbeat, dilate our bronchial tubes in order that we can take in more oxygen and generally place our bodies on 'red alert'.

Death of a spouse is considered the most stressful event that anybody can be subjected to and doctors have subsequently found that ten times more widows and widowers die during the first year after the loss of their partner, than all others in their age group.

Following a divorce, both partners are more likely to suffer from a disease in the first year than any other time in their lives. Changes of any kind, whether good or bad leave people 'open' to disease, and the older we get the more comfortable in our daily routines and habits we become and therefore changes are even more stressful.

Stressful circumstances can be those associated with rapid cultural changes or emigration.

Research provides quite startling figures on measuring how stressful episodes in our lives affects the rise in our blood pressure which as we all know is 'the silent killer'.

On April 16 1947 a ship containing explosive material blew up in Texas City with a blast which was similar to the force of atomic bombs. Physicians in the area noted a marked increase in the blood pressure of their patients for days after the explosion.

Those who live in cities seem to have higher blood pressures than country dwellers. Those from coloured races are genetically more susceptible to high blood pressure than white people.

The fight-or-flight response is stimulated by the hypothalamus and the physiologic changes associated with this response are quite extensive: our respiratory rate increases, we begin to perspire, fat is extracted from the liver, sympathetic nervous system activity increases, sugar is released to give power to the muscles and extra activity to the brain and our heart rate and blood pressure increases.

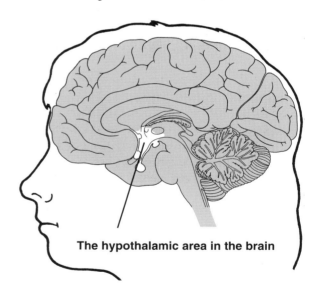

The hypothalamic area in the brain

These are all necessary functions if we were 'running for our life' as the excesses of secretions from our organs and glands would have been burnt up by the activity.

However when we subject our bodies to very stressful situations yet fail to do anything physical other than lifting a telephone receiver or watching a computer screen, we produce the excesses but not the activity. Our body is then receiving very unreal signals: it feels as if it should be 'fleeing' but actually it is totally stationary.

This state of affairs is what raises our blood pressure

and causes the degenerative state of our arteries, and leads to all the cardiovascular conditions and other diseased states of our body.

Although the fight or flight response is stimulated many times a day in those working in stressful business situations where 'deadlines' are a part of every day procedures, and antagonising situations are experienced frequently with working colleagues, a part of the involuntary nervous system called the sympathetic nervous system becomes highly active. It encourages us to 'lash out' physically as we would have done if confronted by a wild beast in a prehistoric life.

We are conditioned by society to suppress our aggressive feelings and so we usually do not punch the boss in the face or run away when stress invades our territory.

To reduce stress in our lives it is necessary to find some physical outlet for our suppressed emotions. Sport is excellent, running in particular or any racquet sport whereby you can bash a ball and release some of the pent-up emotions of the day.

The sympathetic nervous system secretes specific hormones; adrenaline, or epinephrine and noradrenaline or norepinephrine. These combined hormones bring about the physiological changes of increased blood pressure, body metabolism and heart rate.

Many of us revel in stress addiction: jetsetting around the world to business meetings which could quite easily be dealt with by using telephone and fax machines, tearing about on motorways rather than giving yourself sufficient time to get to your destination with as little stress as possible – another cause of breakdown of our mental and physical health. In fact, with the increase of stress in the Western World there is a significant increase in stress-related disease and disorders.

It has been calculated that 75 per cent of absence from work in the West is blamed on stress related illness. In the USA where life is more stressful than in any other part of the world over one third of the population suffers from stress-related overweight problems. Some 1.2 million people in America suffer from a stress related heart attack every year.

Orthodox medicine has a certain difficulty in coping with such an increase in these rapidly spreading stress related diseases and disorders and, therefore, more and more people are turning to alternative and complementary medicine. In fact, books dealing with alternative or complementary medicine are amongst today's best sellers. Stress damages our health because stress, as in any mortal danger or emergency, causes a great surge of blood to flow to the muscles and to that part of the brain which controls muscular activity in order to help individual survival with its 'fight or flight' ability leaving the rest of the organisms starving for food and oxygen.

The more lasting the stress the more our organism is exposed to danger. With chronic stress, sooner or later, our body breaks down. Being mainly self-centred by our mind and its wishfulness, stress can also be placated or eliminated by that same mind. If stress is mainly caused by the gap between our mind's expectations on one side and everyday reality on the other then surely by reducing our wishful expectations we could narrow down or even eliminate the gap thereby leading a much healthier life. Ancient Rome's principle 'Mens sana in corpore sano' meaning 'a healthy mind lives in a healthy body' was the perfect practical guideline, in fact cultivating physical health helps mental sanity. Given the fact that stress is the cause of many physical diseases and given the fact that stress is caused mainly by the mind one could also claim that with a healthy mind we have a healthy body. If mind-induced stress can create psychosomatic disease then mind-induced positive thinking could also create psychosomatic health or wellbeing. In order to allow our brain to reduce its excessive wishful expectations, and in order to widen our reasoning or make it more realistic, we could simply employ the humble gift of gratitude for what we already have.

Most stress and suffering stems from the fact that whatever we have or whatever we have achieved in life we consider our due. What is even sadder is that the more we have the more we crave as Seneca said, 'Is it not the man who has little, but the man who wants more, that is poor?'. Most people are in a position to remember a sense of gratitude for what they have had or for what they have, to recall at least one happy moment in the past on which to build up a spirit of thankfulness. With a sense of gratitude our pretentiousness, our eagerness and our avidity, these very sources of stress disappear opening a way to a richer participation in life. By reducing pretentiousness the efficiency of our senses and of our perception increases, widening our reasoning, enlarging space and time, enriching our life and therefore improving its quality. The idea that things could have been worse or could be worse, can help enormously to develop a sense of gratitude. In our world ruled by uncertainty and instability 'worse' is always a certain possibility. For example we could be dead. Gratitude for just being alive could inspire the joy of living with the exuberance of a playful child. Bearing in mind that every day could be our last might help us to realise that most of our stressful problems are either trivial or even ridiculous. Considering life as a bonus – as a gift for which we should be grateful – could prevent a good deal of stress preventing many stress related diseases or disorders. Most people take good health for granted: it is only when illness strikes that we start appreciating it. If we developed a conscious awareness of our health when we were well, if we started appreciating our health when we have it, we could transform our existence into a joyful one. Much unhappiness and stress in this materialistic world of ours is caused by seeing people around us richer or better off. In our materialistic mentality we assume that money can even buy happiness. A great deal of stress is created by envy, jealousy or malice which are all creations of our mind's offended or frustrated ego. The less an ego is inflated or infatuated the less it is offended or frustrated. 20 per cent of murders in the USA are motivated by jealousy and even a higher percentage of cancers, ulcers, coronary problems and hypertension are generated by envy or hate. The experts claim that envy and jealousy are caused by a sense of insecurity, by doubt in our abilities but we only find ourselves in this situation when our ambitions exceed our abilities, when our pretensions are above our capabilities. By simply reducing our pretensions we could reduce the self-destructive envy or jealousy.

Improving the brain's activity opens up our senses and perception and widens our reasoning. This enriches our life and it strengthens participation in reality: we are then able to realise the problem is not a tragedy the crisis is not a drama. The more an ego is inflated, the more restrictive the brain's activity becomes, the more suffering becomes despair and the more pain becomes agony.

By developing an interest in others we soon realise that most of our stressful problems are really the problems of everyday reality, just the same as everyone else's: a problem shared is a problem solved, as the saying goes.

Governments ought to recognise that the best prevention of disease is an active and persevering promotion of wellbeing and good health. They should not be afraid to spend time and money on this, as the more they spend the less they will have to pay on medical bills.

Quality of life could also be improved by being kind to others which helps not only the receiver but yourself towards raised mental activity, and being kind and civil eliminates suspicion and fear.

There is a technique which could easily be employed by everyone to reduce the irritation from external stress and it is to give endearing names or the names of flowers to the stresser which irritates the most.

CHAPTER 32

Female reproductive system disorders

The uterus – essence of feminity

During the last decade women have become aware of themselves and have searched for more information about the female body, their fertile years and their changing bodily needs.

We hear much about 'female problems' and generally accept that some females have more problems than others in their reproductive system.

A woman's uterus and ovaries represent the essence of her femininity. The uterus represents the beginning of life, while the ovaries produce the ova which, with the help of the sex hormones progesterone, oestrogen and testosterone together with the contribution of the male spermatozoa, allow fertilisation to occur

Today hysterectomy, or 'womb snatching' as it is often referred to, is a common every day surgical intervention which more young women than old undergo. One in three women will have had a hysterectomy before the age of sixty.

In most surgical interventions, the ovaries are also removed to save, so the medics inform us, the risk of ovarian cancer which increases with age.

We could, therefore, have several organs which are subjected to the risk of cancer removed – the breasts, bowels, pancreas to be 'just on the safe side'!

Even when the ovaries are removed, the ovarian tissue remaining can still be an active site for cancer to develop.

'Once the family has been reared, the uterus is of little use'. We hear this distressing statement time and time again, but this really is not so.

Every organ and system in the body serves its owner in one way or another to the end of life. When the ovaries are removed the body has a 'surgical menopause' which causes a radical physiological and psychological change in a woman.

Without your ovaries there will be a higher than normal risk of developing heart disease and osteoporosis.

Premenopausal women will undergo an 'instant menopause' complete with symptoms far more severe than leaving nature to slowly decline the activity of the ovaries over years.

Menstruation and lifestyle

Adolescence is a time of change, not only in the physical body but a change in attitudes and strong emotions emerge from the adolescent about life, living, and loving.

The adolescent forms so many powerful relationships: crushes on teachers, adoration of pop stars, often a dislike of their parents who really do not understand them, and eventually a strong physical relationship with a member of the opposite sex. Unfortunately the adolescent is not yet able to identify 'love' from 'sex'. Time and life's experiences will change that.

Just at a time when the body cries out for good nutrition and adequate minerals and vitamins the teenager decides to go on 'crash diets' and consumes large quantities of 'junk foods'.

Junk foods are alright once or twice a week but if they become the main source of nutrition the result will probably be disfiguring spots and low energy.

At this critical time in the life of the teenager, when the body needs lots of loving care, abuse in the form of late nights, disco-dancing into the early hours and experimenting with too much alcohol and cigarettes, are the norm and this puts the body under excessive stresses.

The teenager needs body fat in order to be able to store oestrogen in preparation for pregnancy later on in life. You should eat three servings of protein per day. You need about 55g in the morning, 110g at lunch time, and another 160g in the evening. Protein can be

in the form of cottage cheese, hard cheese, eggs, fish meat or chicken. If you are vegetarian it can be in the form of nuts, beans, lentils or cheese. Drink plenty of water: it will help flush out your system and cleanse your skin as well as your inner organs.

The body needs at least four pieces of fruit each day plus a serving of vegetables or salad. You can make a vegetable soup if you don't like vegetables in their solid form.

The first period, which is known as the menarche, arrives at about the age of 12 or 13 years. From that time the cycle is repeated 400–500 times throughout a woman's life.

Exercise is essential. Walk, run, skip, cycle or swim: you will feel much better if you exercise regularly. Exercise is great when emotions run riot, relationships become complicated, and studying for exams creates emotional stresses. A good run or hitting a ball against a wall in a squash court will get rid of built up emotions far more effectively than sitting about feeling angry!

During life in the uterus before birth, when we are about 28 weeks in our development, our ovaries already contain about one million eggs. By the time we are born that figure has dropped to about 500,000 by birth and to about 75,000 at puberty.

By the time we are about fifty years old there are very few fertile eggs in our ovaries.

Our menstrual cycle follows a regular pattern which is controlled by our hormones (chemical messengers stimulated from the pituitary). There is a build up of hormonal activity (pre-ovulation), hormonal stimulation which reaches a peak (ovulation) and a diminished activity as menstruation commences.

The thickened lining of the uterus, the endometrium becomes engorged with blood, and when the ovarian hormones reach their low point, the capillaries burst and our menstrual period commences. Most of us lose between two and four ounces of blood during each cycle and the flow usually lasts for three to seven days.

Perhaps our mythological relationship with the moon accounts for our attachment to the 28 day cycle, but even this varies from woman to woman. As we reach the menopause our periods become irregular, varying from three to ten weeks apart. Generally the ovaries rest and are dormant from one cycle to the next.

When menstruation first occurs there is usually no production of ova for the first six months, the same situation occurs when the menopause commences, and although there is bleeding it is inconsistent.

Some women experience quite painful menstrual cramps, but this pain is usually associated with ovulation. It is called *mittelschmerz,* a German word for mid-pain. Some women notice that they suffer a distinctive pain in just one side of their low abdominal region, one month it seems to be on the right side the other the left. As we ovulate from one ovary on alternate months, this would explain the discomfort. Other women experience breakthrough bleeding during ovulation. This is caused by the high levels of oestrogen in the circulation.

Hormonal activities which are produced during our cycle affect us emotionally as well as physically. Some women say that they become over sensitive to tastes and smells during their cycle, similar to the sensitivity experienced to foods etc. when first pregnant. Hormones and our metabolic rate are very united. We get the middle age spread when we consume the same amount of calories but cease ovulating.

The process of ovulation, the building and shedding of the endometrium if pregnancy does not occur, burns quite remarkable amounts of 'bodily energy'. The body actually uses between 300–500 calories per day from ovulation to menstruation.

Unfortunately menstruation is not the smooth or painless experience we wish it could be. Dysmenorrhoea, or period pain, usually starts at the commencement of a period, and comes and goes in sharp waves. The congestive or dull ache often begins prior to menstruation.

Most menstrual pain is due to deficiency, excess or improper metabolism of the female hormones. An imbalance in the production of prostaglandins is often the cause. Prostaglandins are hormone like substances which are produced by the cells.

A low fat low protein diet helps menstrual problems considerably and should be the first change to make in an attempt to relieve the discomfort.

Evening Primrose Oil, zinc, magnesium and calcium are to be recommended. Magnesium and calcium help muscle tone and therefore stop the cramping spasms in the uterine muscles.

We read many articles about the absence of menstruation caused in young girls who become anorexic or who indulge in excessive physical training. It seems that a critical body weight must be obtained for menstruation to commence. A small number of women find that their periods do not return when ceasing to take the contraceptive pill.

Excessive menstrual bleeding can be caused by a

thyroid deficiency, so if this is a problem do ask your doctor for a thyroid function test just to make sure that this is not the underlying cause. Kelp tablets are excellent if the thyroid is imbalanced.

Anaemia is another cause for excessive menstrual bleeding.

Many women suffer from fluid retention either before or during a period. Oedema is distressing and makes the sufferer feel bloated and uncomfortable. Alfalfa leaf tea is recommended, 28g of this herb contains magnesium and calcium, two minerals which are vital for our reproductive health.

Another painful condition of the menstrual cycle is fibrocystic disease of the breasts, often referred to as cystic mastitis. The breasts swell, appear very lumpy and are extremely painful. Do avoid caffeine and chocolate as this is one of the main causes. Don't expect an instant result, but persevere and within three months there should be a dramatic improvement.

Premenstrual tension

Menstruation is a natural event: premenstrual tension is not. Symptoms are signs that all is not right in the functioning of our bodies, and inadequate nutrition is a prime suspect.

Menstrual difficulties were in the Victorian times referred to as 'moon madness'. We also refer to the word lunatic when expressing emotional dysfunctions of some people, linking up the moon – lunar – to its control on our emotional states. We are all aware that our menstrual cycle has a very regular monthly (lunar) connection.

With any illness or symptoms we need to look at the stress factors in our lives and to consider just how we deal with the stresses and strains that confront us all in our daily lives: we need correct mineral and vitamin balances to help our emotional as well as our physical health.

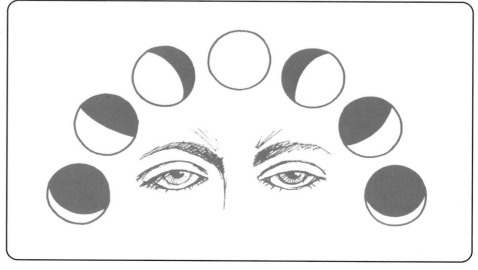

The uterus, ovaries, hypothalamus and pituitary are all linked with the efficient functioning of the reproductive system. We need vitamin B_6 to help us through all stressful and emotional situations in our lives. The female hormone oestrogen, if it builds up in the bloodstream can have an irritating effect on the nervous system.

So many women dread the feelings they experience often as long as 12 days before their menstrual period commences. Symptoms such as irritability, depression, food binges, backache, and swelling and sensitivity of the breasts are just some of the sufferings.

It is the job of the liver to prevent the build up of oestrogen. The B-complex vitamins, in particular B_6 neutralise oestrogen. Both the liver and the B-complex vitamins need magnesium to be present in the system to activate the combined functions, an enzyme process that takes on the excess oestrogen.

Remember that in today's world with high chemical contents in our diets, high fat consumption, too much sugar and probably excesses of alcohol too, the liver's activities are already overburdened, so the chemical factory is having quite a job in fulfilling all its expectations, hence the increase in the symptoms of premenstrual tension. It takes many years of poor nutrition to upset the balance of the endocrine system and only a few months of good nutrition to bring it back to normal.

In many trials carried out recently it has been discovered that most women suffering from premenstrual tension are deficient in magnesium, and the nutritional approach is to put a woman on a diet high in foods containing magnesium. Whole grains, millet, rice corn legumes, potatoes too are a rich source.

Do cut down, or preferably cut out sugar and salt from your diet. Sugar is a metabolic thief, it robs the body of essential vitamins, drains out magnesium and the B-complex vitamins, consequently the oestrogen levels then soar. The sugar/salt excess contributes to premenstrual swellings.

Apart from depleting the body of minerals and vitamins sugar also triggers the release of insulin from the pancreas causing the blood sugar level to drop. This in turn can cause tremors, increased appetite, headaches, fatigue and an increased desire for sweet foods. Excesses of insulin cause excessive levels of salt to remain in the body and salt retains fluids.

Excesses of fluids retained cause the 'mood changes' breast tenderness and bloating of the abdomen. Even your hands and feet may swell!

The week before your period starts, the effect of insulin on blood sugar levels is more pronounced that during the rest of the month. You can help this by including safflower oil in the diet. Safflower oil contains linoleic acid which helps to produce a hormone called prostaglandin. Two tablespoons a day added to salads is a good way to take it. Heating destroys much of its effectiveness.

B_6 is a natural diuretic, so it will help reduce water retention and relieve headaches and breast tenderness.

Cut down on dairy products, the calcium in them blocks the absorption of magnesium. Keep your protein intake to a moderate amount. Chicken, turkey, fish and eggs are preferable to red meats and offal. Magnesium helps the body bring calcium to the bones.

Caffeine aggravates breast tenderness and fluid retention by stimulating the activity of hormones. Reduce your coffee and tea consumption. Chocolate contains large amounts of caffeine as do all cola type drinks.

Nutritional supplements

Try to change your eating habits by following the advice offered above. If you do not achieve the result you expected then the following supplements may be of help: vitamin B_6 and B-complex, magnesium and vitamin C.

If you suffer from lumpy breasts before periods vitamin E has been found to be very effective also.

Exercise is a must not only to relieve premenstrual tension but also to help menstrual cramps.

Walking fast for thirty minutes each day, swimming, aerobic exercises all complement a better health regime. Exercise changes the way the body uses nutrients, it helps the metabolism of the body, increases the level of beta endorphins in the brain. In particular it improves the abdominal and pelvic circulation which aids the working of the reproductive system. Exercise also encourages regular elimination of waste products from the bowel. A retention of waste causes congestion and obstruction in the pelvic area which all contribute to painful periods.

Painful periods — dysmenorrhoea

These symptoms are experienced by most women at some time or other during their menstruating years. Sociological research shows that menstruation does not induce uncontrolled emotions but it lowers a woman's ability to express difficult feelings about her self or her relationships which are already there.

Menstrual bleeding which is either too light or too heavy can be caused by fibroids, endometriosis or ovarian cysts.

In the late 1970s it was discovered that women with

painful menstrual cramps often have high levels of the hormone prostaglandin in their blood and it is this hormone that causes the problem. Many women take antispasmodic drugs from their doctors to help pain levels and these sometimes are effective.

In extreme cases where the pain levels are so high that quality of life is grossly affected women opt for a hysterectomy, but everything else should be tried first before taking this serious step.

Cut down on red meat and milk. Both contain arachidonic acid which contributes to the production of series two prostaglandins.

Nutritional supplements

Linseed, borage and blackcurrant seed help to control heavy bleeding and period pains. Evening Primrose Oil helps all menstrual problems.

Take a natural form of iron, heavy consistent bleeding can grossly affect your iron levels and cause anaemia. Back to the all important vitamin C which can be helpful in the control of heavy bleeding.

The herbal remedy Bromelian reduces pain together with Feverfew, and Agnus Castus is an effective hormone regulator

Pelvic inflammatory disease

Pelvic inflammatory disease is a categorical name for a range of pelvic inflammations and infections. Salpingitis is one which is an inflammatory state of the fallopian tubes. The risk of an ectopic pregnancy increases sixfold after one single episode of pelvic inflammation.

The use of oral contraceptives increases the risk of the disease, as does cigarette smoking.

Symptoms such as a heavy discharge which often causes irritation of the vaginal area, severe cramp-like lower abdominal pain radiating as low as the pubic area, chills with moderately high intermittent fever. Painful or difficult sexual intercourse is yet another symptom.

Inflammatory states of the uterus, fallopian tubes and ovaries are always entirely involved, and women who have had multiple partners are at greater risk. Those who have had surgical intervention involving the reproductive organs such as cervical dilation, abortion and curettage have an increased risk.

Long term antibiotic treatment is usually the treatment offered, but does not usually offer a long term solution.

One of the main causes is the use of an IUD, which is an intra uterine device which is inserted into the uterus to deter fertilisation. Many women become infertile after pelvic inflammatory disease.

Nutritional supplements

Chlorophyll derivatives are cell stimulating agents which aid in building new healthy tissue and enhance the production of red blood cells and erythrocytes. You should take this supplement by mouth as well as using chlorophyll vaginal douches.

Vitamin C is recommended as its anti-inflammatory properties help to decrease tissue destruction.

Bromelain has antimicrobial properties and can reduce the general inflammation and support the natural healing abilities of the body.

Why do we have hysterectomies?

Hysterectomies are offered for a variety of conditions: fibroids, endometriosis, the slackening of the uterus into the vagina due in the main to having several pregnancies, maybe a forceps delivery or an extremely heavy baby.

According to Dr. Stanley West who is an outspoken critic of the gynaecology professions, only ten per cent of all hysterectomies are performed for cancer, and this, according to Dr. West, is the only true reason why the surgery should be performed.

The after-effects of a hysterectomy are most dramatic, with the removal of the ovaries, severe symptoms may be experienced such as fatigue, insomnia, urinary problems, headaches, vertigo, nervousness, anxiety, heart palpitations, vaginal dryness, difficult or painful intercourse, hair loss and a variety of skin problems.

There is a true history of post-hysterectomy depression. Some 30 to 50 per cent of women suffer from this condition. While there is no doubt that some women grieve for the loss of their wombs and cessation of their child bearing abilities, there are also biochemical reasons for this depression.

The hormonal disruptions brought on by the surgery can be far reaching, affecting the nerve and hormone interactions responsible for a sense of emotional well being.

The system in the brain which governs our feelings of wellbeing are dominated by the endorphins. The endorphin centre in the brain is influenced by a change in the levels of the ovarian hormones, oestrogen and progesterone. Oestrogen actually stimulates the release of endorphins from the hypothalamus.

In a similar way the reproductive system responds to the influence of the endorphins when labour commences, how exactly nobody is quite sure, but in some profound way either the baby signals to the hypothalamus to release oxytocin which is the hormone that initiates the contractions of the uterus, or visa versa.

You can see how the brain and our hormones are so involved, and it is not at all surprising that depression is very common after the removal of the uterus and ovaries.

Since the uterus is the key pelvic organ because it sits comfortably in the middle with the bladder in front, the back of the bladder actually being attached to the uterus, and the bowel behind, it is hardly surprising that when the removal occurs, which involves cutting the pelvic floor muscles and ligaments a 'sagging' of the bladder and bowel must occur, leading to an eventual prolapse into the vagina.

Vaginal and bladder repairs are so very common within five years of a hysterectomy.

A woman's vagina is shortened, scarred and dislocated by hysterectomy, not only that but there is frequently displacement of the bowel, bladder and other pelvic organs. Chronic urinary tract infections, frequency and incontinence – these conditions are the price we pay for the removal of the uterus.

The medical professions still continue to reassure women that the uterus is a 'disposable organ' that one can live quite happily without, once the child bearing years are gone, and if menstrual problems are a 'curse' each month, then living without the inconvenience of monthly periods, premenstrual aches and pains, and the freedom from worries about pregnancy and uterine cancer would seem like 'a gift from the Gods'.

We do however pay quite a high price for our so called 'freedom'.

The uterus is the main site for the production of the hormone, prostacyclin, which protects women from heart disease and unwanted blood clotting. Prostacyclin cannot be synthetically manufactured in a laboratory, therefore the loss of the uterus will ensure that production of this vital hormone will cease forever.

The uterus is also an important sex hormone. The well known researchers on human sexuality Masters and Johnson reveal that the contractions of the uterus are greatly involved in sexual excitement and female orgasm relies on these contractions.

During hysterectomy nerves that supply the uterus, the abdomen, the clitoris and the upper thighs are severed, this can cause a loss of tactile sensation from the waist to mid-thigh region.

We are ensured that the ovaries become 'redundant' after menopause. As an endocrine gland they produce hormones before, during and after the menopause.

The outermost covering of the ovary where the ova develop is known as the theca. The inner part is known as the stoma, and it is the stoma that becomes active at menopause for the very first time in a woman's life. After menopause the ovaries still continue with this function hand in hand with the skin, liver and fat to produce hormones.

These postmenopausal hormones promote bone health and skin suppleness, support sexual functioning and protect against heart disease.

The uterus in the female is equivalent to the prostate gland while the ovaries relate to the testicles. If a man has his prostate and testicles removed, the results are total castration. The same applies to a woman.

We just cannot 'cut out' any part of the human body without paying the penalty, nor can we suppress any vital function without there being 'side effects'.

It does not mean that with the removal of the ovaries and uterus we are doomed for the rest of our lives and face the prospect of heart disease, osteoporosis and chronic depression. By choosing a healthy diet, taking minerals and vitamins, along with the guidance from qualified complementary practitioners, much can be done to restore and improve health.

However, we do need to respect the fundamental procreator of life, The Uterus.

Pre-eclampsia

What actually is pre-eclampsia? We hear it referred to as something extremely serious, a disorder that affects pregnant women and if left untreated, can cause 'fits', and has lead in many cases to a stillborn baby, and a sick mother with damaged kidneys.

Some medical authorities call it toxaemia of pregnancy or pregnancy-induced hypertension.

Most antenatal tests are designed to look for signs of pre-eclampsia but many cases are not detected until the patient is actually in labour.

Symptoms of high blood pressure, high levels of uric acid in the blood and swelling of the face, hands and feet are symptoms which raise 'alarm bells'. Individual symptoms are not regarded as serious, but a combination of several certainly are treated urgently.

The rise in blood pressure and fluid retention puts a great stress on the renal function and protein found in the urine are symptoms of the kidneys' distress.

When protein appears in the urine during pregnancy, clots and fatty acids build up in the placenta causing it to eventually cease acting as a 'second liver' altogether. Without the efficient functioning of the placenta the baby is denied sufficient oxygen and nutrients, so the growth of the baby is affected.

Most babies born of mothers who suffered pre-eclampsia are premature. Sometimes 'Mother Nature' induces an early labour in an attempt to save the baby. In many cases labour is induced early to prevent damage to the mother or child.

The biggest factor which has been linked to pre-eclampsia is 'extreme stresses' during pregnancy and poor nutrition. Pregnant women need high protein in their diets in the form of milk, eggs and meat and their calorific intake should be around 3,000. They also need fruit and vegetables, but protein is an essential during pregnancy and breast feeding.

An excessive weight gain in the latter half of pregnancy is another indicator of pre-eclampsia. However a weight gain of a mother who is on a good high protein balanced diet is not such a worry as one who is living on chips, sausages, pies and chocolates.

Pregnant women need to drink plenty of water in order to flush out the kidneys. Some doctors prescribe diuretics to treat oedema. Diuretics deplete the body of essential salt and minerals which can cause even more problems, and we do need salt. Salt helps to regulate the correct fluid balance in the body provided sufficient water is being taken to regulate the salt.

The entire body is made up of a watery salty fluid, and every cell in our bodies relies on this substance to function. The renninangiotensin system activity is a subordinate mechanism to histamine activation in the brain. This system is activated when there is a restriction in the body's fluid volume. It is activated to retain water and it also promotes the absorption of more salt.

Until the salt and water levels reach a correct level the renal system brings about the tightening of the capillary bed and the vascular tension of the arteries. This tightening causes the blood pressure to rise. If there is sufficient water taken to weaken the salty solution there is no need for the tightening of the

arteries to occur, then blood pressure levels will drop.

The kidneys produce urine, a straw-like fluid. If urine is dark and smelly then you are surely dehydrated and need to drink more pure water. When the urine that is passed is only lightly coloured and the flow is unrestricted, you can feel content that your fluid intake is improving. Most of us are dehydrated.

This advice should also be followed for men suffering from urine retention due to enlarged prostate glands, or kidney stones. Drink more water. At least six, eight ounce glasses per day, and this does not include the water contained in tea, coffee or mineral waters.

Remember alcohol dehydrates the body, and constantly substituting water and replacing the fluid intake with alcohol and caffeine laced drinks, will deprive the body of energy in the brain as well as the body.

The kidneys excrete excess sodium, hydrogen, potassium, and waste materials, they need sufficient fluid to excrete these waste products. So much kidney damage is caused by long term dehydration and salt damage.

Miscarriage

Miscarriages are often blamed on 'deficient eggs', 'an allergic reaction to the male sperm', 'stress' and so on but more often than not we hear that the cause of the problem has not been defined.

One in four women miscarry, and some miscarry many times. Although there are only a few days each month when you can conceive the quality of sperm deteriorates the longer they remain in the body.

Many women are put through the untold misery time and time again of miscarrying until 'possible causes are looked into'. It is not always the woman who is lacking when there is repeated occasions of miscarriage, sometimes it is the male who is at fault, the cause being abnormalities in the sperm.

It is estimated that a normally fertile woman under the age of 25 will need an average of two to three months to conceive. Over the age of 35 she will need six months or longer.

As she ages the quality of egg production deteriorates and fewer are released. Age is of course far less of a factor in male fertility. Few doctors

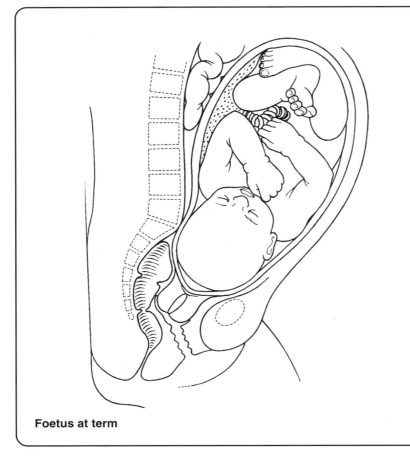

Foetus at term

will consider that the infertile couple needs investigating until eighteen months of unprotected sex has taken place.

Miscarriage is a multifactorial problem and must be looked at in this way. Conditions such as pesticides, smoking habits, alcohol, genitourinary infections, all these factors must be considered. If you have suffered pelvic inflammatory disease or have had abdominal surgery in the past, these are all possible factors affecting conception.

Getting to know your body and understand your fertile times are important. The usual white discharge from the cervix is similar to egg white. At your fertile times the mucus changes, it becomes elastic and forms a string or a 'shute' which encourages the sperm to attach itself and swim towards the uterus. Many women experience a surge in their libido around the time of ovulation.

Temperature rises are common prior to ovulation, so if you wish to check your ovulation time take of your temperature every morning, before you eat or drink anything, you should certainly see a surge in temperature around the middle of your cycle which denotes your fertile time.

Some miscarriages are thought to be due to a genetic abnormality. Selenium is known to protect against chromosomal damage. Selenium protects the body against toxins and pollutants. It would be advisable for couples to take good levels of this mineral in the months before conception is anticipated.

Obesity is another factor which is thought to encourage the risk of miscarriage. Alcohol and smoking should be ceased even before you intend to try and become pregnant, and is disastrous during pregnancy.

Acupuncture can stimulate the body's natural hormone production and may help if the failure to conceive is due to a hormonal disorder, and is certainly to be recommended rather than following drug therapy treatments to stimulate the ovaries.

Asparagus, fenugreek, garlic, onion and liquorice are known to invigorate the reproductive organs and there are many old fashioned herbal remedies including natural yam, true unicorn root, false unicorn root, black cohosh, and squaw vine. Red clover and raspberry leaf contain good levels of minerals, in particular magnesium and calcium is thought to aid conception.

False unicorn is centuries old and stimulates the ovaries themselves: natural plant hormones work in conjunction with female hormones to maximise the chance of conception.

Did you know? **Aromatherapy and the menopause**

Around the time of the menopause, production of the hormones oestrogen and progesterone slow down and the symptoms experienced are due to reduced levels of these hormones in the body.

In general this occurs between the ages of 40 and 48 with the symptoms usually reaching their most irritating at around the ages of 48 to 51 years.

Physical symptoms

Physical symptoms that may be experienced at this time could include hot flushes, night sweats, and aches and pains in the joints and limbs.

Psychological symptoms

You may feel psychologically different and be more prone to one or more of the following: depression, tiredness, loss of sex drive, inability to make decisions and forgetfulness.

It has been proved that essential oils, together with regular reflexology treatments can help bring about the relief you may be seeking.

Aromatherapy oils

The following oils may be of help:

Clary Sage, Geranium and Fennel as these are oestrogenic, hormone balancing and stabilising.

Rose, Neroli, Jasmine, Chamomile, Sandalwood and Ylang Ylang.

Sandalwood and Ylang Ylang in particular are excellent for use in treating depression and are aphrodisiac and tone the uterus.

Peppermint and Spearmint have the ability to control hot flushes.

Blending

You should blend the oils into a cream base such as Calendula in a ratio according to body weight. For example, a patient weighing 9 to 10 stone needs one drop of essential oil to 5ml of carrier oil.

Application

The oils, in whatever base is used, should be applied to the back of the neck, the low abdominal area near to the ovaries, and to the vertebral column from the coccyx to the back of the neck.

Female reproductive system disorders

Reflexology and the female reproductive system

If you are a Reflexologist and are working on patients suffering from the illnesses associated with the female reproductive system, the areas identified below in the chart will give you some guidance of the most important reflexes to work upon.

- Work out the liver area: helps detoxification.
- Work out the entire intestinal area. Remember that 85 per cent of our immunity stems from the intestine which is rich in lymphatic tissue.

Reflexology will help to rid the body of unwanted waste material and balance the ecological flora of the bowel. This will encourage the body to heal as it is not possible for healing to take place when there is toxic waste in the system.

- Work out the endocrine system, the pituitary, thyroid, pancreas, adrenal glands and ovaries.
- Work out the breast, uterus and fallopian tubes.
- Work out the central nervous system, spine and brain.

Do not use Reflexology on a patient who is having IVF – always wait for a week following this treatment.

There is 'no danger' attached to this but working on the feet after these treatments could cause 'side effects'. The patient would then suffer the side effects of the hormonal treatment plus the after effects of the reflexology treatment which could create a 'combined reaction' and make the patient feel extremely unwell.

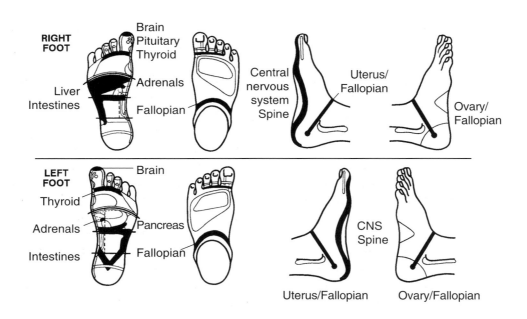

CHAPTER 33

Endometriosis

This strange condition involves the development of growths of tissue around the ovaries, uterus, fallopian tubes and the bladder. Sometimes the tissue even attaches itself to the bowel and can cause pain, menstrual problems and infertility.

By 1920 this set of symptoms was found to be an increasingly common problem for young women. If abdominal surgery had been performed for any reason it increased the likelihood and sufferers of endometriosis were often found to have a low thyroid function. Consequently it is always best to have a thyroid function test carried out first, before seeking relief for the condition.

In many cases old tissue became adhered to ovaries and rectal ligaments and caused abdominal organs to become twisted out of place by the contortions of the strange tissue.

The tissue reacted to the hormonal cycle, just like uterine tissue, when stimulated by oestrogen and sometimes had a 'bleed' during menstruation.

The pain of endometriosis can be very similar to appendicitis, in fact many operations have been performed, without need, for the removal of the appendix, only to discover later that the condition was gynaecological.

The medical treatment is usually with hormone blockers, if they do not work then many young women end up with a total hysterectomy and removal of both ovaries. This is not the answer as the excessive tissue growth can, as stated, attach itself to other organs

As with all operations, complications can result from a hysterectomy. The most common is chronic urinary tract infections, wound infections, and because the uterus, bladder and rectum are so close together, there can be damage to either or all of these.

There are also long term effects. 30 to 50 per cent of women who have hysterectomies suffer from depression; others complain of weight gain, hot flushes and a lack of interest in sex. You can't remove any organ in the body without there being a price to be paid. It is crucial therefore to have a second or even third opinion before you resort to a hysterectomy for endometriosis. It may be the only way to stop heavy menstrual bleeding, but there are other alternatives.

The common clinical symptoms are: extreme tenderness in the abdomen and cramp like pain before menstruation as well as pain which radiates into the rectum during menstruation and a burning sensation along the fallopian tubes and into the ovaries.

If you have endometrial tissue which has built up on the ovary itself, the ovary will become strangled and ovulation will cease to take place.

Sometimes endometriosis can prevent menstruation altogether. For others there is a very irregular menstrual cycle or there is excessive bleeding. Each case is unique. Some women report no painful symptoms whatsoever whilst others suffer seriously.

The incidence of endometriosis is increasing and there are questions being raised as to whether the use of so many hormonal preparations in our lives today – the contraceptive pill, artificially induced ovulation, hormone replacement therapy, the use of IUDs and the hormones we absorb through our foods – is encouraging this illness. I personally feel that these are very likely contributing factors.

Pregnancy usually helps the problem, which may at first seem a strange solution. The main hormone involved in pregnancy is progesterone, indeed progesterone stabilises pregnancy and modulates the effects of oestrogen.

Women of earlier generations had less endometriosis, because they had far more pregnancies and so their oestrogen levels were 'turned off' during the gestation period and also during breast feeding. Breast feeding suppresses ovulation and therefore keeps the oestrogen levels down.

A modern alternative is to induce a false pregnancy by giving synthetic male hormones and pure progesterone to create a 'chemical menopause' which stops the ovarian hormone production.

Some physicians consider that endometriosis could be a premalignant disease; that endometrial cancer has risen 80 percent in some segments of the population and that endometriosis is linked to ovarian cancer as well, so the decision to use drastic control methods is not entirely ill-conceived.

Under no circumstances should truly uncomfortable or worrying symptoms be ignored.

A Case History

The holistic approach to endometriosis

Shirley was an attractive, slim young woman with a strong physique. She was physically active and involved herself in dance classes each week apart from teaching in a school during the weekdays.

Four years ago she went from doctor to doctor to seek help for her diagnosed endometriosis. Shirley was under a lot of stress but was unaware that she was not coping as well as she hoped.

To make matters worse she was dieting stringently. Her daily calorie intake was 500, which was ridiculously low. Her main food intake was grapefruit and lots of black coffee. In spite of two jobs to cope with plus her home life and two children to raise Shirley felt the need for excessive exercise, as her abdomen looked and felt swollen. Her periods stopped and she felt pregnant.

In addition to the bloating she was aware of a burning sensation on the right side. Shirley contacted her doctor who confirmed that she was not pregnant but had considerable swelling in the fallopian tubes and referred her to a gynaecologist but he advised to just wait and see how things proceeded.

Six months later and with still no sign of a period and with constant pain in the right side she resorted to continuous pain killers and bed rest.

The gynaecologist advised that she take the Pill but all that happened was that she gained a lot of weight.

A second opinion was sought with a general physician who said that her lifestyle, poor diet and stressful life was affecting her health and considered she was suffering from mal-nutrition. Bloating evidently is a sign of malnutrition. Shirley increased her food intake and gained weight but the pain continued.

A surgical investigation showed adhesions and active signs of endometriosis. Her main problems were caused by 'near starvation diet' and lots of stresses.

Shirley discharged herself from the hospitals and waved a fond goodbye to doctors and decided to have some reflexology treatments.

She changed her diet and ate fish and chicken, vegetables, fruits and grains. She ceased the coffee drinking which made her 'more stressful', cut out sugar altogether and found that rice, instead of bread was more satisfying and seemed to help the bloated feeling.

She started swimming which she found relaxing and eased the pain in her side. Reflexology certainly relaxed her and her menstrual cycle commenced and became more regular.

Vitamin B-complex is recommended. One of the first signs of B-complex vitamin deficiency will be heavy, painful periods.

Vitamin E has a very important role to play in the management of oestrogen levels. This nutrient is a natural antagonist of excess oestrogen and helps normalise all reproductive organs and balance hormone levels. Vitamin E is also important to the endometriosis victim because it keeps scar tissue soft and flexible and minimises adhesion. This can reduce the twisting and painful contortion of pelvic organs damaged by endometrial lesions. Exercise also keeps adhesions flexible.

More recently it has been discovered that aerobic exercises such as jogging, bicycling and cross-country ski-ing stimulate the release of endorphins. These are natural opiates that produce a sense of well-being and block pain perception. It is believed that body-produced endorphins are instrumental in the positive addiction most 'exercise addicts' experience.

Nutritional measures to manage oestrogen do not work overnight, but they gradually coax the system back to normality – but the initial response may seem contradictory. Occasionally women who eliminate sugar, alcohol and refined foods while adding B-complex supplements may, at first, experience a worsening of symptoms. This is because the ovaries are the first to respond to improved nutrition and promptly speed up oestrogen production. In time, the liver catches up and degrades the oestrogen as the ovaries produce it.

I thought oestrogen was necessary to keep a woman's body healthy, you may say. The answer is 'yes' and 'no'. Oestrogen is necessary to proliferate tissue but only at the appropriate time and place.

The oestrogen produced by the ovaries and fat cells is ordinarily broken down by the liver into oestriol, a variant form that maintains femininity but does not make cells grow inappropriately. This means it will not stimulate endometriosis in the same way that undegraded oestrogen, called oestradiol, often does. Too much oestradiol compared to oestriol has been linked to cystic mastitis, uterine fibroids and breast cancer. Heavy menstruation and chronic endometrial inflammation are all diseases of oestrogen-sensitive tissue. Before giving in therefore to pills and surgery, recommend the information contained in this article to your patients and friends. You will be amazed at the results that can be achieved in treating the natural way.

Reflexology and endometriosis: Shirley's sensitivities are shown in the reflexology chart overleaf.

Did you know? Water – the essence of our being

We are all salty watery beings, every cell in the human body relies on being saturated in water to perform its functions. We developed from species that were given life in water and so the dependency on the life-giving properties of water was inherited. The necessity of water for life has not changed.

The human body is composed of 25 per cent solid matter and 75 per cent water. Brain tissue consists of 85 per cent water, our brain actually floats in water. Water distribution is the only way of making sure that essential hormones and nutrients reach vital organs. We can all live for a long period without food but only for a few days without water.

Without adequate supplies of water our kidneys fail very rapidly. We all need at least three litres of water per day, that means pure filtered water, if possible, and does not include the water in soft drinks, herbal teas, tea or coffee.

However, it is not always pleasant to drink this life sustaining liquid because millions of people in Britain are currently drinking water that is contaminated with levels of toxic chemicals far in excess of the 'allowed' standards. There are over 350 different man made chemicals in our drinking water: some areas have a worse record than others.

City dwellers are likely to have more contamination with lead in their water supply, as the water could be flowing through old lead pipes.

The leakage of waste products into our rivers in Britain is the fastest growing form of pollution and industry is responsible for 37 per cent of this. The problem is insidious because the chemicals are invisible and the only time the pollution comes to the notice of the public is when fish begin to die in our rivers. The situation is then investigated. Industry is responsible for much of this poisoning.

As the farming industry uses twice as much fertilizer on farm land than it did 12 years ago, its leaching into the water supply takes years before any damage as to the concentration of nitrate in the supply is recognised.

What can we do about this sorry state? The first recommendation would be to buy an under-sink water filter. This would reduce aluminium, lead, organic chemicals and chlorine. There is a connection between the intake of chlorine and high blood pressure, anaemia and diabetes and it is also a contributor to heart disease.

If you prefer a jug filter make sure to clean all parts weekly and keep the filtered water in the fridge. If you soak the filter in a mild solution of bicarbonate of soda once a week this will ensure that the filter has been rid of all offending chemicals.

Lead is a neuro toxin and therefore affects our brain and central nervous system. High levels of lead have been found to affect the intellectual development of children.

The next time you suffer from an attack of heartburn or indigestion drink a glass of water every half hour – your symptoms will soon subside.

You must take sufficient water for the bowel to be able to conduct its activities efficiently, insufficient fluid is often the cause of constipation which can be the root cause for so many health conditions.

Remember that every function of the body needs an adequate supply of water to perform its functions, water is a transport system for hormones, chemicals and nutrients to reach vital organs, without water the body is denied the ability to perform efficiently.

Reflexology and endometriosis

For your interest here is a copy of the sensitivities found in Shirley's feet with the reason for each sensitivity explained.

1. As the liver serves a vital role in the breakdown of oestrogen, this was giving a reaction due to the excess of oestrogen in the blood stream.
2. The descending and sigmoid colon were extremely sensitive; I rather feel that there must have been endometrial tissue adhering to this part of the bowel.
3. The fallopian tube on the right was over-sensitive. No doubt there was congestion here also.
4. The fallopian tube on the left reacted as well.
5. Fallopian tube reaction.
6. Fallopian tube reaction.
7. Fallopian tube reaction: excessive on the right side.
8. Fallopian tube reaction: excessive on the left side.
9. Hip and pelvic area. As the patient did not suffer from any skeletal or arthritic condition, I felt that the sensitivity here must have been due to endometrial tissue adhering to the pelvic floor.

10. The same occurred on the hip and pelvic area on the left.
11. The breast area on the right foot was sensitive, again due, I felt, to the excess of oestrogen which was giving symptoms of mastitis.
12. The same sensitivity occurred on the left foot. Shirley had twelve treatment sessions in all. The first eight were on a weekly basis and the last four, fortnightly.

The sensitivities did not start to reduce until the eighth treatment when her symptoms also started to reduce.

There was no sign of endometriosis when she went to see her gynaecologist six months later. However, we must take into consideration the fact that apart from the reflexology treatments, Shirley changed her eating habits, her exercise pattern and took the recommended doses of vitamins.

It was the combination of all aspects that gave her the maximum result.

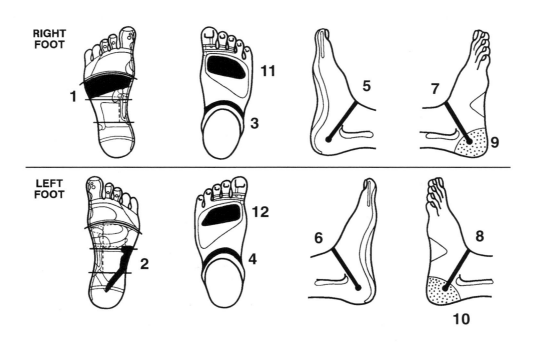

CHAPTER 34

Facts about Candida albicans

Candida albicans is a yeast, naturally present in every one of us from around the age of six months. Candida is so old in its origin that it has probably been present in the human body for as long as we have been around.

Yeasts derive their nutrients from a wide range of sources and in the right environment can multiply at an explosive rate. When we are in a state of good health and balance, and eating a natural diet, the Candida gets little chance to grow to an extent where it can cause problems.

The twentieth century has, however, brought radical changes in lifestyle and a move away from a natural diet. There are chemicals and other pollutants unthought of by our grandparents, changing our environment and capable of causing many allergic reactions

Our foods

Today we eat foods that have been processed through heating, refining, pressurising and chemical preservation. Foods are treated with fertilisers, herbicides, pesticides and mould inhibitors and after processing often contain a range of additives to enhance taste and smell, colour and preservation.

Additionally sugar has become a major part of today's diet and every cook knows that if you want yeast to rise you need to use sugar.

The average person consumes around 125 pounds of sugar per year. Apart from the sugar we add consciously to our foods, just consider the amount of hidden sugar in packets and tins.

The wholly unnatural diets that most people eat today coupled with vitamin and mineral nutrient deficiencies from overcooked denatured foods, encourage the growth of Candida and this consequently weakens our immune system.

Antibiotics and hormone treatment are other influences which encourage the proliferation of Candida.

Antibiotics

With the advent of antibiotics, penicillin in particular became very popular in the 1950s. It was called 'a wonder drug' and indeed it was when used sparingly for life-threatening situations such as pneumonia.

It is not unheard of for a patient to be prescribed an antibiotic following a kidney infection for as long as six months after the initial illness.

Toddlers frequently have as many as six courses of antibiotics in their first year for ear, nose, throat and bronchial infections, and many from the teen years onwards have long-term courses to treat a wide range of infections, including acne.

Whilst antibiotics destroy the offending bacteria, they also destroy the body's friendly bacteria, and particularly those of the digestive tract and consequently upset the balanced ecology of the intestinal system allowing the Candida yeast to flourish.

Apart from being used in medical treatments, we can find antibiotics at low levels in food, having been added to the feed of intensively reared livestock. They are found in meat, poultry, eggs and dairy products unless you are able to obtain your foods from an 'organic source'.

Hormone treatment

Commonly used hormonal treatments including the contraceptive pill are known to encourage the growth of Candida.

Where would you find Candida?

It is found mainly in the intestines and digestive system. It can also be found in the vagina, mouth (as thrush), the skin and nails.

A serious overgrowth of Candida can lead to one feeling 'sick all over' but symptoms such as depression, anxiety, heartburn, indigestion, bloating, fatigue, allergies, migraine, cystitis, thrush, vaginal infections, joint pain, nasal stuffiness, sore throats, and wheezing are common. Quite an alarming selection of illnesses!

There are, of course, other reasons for suffering the above maladies, but Candida is so frequently at the root cause of the condition.

However, it will be interesting to note when treating patients who have been unwell, to see if they have been on antibiotics recently.

The structure of Candida

It is important to understand that Candida can exist in two different forms: as a simple yeast which is relatively less harmful and as a mycelium or mass of filaments, which can break through the digestive system wall and invade the body. It is now thought that this penetration leads to only partly digested food, particularly proteins, passing through the intestinal wall into the blood stream, where they are recognised as foreign bodies and become allergens.

Help from nutrients

A number of nutrients have been shown to be helpful in preventing the yeast branching into a mycelium. A good starting point would be supplements containing biotin, cold pressed oils from which you will get essential fatty acids and immune strengthening nutrients to boost your immune system and your mucous membrane.

There is an acid which is a natural derivative of coconut oil, called caprylic acid which has been used successfully for over 30 years. *It is not advisable to take this if you are pregnant or have ulcerative colitis.*

Garlic is an excellent inhibitor of Candida, used either fresh or as a supplement. Do make sure that the garlic that you take in tablet form is pure and not combined with other oils. It is also recommended that you take a probiotic supplement and eat regularly live yogurt.

Psyllium husks and herbal intestinal cleansing tablets are a gentle way to remove old sticky putrefying deposits and impurities, and to tone and condition the whole intestinal system.

Massaging into your abdominal area with olive oil also helps the circulation and muscle tone of the bowel and encourages elimination.

Changing your diet

A special diet is the most important factor in the control of Candida. It does need to be free of all refined sugar as the Candida organism thrives on it. So avoid it like the plague. Fruit juices, unless you juice your own fruits, are full of added sugar. Don't eat mushrooms or milk products either.

You should eat vegetables, seeds and nuts (not peanuts), lentils, pulses, whole grains and fish. Eggs, meat and poultry are fine in moderation, particularly if you know where you can buy them hormone and antibiotic free. Avoid foods that contain yeast, bread, rolls, buns and biscuits and, of course, alcohol, mayonnaise and salad dressings.

The change of diet is really a tough one, but if you are feeling so unwell there may be little choice, and it may be best to leave a few foods out at a time, rather than eliminating so many foods in the same week

Sugar is the greatest culprit, and any foods containing yeast. With those two items removed you should be on the road to recovery.

CHAPTER 35

Tinnitus and reflexology

What is the cause of this disabling condition, often referred to as 'ringing in the ears'? The noise can be so loud that it prevents sleep, and in many cases patients have been reduced to a severely depressive state because of this illness. This was the case with Mary who came with symptoms of ringing in the ears, which started one morning right out of the blue and apart from a few hours here and there when the condition abated the ringing was continuous.

Mary was in her late thirties so that ruled out poor circulation to the ears which is often the case in elderly patients with this problem. Taking aspirin and beta-blockers over a prolonged period can also be the cause.

Therefore, if you ever have to treat the condition, look into the medical history of your patients and just see if they are suffering from angina, a heart condition

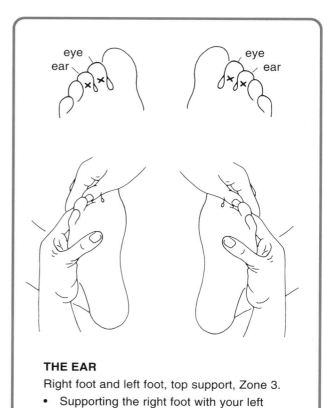

THE EAR

Right foot and left foot, top support, Zone 3.

- Supporting the right foot with your left hand, use a gentle rotating movement with the right thumb.
- Reverse procedure for the left foot.

or high blood pressure and are being treated with aspirin or beta- blockers. (It has been discovered that daily doses of vitamin E are far superior in the treatment of all vascular disease than aspirin!)

If your patient complains of excessive wax in the ears, check on whether his or her diet contains a high content of dairy foods such as full fat milk, cheese and chocolates: also shop bought pies and pastries which are high in saturated fats and sugar.

Yet a further cause can be a zinc deficiency and sometimes a neck injury can interfere with the lymph nodes which can prevent lymphatic fluid draining properly.

Mary had seen all manner of specialists who had all concentrated their findings on something wrong with the ear, and that was as far as things went.

She was amazed when I told her that the problem could be an intolerance to dairy produce, and she did confess to a high intake of chocolate, particularly pre-menstrually.

Another 'clue' to the cause was a neck injury that Mary suffered two or three years before after falling from a horse.

She had actually told the specialist at the hospital about this incident but this event was dismissed and still everyone concentrated on the ears, which was probably why they never got to the root of the problem and why Mary was still suffering some three years later.

Reflexology treatment

On working through the reflexes, when I came to the area at the base of the first three toes on the right and left feet (illustrated below) she cried out as the sensitivity was so acute. "It feels as if you are working on my feet with red hot glass", she exclaimed.

Here, I was sure, was the problem. Congestion and inflammation in the neck due to poor lymphatic drainage due to that accident.

After just six treatments on a weekly basis, concentrating on the entire spine, particularly the cervical and the neck/thyroid area, the ringing in the ears stopped and to date, and that is one year later, Mary is still symptom free and enjoying her life once again.

She did stop the chocolate, so maybe that helped, but I am confident that the cause of the condition was that neck injury – and don't forget what we always say during the reflexology training, 'Structure Governs Function'.

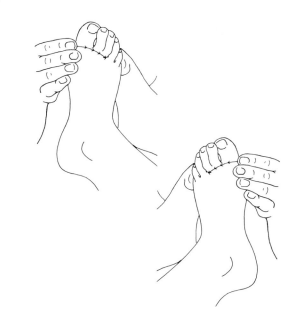

THE THYROID/NECK AREA

Right foot and left foot – dorsal view – medial to lateral, top support, Zones 1,2,3.

- Supporting the right foot with your left fist and using the right index finger, work 3 times across the join of the toes.
- Reverse the procedure for the left foot.

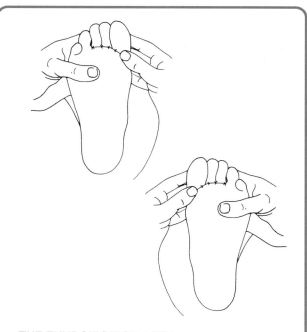

THE THYROID/NECK AREA

Right foot and left foot – plantar view – medial to lateral, top support, Zones 1,2,3.

- Supporting the right foot with your left hand and using the right thumb, work 3 times across this area.
- Reverse the procedure for the left foot.

CHAPTER 36

It's not all in the mind – diseases of the psyche

Autism

Autism was originally considered to be primarily a psychiatric condition, genetic in origin, but recent studies have led to the belief that the disorder is due to an organic defect in brain development. Abnormal levels of serotonin metabolism have been found in the brain.

Far more males suffer this condition. In fact the ratio is male to female 4:1. Strange behavioural symptoms are usually recognised no later than 30 months. Symptoms are poor communication levels, lack of expression, a seeming inability to feel pain or pleasure and a ritual of repeating words over and over with little understanding of meaning.

The prognosis medically of the autistic child is poor, and some develop temporal lobe epilepsy in later life.

However, a big question mark hangs over the link between the increase in vaccinations and the escalating rise in autism. Connections with the MMR vaccine are alarming as many parents are reporting that after the MMR vaccine their child spent hours of high pitched screaming, was impossible to console and started exhibiting strange emotional behaviour 12 days or so following the vaccine.

Trials at the Royal Free Hospital in London revealed that examinations of autistic children showed gross abnormalities in their bowel.

It is thought that the vaccine could damage the gut wall and that the vaccination affects the body's ability to process certain foods. The most frequent causes are gluten from wheat, cereals like rye, barley and oats also milk and dairy products Other environmental toxicities such as pesticides could also be involved in damaging the intestinal wall.

There is a huge increase in behavioural problems in children which were unheard of prior to the war, and before the introduction of vaccinations for now, nearly everything.

We hear of dyslexia, attention deficit, learning difficulties, violent and aggressive behaviour in young children, sleeplessness, and anxiety states. Despite all the array of 'learning aids' that are around today so many children are having problems in being able to read and write.

Each vaccine is a toxin – a toxic compound which is introduced into the delicate blood stream of an infant who is 'usually perfect' in all aspects. Vaccinations are not lifelong immunity to diseases, they give very short term protection and then have to be repeated again and again.

Apart from the toxins introduced by immunisation today's child is subjected to a variety of strange concoctions in diet, from the air he breathes and even in the water he drinks, so the body is under excessive stress in being able to 'defend' against all these invasions.

Utilizing lifestyle modification to treat and prevent illness is one of the few approaches that have begun to make inroads into conventional medicine. The fact that many physicians are advising their patients to try to make changes in the area of diet and physical activity, demonstrates how traditional medicine is being forced into areas that were formerly recognised as the province of the holistic therapist. The key to treating illnesses must ultimately be determined by our ability to comprehend how the illness came about in the first place.

Instead of shutting out all possibilities of causes of diseases such as the damage that can be sustained by vaccination and drugs and looking at prevention and lifestyle changes, there will never be a true revelation of the understanding of illness, whether of the body mind or spirit, until we look at the body as 'a whole' and not separate parts all needing to be treated differently.

Measles is not the 'terrifying killer' disease that medicine would have us believe. In America in 1990 at the height of a measles epidemic when 27,000 cases of measles were reported, 89 people died. (Statistics taken from *The Vaccination Bible - What Doctors Don't Tell You Series* page 51.)

What the Government failed to reveal was that the deaths occurred mainly in young children of low income families where poor nutrition played an important part with failure to seek medical help when complications arose. These children died as the result of complications of measles such as bronchitis and pneumonia.

Surely it would be far safer to allow a child to get measles, mumps or general childhood illnesses, which in the 1950s children were 'encouraged to catch' than to take the risk of a life long disability of emotional, learning and behaviour problems, and even worse epilepsy.

Who knows what other diseases have their origin in vaccinations. Could it not be that as children are vaccinated against everything, the immune system never gets a chance to mature and protect as it was meant to? Maybe when a cancer cell arrives on the scene – perhaps leukaemia – the immune system just does not know how to respond!

Vaccinations are themselves an onslaught on the delicate immune system given to babies and young children when their immune systems are immature.

There are many safe homeopathic remedies called nosodes. These are equivalent to vaccinations. One can take these to prevent all manner of diseases that are safe effective and have no dangerous disabling side effects. They are particularly beneficial to use when travelling to far off climes and wishing to avoid the possibilities of contacting hepatitis, meningitis etc.

Unfortunately homeopathic remedies are cheap and therefore are not recommended as they do not return the revenue that the drug industry wants.

Hyperactivity and learning disorders

With hyperactivity (attention deficit disorder with hyperactivity) the child displays signs of inattention and has poor concentration.

Are these conditions caused by 'Nature' or 'Nurture'? I rather feel that the latter is more likely. Far more boys than girls suffer from this disorder which can wreck family life and cause masses of stress in the classroom situation, both for the teacher and the other children.

Dysfunctional behaviour is usually seen by the age of three although the problem is not usually diagnosed until the child commences school.

Some hyperactive children suffer from speech and hearing deficits, are emotionally unstable, and have poor coordination. Their memories are usually poor and in some to retain information in the classroom for more than a couple of hours is usual.

Some children have this disorder which can be linked to a difficult birth, such as a forceps delivery, or a restrictive oxygen supply during labour, when the infant would obviously have been 'in distress'. These causes are rare and if either of these conditions are suspected cranial osteopathy would be highly recommended. Excellent results have been achieved with this cranial work.

However considerable evidence points towards food additives, food sensitivities and high sugar consumption being the main causes.

I knew of a young child who I treated with reflexology who suffered a complete change of character when she drunk cola drinks. From being a normal pleasant child who was in no way hyperactive, she would become very excitable, racing about uncontrollably, jumping off furniture, and screaming.

This reaction would occur within 15 minutes of a glass of cola. Once cola was forbidden and never entered the house again, she suffered no further episodes of hyperactivity, other than the occasions when she visited friends houses or went to parties and 'broke the rules'.

The term food additives covers thousands of chemicals, all of which should never have arrived on this planet, let alone to be taken into our bodies.

There are additives that act as bleaching agents to give the whiter than white loaf, artificial colourings, flavourings, emulsifiers, preservatives, thickeners and vegetable gums.

So many children are sensitive to the food colourings found in sweets, fruit squash drinks (which have seldom seen any fruit) and the huge variety of flavoured crisps.

Other symptoms are headaches for which no real cause can be found, abdominal pains, fits and bed wetting. Eczema and asthma are frequently found in hyperactive children, a sure sign of a toxic overload.

All these symptoms can and often are the result of food additive sensitivity, which grossly affects the function of our liver.

Numerous studies have demonstrated a relationship between learning difficulties in children and heavy stores of lead in the blood stream.

It is important that the patient is removed from sugar first for three weeks at least and then observations made on any improvement, if any. It seems that sugar taken in place of a meal, such as a bar of chocolate, has more exaggerated effects on the hyperactive child than sugar consumed with a meal.

Sugar in any case depresses the immune system and just one chocolate bar can affect immunity for up to five hours.

The next port of call would be the colourings and additives in crisps and sweets, again leave out these possible offenders for another three weeks and observe very closely the changes in the child.

Nutritional deficiencies can play a major part in impaired brain function. So many children today eat a very poor diet, junk foods forming the basic part of what they do eat. Most parents notice a positive change in their child's behaviour when cutting out all junk foods, colourings etc. This has to be strictly adhered to, there can be no half hearted attempts. After all none of us would willingly place a spoonful of dye into our child's mouth. Colourings, additives sugars and various other external pollutants do act as a 'poison' to these children.

The standard therapy for hyperactivity particularly in America, is drugs. One in particular is Ritalin, which produces a calming effect on the nervous system. This drug is not without its side effects and insomnia, anorexia, blood pressure changes and heart palpitations are just some.

It is well worth trying every possible avenue before resorting to drugs, elimination first and attention to supplementation B vitamins like niacin and thiamine may help. Calcium has a calming effect and should be taken. Magnesium deficiency causes anxiety and restlessness and learning difficulties even among children with a normal IQ.

Daily doses of cod liver oil and linseed oil are an excellent promoter of general health too.

Health is a total balance of our subtle energy systems with the forces of the human body combined with respect for Mother Nature, and is not just the absence of disease.

Alzheimer's disease and senile dementia

This disease of the brain creates a gradual mental deterioration, loss of memory and inability to carry out even the simplest tasks. Is memory loss just a part of the ageing process and can anything be done about this upsetting condition?

Psychologists feel that the illness could go back a long way, probably to childhood and suppression of emotions can be the root cause of the deterioration later in life. That Alzhemier's disease is often genetic in nature is a fact, but family standards and ways of dealing with emotions also have familial tendencies.

Dementia refers to a general marked deterioration in the elderly which is often referred to as senile dementia. Alzheimer's disease is a condition where there are marked changes and atrophy of the actual brain. Apart from the memory loss, the sufferer is often moody, self centred and exhibits childish behaviour. Currently 1.3 million elderly in the US suffer severe dementia.

Alzheimer's disease is most common after the age of fifty. There seems to be some link with neck conditions and Alzheimer's disease. It is thought that any trauma to the neck as in the case of a road accident could affect the blood and nerve supply to the brain. Symptoms associated with trauma are short-term memory loss, vertigo, ringing in the ears, and depression. An extract from the leaves of a remarkable tree Ginkgo Biloba offers some hope for dementia as it seems to improve the vascular supply to the brain.

Ginkgo Biloba is the world's oldest living tree species and can be traced back more than 200 million years to the fossils of the Permian Period and for this reason it is often referred to as 'the living fossil'. Ginkgo's use can be traced back to the most ancient of Chinese medicine (2800 BC). Records state that the leaves were used for 'the benefit of the brain'.

Its potency in relieving dementias is gaining ground and it is thought that its benefits are in improving the circulation to the brain by stimulating the lining of the blood vessels, the vascular endothelium. Its vasodilating action is explained by a direct stimulation of the release of endothelium derived relaxing factor and prostacyclin, a beneficial prostaglandin..

Apart from the benefits in improving cerebral vascular insufficiency and impaired mental performance Ginkgo Biloba is also recommended for any type of vascular insufficiency, peripheral arterial insufficiency being one,

In addition to trauma it must be considered that so many elderly people take a concoction of drugs over a long period of time and this long term use of drugs could also be a cause of mental deterioration.

High body aluminium and silicon levels have been found in patients with Alzhemier's. Aluminium and silicon are included in many indigestion remedies, processed foods, underarm deodorants, cooking pans and drinking water.

Sufferers have been found to have low levels of Vitamin B_{12}, so this vitamin should be taken as a daily recommended dose for all those over 10 years of age.

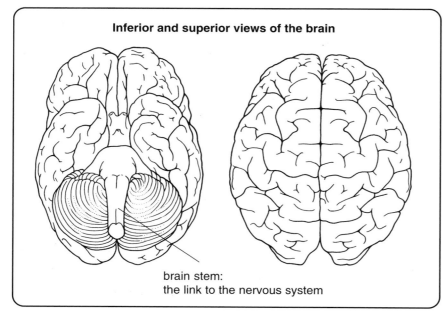

Inferior and superior views of the brain

brain stem:
the link to the nervous system

Epilepsy

Epilepsy is a symptom rather than a disease and the condition often remains a mystery. There is an exaggerated response in one side of the brain causing fits. There are three types of epilepsy – grand mal, petit mal and temporal lobe epilepsy.

Grand mal

This is a form of generalised but temporary convulsion which in some can occur several times a day. Some epileptics are aware that a fit is about to commence and will experience 'an aura' – a definite sensation. In some it is increased sensitivity to smell or taste, or feeling very anxious and nervous.

The tonic phase is when the patient falls to the ground totally unconscious remaining rigid. Epilepsy is triggered in some cases by changes in the atmosphere, thundery conditions are common, or extreme heat. Flashing lights and loud noises are also initiators of an attack.

The clonic phase is the jerking stage of the condition. The whole body goes into a convulsive

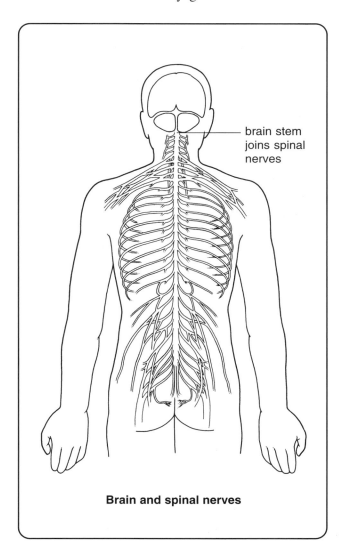

Brain and spinal nerves

brain stem joins spinal nerves

state. Sometimes the tongue is bitten and there is often frothing of the mouth, and incontinence.

The relaxation stage is when consciousness returns and the patient feels extremely tired and usually sleeps for long periods.

Petit mal

A much milder form of epilepsy: many children have this condition. It is a situation that causes the child to 'drift' or to become 'absent' from his or her surroundings for a few minutes. The child who 'daydreams' in the classroom is often having an attack of petit mal, but will be accused of lack of concentration.

Temporal lobe epilepsy

As the name suggests, this is localised in the lobe where memory and some sensations are coordinated. The sufferer may experience hallucinations, or revert to dream like states.

Patients suffering from temporal lobe epilepsy are not permitted to drive if they have suffered from day time fits in the previous two years.

Febrile convulsions

These frightening 'fits' are common in young children under the age of five and usually occur during a feverish illness, and it is the rise in temperature that excites the brain that is the cause. They rarely cause any harm and the child usually outgrows these attacks.

There are various therapeutic considerations that need to be looked at when seeking out possible causes of fits. Heavy metals such as lead, mercury, cadmium and aluminium can induce seizures by effecting nerve function A hair mineral analysis provides the most cost effective screening method for the detection of heavy metals.

Another possible cause is hypoglycaemia. In fact many researchers believe that this is the most important metabolic cause of seizures. 50 to 90 per cent of epileptics were found to have periodic low blood sugar and 70 per cent were found to have abnormal glucose tolerance tests.

Food allergies

Do not rule out the possibility of food allergies being the cause of convulsions or seizures. The body is an integrated organism and food placed into the mouth enters the digestive system and eventually circulates through the entire body, including the brain. Irritants in the form of colourings, preservatives and high levels of sugar in the diet could just as easily irritate the brain in some as it does the skin in others.

Simplistic changes in diet and supplementation are always advisable and well worth trying. All medications for epilepsy, or anything else have side effects which are often very unpleasant.

Bell's Palsy

This condition affects the seventh cranial nerve and this nerve affects the facial muscles so expression and taste are involved.

The seventh cranial nerve runs within a narrow bony canal where it exits from the middle ear. It is thought that if this delicate canal is exposed to a cold draught swelling of the nerve can occur which would then cause the disabling symptoms. The patient suffers extreme embarrassment as the expressions are affected. The patient is unable to smile, the mouth will droop so speech will be affected. There will be no control over the mouth so eating and drinking pose great difficulties and the eyes will droop. It is therefore a most disfiguring condition. Occasionally Bell's Palsy occurs following an acute ear infection. Thankfully most of those suffering will recover completely within six weeks or so.

Reflexology

If you are a Reflexologist and working on patients suffering from any disease affecting the mind and brain function, the areas identified below in the various charts will give you some guidance of the most important reflexes to work upon.

AUTISM

- Work out the areas of the entire intestinal area very thoroughly and repeat as often as eight times on each foot at each treatment session.
- Work out the area of the central nervous system, spine and brain.
- Work out the endocrine system.

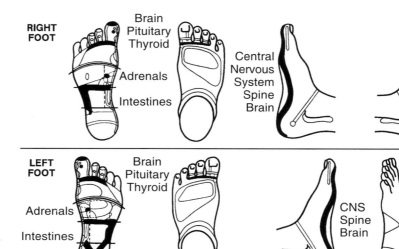

HYPERACTIVITY

- Work out the lung and solar plexus area to try and bring about some relaxation. Helping the lung function and solar plexus will assist.
- Work out the entire digestive system, again paying particular attention to the intestines (the likelihood is that food allergy is the cause).

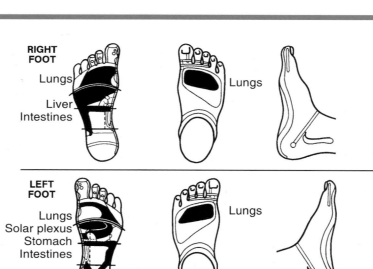

ALZHEIMER'S DISEASE & SENILE DEMENTIA

- Pay particular attention to the neck area, the area marked with a cross is the direct contact point to the carotid artery which is situated in the neck and will improve the blood supply to the brain.
- Work out all the toes and work down the lateral sides of each toe also all head and neck related areas.
- Work out the central nervous system, spine and brain.

RIGHT FOOT 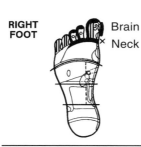 Brain Neck  Central Nervous System Spine Brain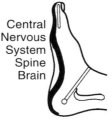

LEFT FOOT  Brain Neck 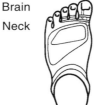  CNS Spine Brain

EPILEPSY

Before treating the epileptic sufferer one must find out whether the patient has suffered a head or neck injury at any time. If trauma to the head and neck are the possible cause, then the approach to the areas to treat are different than those necessary to work upon if the cause could be a food related problem.

RIGHT FOOT  Head/ Neck related Central Nervous System Spine Brain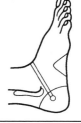

LEFT FOOT Head/ Neck related   CNS Spine Brain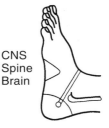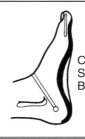

1. EPILEPSY: HEAD OR NECK INJURY

- Work out the entire head and neck area, particular attention must be made to the cervical spine, the entire central nervous system and brain.

2. EPILEPSY: FOOD ALLERGY

- Work out the endocrine system, the digestive system, the intestinal area and again the central nervous system spine and brain.

RIGHT FOOT  Brain Pituitary Thyroid Neck

Liver Adrenals

Intestines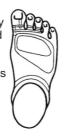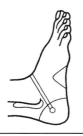

LEFT FOOT  Brain Pituitary Thyroid Neck

Stomach Adrenals Pancreas 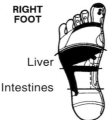 Intestines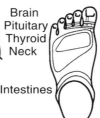

Continued..Bell's Palsy

105

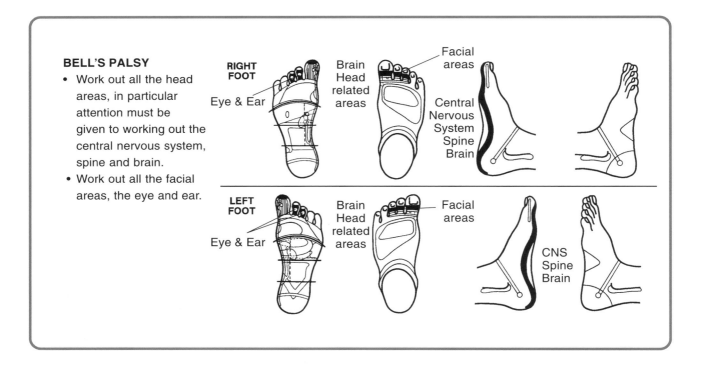

BELL'S PALSY
- Work out all the head areas, in particular attention must be given to working out the central nervous system, spine and brain.
- Work out all the facial areas, the eye and ear.

Did you know? **The Miracle of Selenium**

Selenium is a mineral element, unfamiliar to most people but it is a mineral that we are unable to handle in its natural form, unlike other elements such as copper, iron and zinc. Some chemists call it a non-metal because it is somewhere between the two: maybe it is more like a sulphur.

Selenium was discovered by the Swedish chemist Berzelius in 1818 and named it after the moon (selene). It is the fortieth most abundant chemical on earth – only just more abundant than gold – and is found in sedimentary rocks.

This element offers vital supports to the body as it helps to protect tissues from the highly reactive and destructive chemicals called 'free radicals'. These are highly active forms of oxygen. Being subjected to the hazards of free radicals is a price which has to be paid by any organism living in an atmosphere of oxygen.

Selenium seems to play a significant role in removing damaging toxic substances in the body and, after all, high toxic levels in the body are invitations for disease to manifest. The toxicity that builds up in the body as the result of drug therapies is quite immense, plus all the foreign substances which are used, such as food colourings, pesticides and household chemicals.

The daily requirements are quite high – 150mcg/daily. In a study of cancer victims in 27 different countries, it was concluded that the higher the blood selenium level, the lower the cancer incident.

A diet high in polyunsaturated fats, unprotected by plenty of selenium, caused rats to become especially vulnerable to breast cancer.

High levels of heart disease are seen in China where selenium-deprived children are much affected. The deficiency of selenium levels in the soil caused the low selenium levels in crops. When selenium supplementation was given to children in China, the statistics of heart disease dropped quite dramatically.

Sufferers from arthritis were found once again to have lower than normal levels of selenium. It was thought that the high levels of toxicity which present themselves when selenium deficiency is found could be one of the main causes of arthritis.

Some of the best forms of selenium are cereals, organ meats, sea foods and brown rice. If it is not possible to include these foods in your daily diet, then a daily supplement could be beneficial in treating all manner of disease.

Therefore, consider selenium as your body's protective mineral.

CHAPTER 37

What is M.E?

Myalgic Encephalomyelitis – M.E.

M.E. is at present a poorly differentiated disease, largely due to the multitude of symptoms associated with it. It remains uncertain whether or not M.E. is precipitated by a sudden viral stress. The major symptoms include:

- Fatigue (not relieved by rest)
- Aches and pains (generalised throughout the body)
- Poor concentration
- Digestive disturbance
- Temperature control disturbance
- Mood disturbance

What causes Myalgic Encephalomyelitis?

The actual cause remains unknown, but the feeling that a number of doctors working in the field and, certainly, I have for the illness is that the problem lies within the individual's immune system and their inability to handle some particular viruses, and is not related to the specific virus involved.

Picture the immune system as a ship, which is sailing around getting more and more laden with cargo and sailing lower and lower in the water. Then the ship is holed in the side and begins to sink. The ship will sink unless the damage is repaired. The analogy works very well for M.E., as there is an immune system with a hole probably caused by a virus which we are unable to treat, and the only way of treating the sinking body is to unload the immune system enabling it to carry on with the hole still present but above the water line.

Glandular fever or infectious mononucleosis is a more common illness, but similar to M.E. in its clinical picture. It is caused by the Epstein-barr virus and usually causes illness for one to six months. Stimulating the immune system to recover from the viral illness in glandular fever can promote a far quicker and more complete recovery.

Unfortunately, in this day and age everyone faces unnecessary health hazards, such as allergies, candida, toxic overload problems, stresses and difficulties with self image and social support networks, and, in particular, nutritional problems – deficiencies in vitamins, minerals and other nutrients.

Allergies

It is unlikely that allergies actually cause M.E., but they play an important role in the illness. People may be allergic to food or inhalants or both, and ridding the immune system of the same can make an immense difference by greatly enhancing the body's defence mechanism.

Allergies can be treated by either avoiding the things one is allergic too, once it is established what the allergies are, or by desensitisation. A helpful test (this test is reliable and reproducable in good centres), would be followed with an elimination diet based on the cytotoxic test, or using a very stringent elimination diet avoiding many foods for several weeks.

Hyperventilation is closely associated with allergies. When the breathing gets out of control, the body is far less resistant to allergy.

Enzyme Potentiated Desensitisation (E.P.D.)

E.P.D. is an extremely successful allergy treatment. It was developed about 20 years ago, and uses very small homeopathic doses of foods and does not require the individual to work out what particular foods cause an allergic reaction. The same treatment applies for every patient and it stops recruitment of new allergies and consequently it is much less complicated to work out than any previous form of desensitisation or neutralisation.

Candida

Candida is a yeast, a mould, that grows in the human intestine. It is the yeast that causes thrush. The yeast in the bowel does not cause itching and discharge as it does with vaginal or oral thrush. It tends to produce symptoms like bloating, constipation, diarrhoea, with the sort of digestive symptoms that doctors put down to irritable bowel syndrome and, in many people, it is candida infestation of the bowel. The candida yeast releases toxins and these toxins can affect the immune and endocrine systems and actually paralyse the T cells, so preventing them from working properly, so it is very important to unload the immune system of candida in order that the T cells can have an opportunity to recover.

Candida can also release toxins that affect the brain

107

and hormonal system, it tends to make people tired, depressed and forgetful, and gives hormonal problems such as premenstrual tension, menstrual irregularities, etc.

The American doctor, William Crook revolutionised thinking on the treatment of candida when he published his work on the ill effects of these yeasts on the body. He said that the yeast has to be starved out of the body.

Yeasts ferment carbohydrates: consequently, if the yeast is deprived of carbohydrate it will not be able to survive. Therefore, people with this condition need to eat a high protein diet for some time. Obviously this goes against everything ever written about heart disease, but, whereas an individual may need to cut out sugar for many years, the yeast is starved out of the system after about six weeks on a low carbohydrate diet.

Toxic substances

- Pollution
- Mercury
- Other environmental toxins

Avoiding toxic substances is important for the 'unloading process', and the rebalancing of the immune system.

It is very difficult in our present environment to avoid pollution so greater efforts need to be maintained.

Mercury is probably the toxic metal receiving the most publicity at present. Jeffrey Bland, President of Health Comm Inc, and former director of the Linus Pauling Institute in the United States, suggests the elevated mercury levels decrease the conversion of thyroid hormones from T4 to T3. T3 is the active hormone and T4 is what the thyroid actually produces. Even when the thyroid gland secretes the normal amount of T4, if this is not converted into T3 the results are fatigue, constipation and feeling cold even when thyroid function test results are within normal limits.

Self image

People's perception of themselves is an important aspect of any illness. In one's quests for health there are spiritual and mental principles that can be applied.

Creative visualisation also proves helpful in the environment of healing. The Cancer Centre in Bristol is having notable success in treating cancer in this way.

Useful blood tests show:
- IgM often elevated
- T4/T8 ratio, usually 2.0
- VP1 protein present in blood

IgM is a particular kind of antibody present in an acute infection. It tends to remain elevated in people with M.E.

T4/T8 ratio Different kinds of lymphocytes are called helper cells or suppressor cells and, in health, the ratio should be 1.7 times as many helpers as suppressors. In people with M.E. it is a case of too many Indians and not enough chiefs, and the T4/T8 ratio is usually >2, i.e. too many helpers and not enough suppressors, with the result that the immune system is out of balance.

Virus Protein One (VP1) is a protein found in an individual's blood which indicates that there is chronic Coxsackie infection. However, the role of this virus in M.E. is unclear.

The above tests are not specific

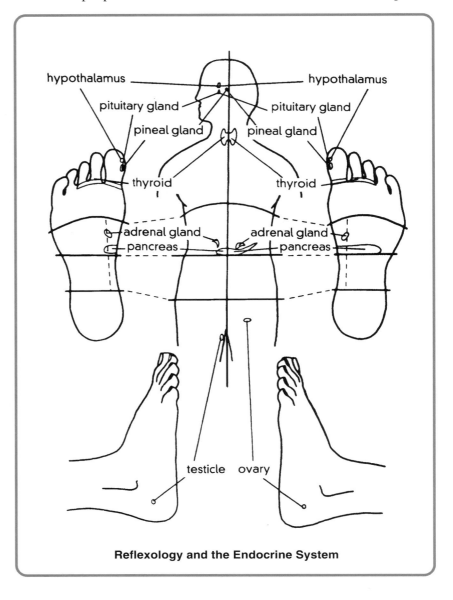

Reflexology and the Endocrine System

Reflexology and M.E.

In helping myalgic encephalomyelitis concentrate on the Endocrine System for hormonal balancing; the Digestive System to help the possibility of candida, and the spleen to improve immunity.

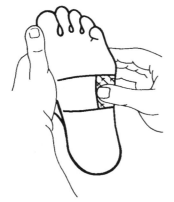

Working the spleen
(left foot only)

Supporting the left foot with your left hand, place the right thumb on the lateral side of the foot and work diagonally in the direction illustrated.

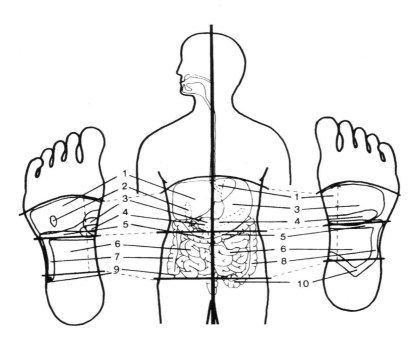

Key

1 Liver
2 Gall bladder
3 Stomach
4 Pancreas
5 Transverse colon

6 Small intestine
7 Ascending colon
8 Descending colon
9 Ileo-caecal valve
10 Sigmoid colon

Reflexology and the Digestive System

to M.E. However, when consistent abnormalities are determined or there is a discernible illness pattern, M.E. may be diagnosed.

What is actually wrong with these people? Is it a bizarre virus leading to a single bizarre illness? I personally think not.

Professor J. Mowbray of St. Mary's Hospital is researching the virus and is finding a particularly high incidence of Coxsackie virus. I think it will be a long time yet before really clear virological evidence is available, but research is currently being conducted in several centres of excellence.

My feeling is that the problem lies with the individual's immune system and the individual inability to handle that particular virus.

Nutrition

One of the main imbalances causing immune dysfunction is sub-optimal nutritional status, and in good nutrition control can be very effective in boosting an impaired immunity.

Vitamins

Vitamin B_6, folic acid and B_{12} levels are often low in people suffering from M.E. Many people are lacking the enzyme which is called pyridoxal 5 phosphatease which converts B_6 into pyridoxal 5 phosphate, which means the B_6 level is normal but cannot do its job. This is important because the signs of B_6 deficiency are tiredness, mood swings, and a number of other symptoms suffered by people with M.E. Patients expect to improve when taking B_6 but, as they are unable to convert it to the next stage, what they need to use is a supplement of pyridoxal 5 phosphate.

The antioxidant vitamins A, C, and E

Gluthione peroxidase levels, platelet aggregation and red and white cell fragility (the antioxidant parameters) are often within the normal range, and M.E. patients on the whole seem quite unaffected by anti-oxidant problems. However, vitamins A and C have crucial immunological functions.

High doses of vitamin C are particularly helpful, partly for its anti-candida effect and for its antiviral actions.

At the same time, multivitamins are needed as the B vitamins are required to metabolise the vitamin C or one risks kidney stone formation.

CHAPTER 38

Bones & disorders of support

Bone

Bone is living tissue and as such is constantly on the move in the sense that material is continually being deposited and removed, therefore we renew our skeleton many times over the course of a lifetime.

Bone really resembles fibreglass, in that it consists of a meshwork of collagen fibres bound together with a resin and then hardened with calcium and phosphorus.

There are three hormones which are involved with the density and growth of bones: parathormone, which is produced in the parathyroid glands – four wheat shaped glands embedded in the upper and lower lobes of the thyroid gland, calicitonin and vitamin D.

The regulation of the living 'matrix' of the bone is performed by three types of cells, known as osteoblasts, osteocytes and osteoclasts respectively. All three have to function in unity if bone health is to be maintained. Disease of bone is usually due either to an imbalance in their conduct or much less commonly to abnormalities of hormone production.

Childhood development

During childhood minerals are deposited on preformed cartilage, a process called ossification which is controlled by the osteoblasts at the metaphysis or more exactly the epiphyseal line of the metaphysis. Sometimes due to a fracture or injury in childhood, the epiphysis slips out of position and then the bone does not elongate.

At the end of puberty, growth of long bones terminate with the fusion of the epiphysis to prevent excessive height.

Vitamins and minerals

One of the most vital vitamins that is needed for bone formation is vitamin D. This vitamin is obtained from animal fats and from the action of the sun on the skin. Those who have a poor diet and have little access to sunlight are more likely to be subjected to bone deformities. Softening of the bones, known as rickets was once a common condition and is still found in underdeveloped countries.

Lack of calcium in the blood will have the effect of demineralising bones. In cases of chronic renal failure, excessive calcium is lost due to poor kidney function;

another condition – coeliac disease prevents calcium being absorbed.

Aches and pains in our muscles and joints can be caused by insufficient calcium in the blood.

Osteoporosis

We hear so much about this condition today, mainly due to the fact that we are living much longer and our skeletal systems are subjected to far more wear and tear than say fifty years ago.

Lack of calcium does play an important part, however it is vital to keep the body moving, bone depends on impact to remain intact, so jumping, running, stretching, swimming, any activity is so important for bone health.

If you lay in bed long enough, no matter how fit you are, you will lose calcium from your bones and suffer osteoporosis.

Calcium is the most abundant mineral in the body: bones contain about 99 per cent. Insufficient calcium causes thinning of the bones; an abundance of it can encourage gall stones and kidney stones.

We need magnesium to stimulate the absorption of calcium.

One of the most interesting features of osteoporosis is that it occurs more in cities and in 'first world' countries rather than in rural areas and 'third world' countries.

There is more evidence of osteoporosis in European and North American countries where people consume large quantities of milk products than in the African countries where people drink almost none.

We all know that bone fractures usually occur during the later stage of a woman's life, menopause is not the cause of these problems. The most important aspect is how we treat our bodies and especially what we eat.

The following can adversely affect the condition of bone:

1. A diet high in meat, white flour and sugar products, potatoes and tomatoes.
2. A high consumption of drugs, either over-the-counter drugs or others.
3. Very limited exercise.
4. Sufferers are thin – the incidence of osteoporosis is then high. With a reasonable covering of fat, a woman's body produces small amounts of oestrogen from the fat layer. This is essential as once the menopause occurs the ovaries stop producing oestrogen, so we do need it from another source. When you are too thin there is just nothing for the body to draw from.
5. Acid forming foods, counteract and withdraw the calcium and minerals in bone – so sugar is high on the list here, and just think of the vast quantities of sugar we consume from birth to the grave
6. Another disaster area in decreasing calcium from bone is a high intake of caffeine which encourages the excretion of magnesium and calcium loss from the bones which is deposited in the urine. Consumption of over five cups per day and you are in trouble.

Help with the menopause

To help you through the menopause and to sail through it without replacement hormones, make sure you consume:

1. Dark green vegetables. Plants boost the calcium and mineral content in your body. Carrots, parsnips, cruciferous vegetables, such as broccoli, cabbage or cauliflower are a good source of cholesterol-free protein as well as calcium.
2. Eat the bones of tinned fish such as sardines, herring, salmon and eat them canned in olive oil, not brine.
3. Meat on the bone will give you some calcium.
4. Sunflower oil, olive oil, sesame seeds, are all good sources of natural fats.
5. Drink three litres of water per day.
6. Avoid foods with caffeine, and that includes coffee, cola drinks and chocolate.
7. Take alcohol in moderation.
8. Avoid drugs that contain steroids and antacids as these all decalcify bone.
9. Keep yourself moving.

Arthritic and rheumatic pain

'Arthritic' and 'rheumatic' are words used to describe pains in joints or pains in various parts of the body due to movement. Rheumatic pain tends to move about the body and may therefore emanate from ligaments, tendons or muscles.

Pains in joints arise from the surfaces lining them, the synovium or cartilage. It is the synovium which exudes fluid into the joint which makes it swell.

Our knees in particular take huge amounts of strain during our lifetime, as do our hips, and the process of wear will be greatly increased if the person

A knee joint transmits half of the body's weight

111

is overweight. This process of wearing out of the cartilage is the basis of osteoarthritis and as the cartilage wears away the bone cells beneath frantically try to repair the damage.

Rheumatoid Arthritis

The disease takes its name from the word 'rheuma' meaning a stream of morbid humours flowing through the body, and refers to severe aches and pains throughout the body.

There are many theories as to the origination of the condition. Some people believe that the cause is genetic, others believe that it is food sensitivity, autoimmunity and viral. In 90 per cent of cases an abnormal protein called the rheumatoid factor is present in the blood.

Ankylosing Spondylitis

This distressing condition usually affects young men and can cause severe disability, the main one being a stiffening of the spine. Movement is greatly reduced and the pain can be quite severe. Apart from anti-inflammatory drugs and physiotherapy there is very little than can be done.

Very gradually the intervertebral discs become ossified, and usually the sacro-iliac joints are the first to become affected and this usually heralds the onset of the condition. Pain and stiffness are worse in the mornings and improve as the day continues. Some sufferers complain of undue fatigue and weakness, particularly in the early stages of the illness. Resting is the worst treatment for the condition, remaining as active as possible is essential.

Reflexology and disorders of support

Treatment with reflexology can be very beneficial in treating both rheumatic aches and pains. We obviously need to treat the relative areas that are causing pain, but don't forget the immune system and all systems of elimination: the more toxic waste there is in the body the more chance there is of waste deposits being directed into the joints.

When treating ankylosing spondylitis direct your treatment on plenty of work on the coccyx lumbar, hip and pelvic area. You will be contacting the sacro-iliac joint as you cover these areas which is the very root cause of the condition and needs to be kept as mobile as possible for as long as possible.

Treatment on a regular basis will probably stop the condition worsening, or at least give freedom from pain. You will no doubt find that these areas are extremely sensitive in the feet.

CHAPTER 39

Carpal tunnel syndrome

This unpleasant condition affects more women than men and has been associated with constant use of finger/hand pressures, such as is associated with those who are spending long periods working at keyboards or even spending long periods knitting or crocheting.

The symptoms of numbness, tingling and/or burning pain usually of the first three fingers of the hand, are much worse at night.

The symptoms arise through compression of the median nerve as it passes between the bones and ligaments of the wrist. Compression of the nerve causes weakness, and pain when gripping.

Although not commonly accepted, carpal tunnel syndrome is very common in those taking the contraceptive pill or hormone replacement therapy and throughout pregnancy and the menopause.

During pregnancy, levels of female hormones are increased, the increase in fluids accumulates in various parts of the body, including the sheaths of the nerve fibres in the wrist.

Most women have experienced fluid retention prior to their periods: they feel congested and bloated and hands and feet often swell – again this is all caused by hormonal changes.

The same hormonal changes cause the fluctuations of mood, food binges, anxiety, depressive episodes and the 'bad temper' that can be experienced when a period is due and which rapidly dissipates once menstruation begins.

There are however more serious conditions that can cause this condition: rheumatoid arthritis, hypo-thyroidism and severe injury to the wrist.

Vitamin B$_6$ is very important

Vitamin B$_6$ deficiency is common in carpal tunnel syndrome, in fact, except when due to direct trauma or systemic disease, there seems to be no exception to this rule. A person's vitamin B$_6$ status can be determined by measuring activity of an enzyme in the red blood cells.

Several clinical trials have conclusively demonstrated that vitamin B$_6$ supplementation relieves all symptoms of the carpal tunnel syndrome in patients with low levels of the vitamin. It is necessary to take vitamin B$_6$ for at least three months before seeing a positive result.

Helpful herbs

During the acute inflammatory stage of carpal tunnel syndrome, herbs which limit the inflammatory process may be of assistance.

Turmeric

Also known as Indian Saffron, has been used in both the Indian (Ayurvedic) and Chinese systems of medicine for the treatment of many forms of inflammatory disorders. Benefits are probably obtained from the volatile oil fraction of the spice which have been considered as beneficial as hydrocortisone and phenyl-butazone.

A very old fashioned remedy for inflammations of joints, including sprains and strains, is a poultice made from turmeric.

Curcumin

Even more potent in the inflammatory stage is the yellow pigment of turmeric, curcumin.

Bromelain

For patients whose carpal tunnel syndrome is due to injury and who do not respond to vitamin B_6, and who are considering surgical intervention, the proteolytic enzyme of pineapple may be of benefit.

The effects of bromelain orally administered on the reduction of swelling, bruising, healing time and pain following surgery and injuries has been well documented and its efficacy recommended.

There is no real evidence of 'diet' playing a vital role in relieving this condition, however excessive consumption of proteins is not advisable and any foods high in yellow dyes should be avoided.

As with all diseases, finding and removing the cause is important.

Reflexology and Carpal Tunnel Syndrome

By physically working around the wrist area itself with a deep creeping forward movement you may relieve the congestion.

If you suspect that there may be a hormonal cause to the condition, by working out the entire hormonal system you may well balance the imbalance here.

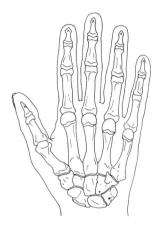

However, I recommend that you suggest your patients follow the advice as suggested in this chapter, combined with a reflexology treatment, before resorting to surgery, since this will not give long term relief if the endocrine system is the cause.

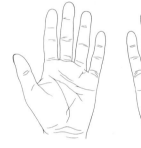

Did you know? **Osteoporosis**

Osteoporosis, or brittle bones, is caused by the slow loss of bone density and is primarily a disease of the elderly. The slow but steady process generally starts at about the age of fifty, particularly in women, and often goes undiagnosed until 'a fracture or break' in a bone occurs.

Bone density increases in our twenties and the minerals involved, especially calcium, are not fixed but are in constant flux. Osteoporosis occurs when more calcium is removed from the bone than is being replaced by the body.

Diet and Lifestyle

It is known that phosphorous, which produces the 'fizz' in drinks, decalcifies bone. Just think of the huge consumption of fizzy drinks in our lives today, such as cola and lemonade.

Maybe if we reduced or preferably removed these drinks from our lifestyle we would have no need for the use of HRT to 'prevent osteoporosis'.

There is some evidence that smoking increases the risk of osteoporosis, as does excessive coffee and alcohol.

Physical exercise can prevent bone loss but it must be 'load bearing' such as walking or tennis so that bones are flexed which encourages calcium to be laid down.

Vegetarians have a lower incidence of osteoporosis perhaps because the diet is lower in protein, since high protein diets can cause calcium excretion.

Useful Supplements

Calcium and Magnesium

Boron reduces calcium and magnesium loss and raises oestrogen, helping absorption.

B-Complex – medium levels as found in a multivitamin product.

Vitamin D is recommended to aid absorption plus **Zinc, Copper, Iron and Manganese** to assist bone formation.

Vitamin C helps to produce collagen, an important part of the bone.

CHAPTER 40

Are you going to sniff through yet another summer?

Do you despair when spring and summer arrives and pollen counts rise drastically, that you will spend most of the time indoors keeping out of the sun and the garden? Think again, you could well do much to help yourself.

Spring in particular is a time for rebirth, but not for allergy sufferers. The beautiful spring blossoms bring misery including smarting red eyes, itchy or streaming nose, not to mention a sore throat. Your best friend at this time is a box of tissues!

Allergies are defined as 'abnormal responses to normal substances' and such malfunctions and other over-reactions of the immune system are far more common these days than ever before. In fact, allergies are almost epidemic.

It is said that the additional burden of chemicals that we consume both from the air and in our diets cause the problem, but as Tokyo is the most polluted city in the world and has little problem with 'allergies' we must think again!

High levels of pollution can cause a burden on our immune systems which will result in malfunctions in the form of an exaggerated reaction to allergens......which can be anything from dust to pollen, animal hair, deodorant sprays, perfume, or some types of food.

A healthy body should be able to cope with pollen dust and other potential allergens. However, in a body already overloaded with toxins, allergens can cause a problem. In hay fever the allergens inflame the membranes of the nose: the membranes swell restricting the amount of space for air to be inhaled and then the inflammation of the membranes increases the mucus in the nose and throat.

Antibodies are then formed by the plasma cells which induce the mast cells (a type of white blood cells) to release chemicals – in particular histamine. It is the excess of histamine that causes the unpleasant symptoms.

Pollution

So many things in our lives today affect our immune system; there are even chemicals and pollutants in our drinking water. If you have a water filter in your kitchen you can reduce these considerably.

We unknowingly ingest antibiotics in our food. The meat industry use antibiotics in the feed of cattle to help prevent infections of one kind or another and our diet could be inadequate with insufficient minerals, vitamins and enzymes which are important as well.

Aluminium in cooking utensils, some packaging in which our food is contained, drugs, alcohol and smoking, these all have a negative effect on our body, in particular our immune system.

How to improve the immune system

Vitamin C is a great detoxifier, increases your resistance and is very good against stress. You need to take 1g of pure vitamin C per day for it to be effective in aiding the miseries of hay fever.

Try and give your body a spring

clean to encourage detoxification. A couple of days on spring water and grapes, if you are strong minded enough, is a good start. Try and buy grapes that do have pips and crunch up the pips as they stimulate the bowel and encourage detoxification.

You can eat three or four pounds of grapes a day if you wish to. The good thing about a grape fast is that the natural sugar in the fruit keeps your blood sugar levels intact and helps prevent the severe lassitude that can be experienced.

Chlorella granules twice a day, in water, are good. Not only is chlorella a good detoxifier, but it is also 60 per cent protein and contains a broad range of nutrients including the all-essential amino acids and is also high in vitamin A. It also contains Quercetin which is a bioflavonoid recently found to have natural antihistamine qualities.

Chlorella granules are available in most health food shops.

If you are very 'stuffed up' try an inhalation of camphor and eucalyptus oil, a few drops in boiling water works wonders. You can now buy a very reasonably priced facial inhaler, this is a small plastic cup with a spout which you simply either put in your mouth and inhale, or there is a facepiece which you can attach to cover your nose and again inhale the vapours.

This little device is available in most large chemist shops.

So don't despair if you are a hay fever sufferer, there are certainly things you can do to help yourself.

One last piece of advice, refrain from taking sugar in any form during the hay fever season. Allergy thrives on sugar, so turn your back as the ice cream van comes into view. You can have strawberries, but forget the sugar.

A Reflexology treatment plan for hay fever and similar symptoms of allergy

You can do more to relieve the unpleasant allergic symptoms with regular treatments of reflexology, which are beneficial in helping all manner of allergic conditions.

We need to go back to basics and begin treating the whole person. Reflexology treatments will help to detoxify the body and improve immunity. Encourage your patient to try to commence treatment approximately six weeks before the 'worst time'.

Give your treatment once a week and then during the attack as well. *Details and diagrams are to be found on the next page.*

One will usually find that the hay fever is far less severe if the treatments are commenced before the hay fever starts.

Did you know? Eye Disorders

There are many eye defects or abnormalities which nutrionists believe can be traced to a lack of vital nutrients in the diet.

NIGHT BLINDNESS Poor vision at night is usually caused by a deficiency in vitamin A resulting from malnutrition. Night blindness is more of a problem the older you become.

Useful Supplements
Vitamin A
Anthocyanidins such as grape seed and bilberry can significantly improve one's adaptation to darkness.

CONJUNCTIVITUS Inflammation of the eyes which become red and are usually caused by an infection or allergy, for example to pollen. Antibiotic drops are usually prescribed but for recurring cases, vitamin C can be useful.

Useful Supplements
Vitamin C
Echinacea purpurea for antibacterial properties.

RED EYELIDS Soreness and cracking of the eyelids can be due to a vitamin B_2 and B_6 deficiency.

Did you know? Cataracts

A cataract is when the lens of the eye becomes clouded leading to a sensitivity to light and gradual loss of vision. Cataracts develop when there is a degradation and oxidation of lens proteins that makes them opaque. In addition to the enzymatic defence system the lens also contains the antioxidant vitamins C and E, and is also thought to contain beta carotene as another line of defence.
Studies have shown that vitamins C and E give protective effects against light-induced cataracts by slowing down the damage process.
Surgical intervention to remove the cataract is reasonably successful.

Diet and Lifestyle
Increase your consumption of carotene rich foods, e.g. broccoli, carrots, and foods which contain vitamins C and E. Be particularly careful and wear sunglasses in bright sunlight all the time.

Useful Supplements
Antioxidant nutrients known to aid in the prevention of free radical damage are
Anthocyanidins such as grape seed, bilberry and pine bark extract.

The Reflexology approach to hay fever and similar symptoms of allergy

Commencing with the right foot.

1. Work out all the toes, these represent the sinuses in the head and will relieve the congested nasal areas. Supporting the right foot with your left hand use the right thumb and work out all the areas of the toes, use tiny forwards creeping movements.

Repeat exactly the same procedure for the left foot.

2. To help the sensitivity in the eyes work out the eye reflex on the second toe on the right foot by making small rotations and repeat the same technique on the left foot.

3. To concentrate just on the nostril area apply pressure to the inside edge of the right big toe. Place your thumb on the point and sustain a deep pressure for up to two minutes. You will find that this will bring about a great relief almost instantaneously, and will free the nasal passage.

Repeat the same procedure on the left toe.

4. If we work out the digestive system this will help any food allergies which will ultimately affect both the nose and lungs, and the skin.

We need first to work out the liver, stomach and intestinal area which will be found on the right foot.

Supporting the foot as shown, work out the areas between the diaphragm line and the heel line with forward creeping small movements of the thumb. Always work in a forward direction, never go backwards.

Change to the left foot and work out the same area, this will however represent the stomach, pancreas and continuation of the intestinal area.

5. We need to work out the lung area which could well be affected by the frequent attacks of hay fever.

Support the right foot with your left hand and use the right thumb and work up the area from the diaphragm line to the join of the toes to the feet.

Repeat the same procedure on the left foot.

6. End your session by using the metatarsal kneading.

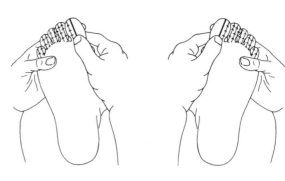

Working the sinus areas

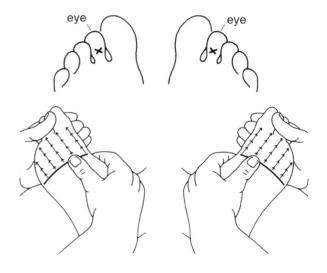

eye   eye

Working the lung areas

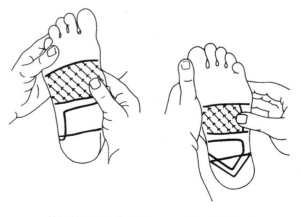

Working the liver area on the right foot and the stomach and pancreas on the left foot: also the intestinal area on both feet.

CHAPTER 41

Understanding psychologies

Psychology means different things to different people. To many people, contacting a psychologist for help means that at least you must be 'nuts'. To sit on a couch and have somebody prying into your life – 'that certainly would not be for me' is what we hear said.

Psychology comes from the Greek word 'psyche' (soul) so it relates to a study of the mind or, more importantly, perhaps the very spirit of man. There are so many types of psychology used in life today.

Many psychologists are employed in commerce and industry to assess suitable candidates for certain specialised jobs.

They are there to assess the psychological make-up of the person about to be employed for a position that maybe requires a certain type of person who copes with 'stresses' in a positive way, rather than employ somebody who one 'thinks' fits the bill only to find that months later their health becomes affected through the demands of the job and they were constantly absent with some form of stress related condition.

The psychologist in this situation can save time, and money to the employer, and distress to the employee and very valuable can his services be.

Then we hear of educational psychologists who study the way people learn. They can play a valuable part in those with learning difficulties and emotional problems that prevent them absorbing information.

Physiological psychology deals with our bodies, our genetic make-up, hormones, and nervous system.

Cognitive psychology deals with our memory and perception, valuable in those treating 'stroke' patients.

Psychology and psychiatry

A psychologist deals with all behaviour both normal and abnormal.

A psychiatrist treats mental illness, and uses medication and other forms of treatment to control mental disease. He would therefore be a fully trained medical doctor who has gone on to specialise in diseases of the mind.

Unfortunately in the fast-track world we live in today when most of us are divorced from the way we were all meant to live, mental illness is on the increase.

Sedatives, tranquillisers and antidepressants are used freely for those who have undergone a period of extreme stress, such as bereavement, divorce, rape or chronic disabling illness. It is all too easy to become 'hooked' on what seemed to be a temporary support during a time of stress.

Some of the stronger drugs that have been used in mental hospitals have been found to cause 'persistent facial contortions'. This is a distressing and ugly disfigurement of the face which no doubt causes more pain and distress to the emotionally disturbed than the reason that first put them into the hospital.

Depression appears to play a large part in our lives today, and all too readily people rush to their doctors for a 'cure' and a return of a happier frame of mind.

The role of diet

Many emotional and psychological disturbances are diet related, particularly in the case of the hyperactive child.

Certain people are acutely affected when they take food additives and colourings, even instant coffee has precipitated an epileptic seizure in those so predisposed, and look what can happen to some who cannot tolerate 'nuts of any type'!

How many psychiatrists ever look to additives, colourings and food allergies before putting their patients on drug regimes?

Ancient skills

Did the healers of ancient times really have some secrets that we are still unaware of today?

Discoveries in early Egypt reveal that surgery was practised with considerable skill and anaesthetics made from the juices of plants were used to relieve pain.

Aside from acupuncture the Chinese have had satisfactory treatments for many ailments including emotional disorders by the use of their Chinese herbs.

Records from ancient India dating back thousands of years mention brain surgery, Caesarean sections and treatments for the rejuvenation of vitality, memory, and more.

As Van Gogh said 'Emotions are the great captains of our lives'.

Historical facts taken from *The Psychology of Healing* – Murray Hope.

CHAPTER 42

The tranquilliser trap

When we hear of drug addiction, images of a degrading state come to mind. We hear of youngsters 'having a fix' and becoming aggressive, violent, or so 'spaced out' that they are totally out of control of their emotions and feelings.

Words such as heroin, crack and cannabis spring to mind. Indeed it is a sorry state to read that 50,000 people are hooked on such illegal substances. But more than twenty times that number, one million, men and women are addicted to prescription drugs: tranquillisers that calm them down and make them sleep and other drugs that help their depressive states.

How can one become hooked on prescription medicines? Quite easily is the answer.

The grim reality is that thousands of men and women have tried to come off medication but have dismally failed. Medication withdrawal can be quite terrifying producing symptoms such as sweating, palpitations, sleepless nights, depression – the list is endless.

Basically drugs are toxins, which means that the body registers them as poisons and they have to be eliminated out of the system via the liver.

Long term drug taking can mean a damaged liver which in turn produces more and more bizarre symptoms as the liver is 'the butler to the brain' – and when liver functions fail, brain functions are also severely diminished – bad news!

The breath of life

Most tranquillisers takers hyperventilate. That is to say, they do not use their total lung capacity but revert to this 'upper chest' breathing which, therefore, does not ventilate the blood sufficiently.

Tranquillisers tend to depress the function of the muscles that control breathing, which are the diaphragm muscle and the intercostal muscles between the ribs.

Hyperventilation can itself induce an anxiety state. Symptoms such as agoraphobia, depression, a pounding heart and palpitations are usual. We, therefore, need to impress upon people the need to know how to breathe from their abdomen.

Better eating

There is also the need to introduce a good eating plan.

Achieving a good alkaline/acid balance in the diet is really first class for people coming off tablets because this better way of eating does instil a state of calmness.

Symptoms are worsened by a vitamin deficiency. Magnesium deficiency is believed to be a contributing factor to a whole range of psychiatric symptoms, so a daily dose of magnesium is essential when trying to come off psychotic drugs of one kind or another.

Reflexology support for tranquilliser addiction

If you are a practitioner you will be able to help your patients who come to you for stress and anxiety, and who are on medications of one kind or another.

Firstly, the relaxation of the diaphragm will give an improved respiratory function. You could ask your patient to assist you by taking in deep breaths as you work upon the diaphragm area.

Working out the entire digestive system will help eliminate the toxins from the body. Again, this is another good step forward in aiding, in particular, the liver to allow some respite from the damage suffered – maybe for many years.

It will take at least six months to completely detoxify and eliminate the need to be 'hooked on drugs'. Reduce any medication very slowly: maybe halve the tablets taken each day, or try to take a dose every other day. Medication remains in our blood stream for far longer than twenty-four hours.

Then reduce the medication to once in three days, and so on. The habit can be 'kicked' if changes are made. The horror stories you hear about people suffering disastrous side effects is generally because they attempted to stop too quickly.

Flu-like symptoms are most common and these will subside in about 72 hours. The benefits of having a clear thinking brain and a better quality of life really make the personal effort well worth while.

CHAPTER **43**

Food is medicine

Few of us would have believed say, ten years ago that we would be encouraged to drink red wine to help the condition of our heart, that garlic was an excellent antibiotic and helped to prevent vascular diseases, yet it was accepted that we needed fresh fruits in particular lemons and oranges, to help prevent scurvy.

Two hundred years ago a flower called the Foxglove, known as 'Digitalis' was found to help heart

conditions and salicylic acid, the natural forerunner of today's aspirin, was discovered in the bark of the willow.

The largest proportion of medicines were herbal based and it is only since the middle of the last century that Western medicine has become so sceptical of the use of plants in healing the body. We must all remember that herbal medicine is about the oldest form of medicine recorded.

Mankind today is so reliant on the use of chemical drugs to relieve diseases of the body and has become dependant upon drugs to achieve good health.

However, we are producing more and more powerful drugs to attack more and more powerful viruses and consequently become drug resistant and suffer from quite unpleasant side effects.

Every form of medication we take has an effect on yet another function of the body, weakening our resistance, creating fungicidal conditions in our bowels, and unpleasant skin eruptions.

As we all have to eat, it is educating ourselves in knowing what to eat to improve our health and strengthen our immune systems to prevent diseases occurring that is a necessary essential to our wellbeing.

Let's look at some of the illnesses that seem to abound today and use foods to aid recovery.

Acne and skin eruptions

Acne is caused by too much oil (sebum) which sits in the pores of the skin. The pores become clogged and get infected. Acne is common in teenagers when an increase in sex hormones stimulates the oil producing glands. Acne is more common in males, and is considered to be exacerbated by stress.

Nutrition

Include broccoli, apricots, carrots and green leafy vegetables in the diet: these convert into vitamin A which is essential for healthy skin.

Take zinc supplements and/or include foods rich in zinc such as nuts and shellfish. A diet rich in vitamin C is important: vitamin C helps general healing and reduces inflammation.

All high fat and high salt content diets are very bad for acne and skin eruptions, the system is already overladen with fat and salt which is one of the general causes.

Alcohol abuse

Alcohol is a drug. It is a powerful intoxicant with the ability to kill and dependency on alcohol is widespread. Three quarters of a bottle of brandy consumed over a short period would produce a coma. Wine is considered to be 'less damaging' to the body if taken in moderation: two to three units per day is unlikely to do you any harm.

An addiction to alcohol is a 'dependency state' with cravings that are not controllable. Headaches, tremors and sweating are some of the symptoms along with poor concentration, poor memory and aggressive outbursts.

If you drink on an empty stomach it will intoxicate you faster than sipping one or two glasses of wine with a meal. A standard glass of wine is 125ml and this is the size you would expect to get in a pub.

It is estimated that 33,000 premature deaths a year in England and Wales alone relate to excessive alcohol consumption.

Alcohol is so easily available in our supermarkets and village stores, quite apart from pubs and restaurants.

Not only does addiction to alcohol 'change personalities' it is also dangerous in that it affects the individual's judgement of the situation, in particular, driving skills, which lead to road traffic accidents. Unfortunately, not only does the drinker sustain injury but also the innocent pedestrian, other drivers or passengers.

80 per cent of suicides are linked to alcohol excesses as well as 70 per cent of violent crimes.

You are likely to be lacking in nutrients if you consume too much alcohol, in particular, calcium, phosphorous, magnesium and zinc.

Heavy drinking causes changes in the heart rhythms increasing the risk of a heart attack, or a stroke (the risk becomes quadrupled if you have already had a heart attack).

There are also increased risks of getting cancer, particularly of the mouth, stomach, oesophagus, liver and bowel.

Most alcoholics have a poor diet and in an attempt to stop their drinking habit they would need to take the nutrients which are recommended in this article and refrain from eating junk foods which cause 'highs' and 'lows' of blood sugar levels.

As the liver will undoubtedly be affected by an excess of alcohol, by increasing fish oils, evening primrose oil and linseed will help 'repair' the liver cells. The liver is a most remarkable organ which can regenerate and do quite a remarkable 'repair job'.

Alcoholics Anonymous give support to those genuinely desiring to stop the habit and the telephone number of a local branch can be found in most telephone directories.

Allergies

What is an allergy? It is the body's over sensitive reaction to a stimulation, either by a food substance which irritates the mucous membranes of the digestive system, an airborne pollutant to chemicals, pollen from flowers or plants, animal fur or feathers.

An allergic reaction can affect different people in different ways. An irritation of the skin, eczema, psoriasis, or urticaria is but one reaction to an allergy. There may be uncomfortable bloating of the abdomen after eating or diarrhoea.

Other more serious reactions are respiratory changes, wheezing and laboured breathing, palpitations, itching swollen runny eyes and nose.

When a person suffers from anaphylactic shock as a result of ingesting an allergen, the immune system releases an excess of histamine within seconds of the substance being ingested. The membranes of the throat swell making it difficult and sometimes impossible to breath which puts the sufferer into a panic state'. This is a serious life threatening condition and unless an injection of adrenaline is given the allergic reaction can cause death.

This shock syndrome usually starts in childhood and can remain with the sufferer for life. Common offenders are peanuts, shellfish – particularly crab, lobster and eggs.

It is believed that one in six people in the UK suffer from some form of allergy, and these figures are rising.

It is also believed that many of the chemicals used in our foods today which give longer shelf life, enhanced colouring and flavouring may well be the cause of the allergy, not the food itself.

Apart from the physical manifestations that allergy can cause, emotional problems such as hyperactivity in children, migraine and depressive episodes are also linked to food and chemical intolerances.

A simple way to identify the culprit which is causing the unpleasant reaction is to go on an exclusion diet.

Remove one group of foods completely for three weeks and see if your allergy abates. As an example remove all dairy products. If there is no change then avoid all wheat for another three weeks. Try to avoid eggs on another occasion and so on. You do need at least three weeks for all traces of the substance to be removed from the system.

Anaemia

This is a condition which affects the red blood cells, causing a reduction in the cells which carry oxygen to the tissues of the body. Anaemia needs to be regarded as serious, as reduced red blood cells cause an extra strain on the heart.

The symptoms of anaemia include breathlessness, tiredness, fatigue, confusion, and sometimes depression.

Women during their menstruating years are particularly prone, especially if periods are heavy.

A haemorrhage, accident or problems in childbirth can result in anaemia.

Pregnant woman are also prone to anaemia which is why blood tests are carried out regularly during the forty weeks.

Elderly people with arthritis who have taken pain killing drugs and anti-inflammatory medications frequently suffer from stomach ulceration. The slow bleeding from these ulcers can cause anaemia.

Nutrition and anaemia

You need to include iron rich foods in your diet, red meat, offal, dark green vegetables, eggs, ground ginger, brown rice. Molasses is rich in iron and should be taken daily. You can add one tablespoon to a small cup of hot water, add a little lemon and take at least once a day

In order to absorb iron you need to take adequate vitamin C. Iron supplements tend to cause constipation and should be avoided unless attention to diet does not bring about the desired effect.

Arthritis

Two main types of arthritis are: rheumatoid and osteoarthritis.

Osteoarthritis normally affects the older age group and most elderly people suffer from some degree of wear and tear in their main joints, particularly in this day and age when many of us are living into our eighties.

A healthy, weight bearing joint is covered by a smooth layer of shiny cartilage which normally allows free gliding movement. As we age, or if we suffer from 'falls' or any other type of injury the cartilage becomes roughened which causes the underlying bone to wear.

When we suffer from arthritis we are disabled by pain, stiffness and lack of mobility.

Rheumatoid arthritis It is determined by blood tests and is most common in adult women. This chronic inflammatory condition can affect most of the joints and is considered to be caused by an autoimmune condition.

Instead of our immune system working efficiently to protect us, it appears to react against some parts of the body.

Rheumatoid arthritis frequently attacks the hands and wrists. Swelling and deformity of the fingers causes the hands to lose power and fine movements become impossible. Sometimes rheumatoid arthritis 'flares up' and then seems to burn itself out for a period.

Nutrition and arthritis

Some positive changes that one can make to help these conditions and have proved beneficial include high intakes of antioxidant vitamins C and E. Cod liver oil is also thought to be protective.

It is worth eliminating potatoes, peppers, aubergines and mushrooms. Watch your intake of coffee and tea. Caffeine is not recommended for any condition of our health as it can stimulate 'attacks'

All fish oils are so beneficial, linseed oil is rich in omega-3 fatty acids and one or other of these oils should be included daily in the diet.

Did you know?
Mouth Ulcers

This common condition can be extremely painful and although ulcers usually clear in 7–15 days, they often recur.

Diet and Lifestyle

There really is no known cause for this problem but food allergies are linked. Gluten, a protein in wheat and flour, is one suspect. Stress is also indicated. Nutritional deficiencies are almost always implicated. In nearly 50 per cent of sufferers in one trial, iron folate or vitamin B_{12} deficiencies were found. When these deficiencies were corrected, the incidence of ulcers was reduced.

Relating to the reflexology principle, it is usually found that with patients suffering with ulcerated conditions of the mouth, the stomach reflex area is very sensitive. It is quite probable that there are also small erosions on the stomach wall which link to the inflammatory state of the mouth.

Useful Supplements
Zinc and a good multi-vitamin

Money will buy...

A bed but not sleep.

Books but not brains.

Food but not appetite.

Finery but not beauty.

A house but not a home.

Medicine but not health.

Luxuries but not culture.

Amusement but not happiness.

A church pew but not Heaven.

Author unknown.

CHAPTER **44**

We are perfectly imperfect

We are perfectly imperfect from the day we were born, and always will be.

Each one of us makes mistakes on occasions: does things which they regret. Everyone is capable of honesty and sneakiness, kindness and hatred, compassion and cruelty. At the same time though you are still a perfect living being. You have been entrusted with a life that is yours to care for, enjoy and learn from. There will never be another YOU for YOU are an individual.

Many people have an unrealistic notion of what it means to be human. They get angry when they misplace their keys, lose their temper and offend other people, or experience fear, and then get frustrated when these events occur.

We think we should be able to stick to a diet, give up smoking, be popular with everyone and wake up each day feeling bright and alert.

If you really feel that this expectation of life is possible, look around you, can you find anybody to fit this description?

If you want to be happy, wave those perfect thoughts a fond goodbye, your expectations of yourself are too high.

We all get lonely sometimes, spill the milk, swear at the dog, and spend far too much on our credit cards, we are human after all and humans have many frailties.

Do you realise just what an amazing body you have been blessed with? Do you think more about how your body looks than how it feels? If so you are missing an important step to joy.

No matter what age you are there are many things you can do to feel more alive in your body.

In Western medicine, health is often seen as nothing more than a lack of pathology, a lump, a fever, sore throat or upset stomach.

It is necessary to understand that many stunningly beautiful people, have often been totally unhappy, suicidal and had few friends.

We observe horrifying reports daily on the suffering of mankind, particularly in the world's poorer countries. The greater tragedy however is surely the misery endured by these people albeit, smaller in numbers who eke out a wretched existence in the back streets of the truly wealthy nations.

Many authorities feel that the answer to social unrest lies in education, but does it? The erosion of human values appears to have increased with the expanding educational opportunities available for young and old. Crime and abuse has increased and morality has declined.

It was not too many moons ago when one could go out and leave one's door unlocked, the money at the side of the empty milk bottle for the milkman and walk five miles to the local village shops without fear of violent attack or rape.

During this period however, there were also those who had no shoes to walk to school, no surety of a good meal every day and little or no care

---

Did you know?
The Negatives About Additives

E220–27
Sulphur dioxides and sulphites
Preservatives found in dried fruit, fruit pie fillings, sausage meat, wine and beer.
Reactions:
Skin rashes in those sensitive individuals and wheezing, especially in athmatic sufferers.

E249–52
Nitrites and nitrates
Preservatives found in processed meats: ham, sausage, cooked meats. Also found in smoked fish and smoked meats.
Reactions:
Cancer in stomach has been linked to this preservative. Greenland Eskimos, who eat a lot of smoked fish, have a high incidence of stomach cancer.

E102
Tartrazine
A yellow dye found in squashes, especially orange squash. Also in brightly coloured sweets, ice lollies, jellies, etc.
Reactions:
Tartrazine has been associated with allergic reactions, skin rashes, hyperactivity in children, runny nose, ear infections and migraine attacks.

E952
Sodium cuclamate
An artifically produced sweetener found in soft drinks, ice cream, instant desserts, etc.
Reactions:
Can induce attacks of asthma, and there are conerns that hormonal functions may be affected.
There have been links with all types of artifical sweetners and certain types of cancer.

when taken ill, other than to rely on natural remedies and 'hope'.

The increase today in longevity in Western society is often credited to the medical profession. Life expectancy has increased but the burden and expense placed on the National Health Service by the growing number of elderly and infirm is beginning to create another set of problems.

Socially related diseases

Many socially related diseases in the young are the result of pressure brought to bear on the individual by society: bulimia, anorexia and depressive illnesses, to name but a few.

Many theories have been put forward regarding the cause of these illnesses which can result in death of the individual if left untreated.

For the teenager, anorexia can be the fear of becoming adult, in particular to conform to a certain size in order to be accepted into the teenage society.

Actresses and models, today's attractive women, wear size eight clothes, no bras and the bones of the ribs and spine need to show. Any ounce of surplus fat is unacceptable.

Women subject themselves to painful surgery in an attempt to create the figure they desire, lipo-suction, plastic surgery, breast reduction or enlargement. However these 'attacks' at the body image can only be made available for those whose incomes allow.

Their male counterparts are broad shouldered, slim hipped, Porsche driving machos.

The mind over matter theme is growing in popularity, even among the medical profession. The market is flooded with books on psychology, psychotherapy, meditation. There are tapes on self healing. Courses on personal development, visualisation, healing and how to overcome addictions and depression.

Those who are unable to involve themselves in self help are looked down upon as having no direction or purpose in their life.

Loneliness and isolation increases

Gone are the days when the problems and frustrations of life were dealt with by elder members of families who gave direction and guidance: the integrated close family group is a rarity and as families divide, split and go off to pastures new, loneliness and isolation increases.

To experience joy a child needs to feel safe. In the womb a child is bonded to its mother by the umbilical cord – the source of food and life. The umbilical link between mother and child is never severed: it is rather like a comfort zone. Small children can survive for a short period without contact with mother, but are drawn back by the invisible umbilical link, to the comfort of the mother figure.

Little children look up to the adults around them and must feel that they are surrounded by 'giants'. Just imagine how terrifying if these giants react by shaking a finger in the face of the small one, or call them stupid, bad or 'impossible'. It must be quite terrifying.

Spread joy

There are many quite ordinary folk who give an abundance of human kindness wherever they go, spread joy and have happy personal lives.

Think about yourself as a spirit that lives in a physical body. True beauty comes from taking care of both your spirit and your physical body which creates a glow of vitality.

Life is often messy, uncertain and unpredictable, sometimes we have a period when there seems to be a string of problems with no ending. That's normal life: ups and downs are normal. Without the 'bads' there would never be any 'goods'.

Low energy days are normal. We cannot be on a 'high' all the time, it is the dominance of advertising which shows perfect people, in perfect homes, living perfect lives, that makes us all so dissatisfied with our lot.

According to Chinese Medicine it is accepted as natural that we fluctuate from being in balance to being out of balance. Peace of mind comes from not attaching a great deal of significance to either state.

It is the essence of life that giving birth, growing, loving, losing, learning, creating, discovering and dying, enables us to experience 'emotions'. Without these experiences we would not understand what 'feelings' were all about.

Just imagine a world where beauty is equated with people who radiate vitality, warmth, peacefulness and joy. Imagine accepting each other just as we are faults and all, without being so judgmental.

Many of us look for the rainbow and are constantly chasing the gold at the end of it. When we get there we find that the gold had vanished and all that was left was just a pile of old rubbish.

There is beauty and richness in 'ordinary things in life' that cost little, but in our rush for financial gain we often pass the simple pleasures of life. We are given life, a precious commodity, and are placed on this earth for such a short while. We are surrounded by incredible beauty, strength and love along with incredible hatred, violence and prejudice.

Each time we involve ourselves in helping another, we are moving away from violence and closer to compassion.

Look for the positive intention

No matter how strange, crazy or cruel a behaviour appears to be, there is a positive intention under every negative reaction. It is usually a desire to be loved.

All people make mistakes: it's human to make mistakes – that's why lots of pencils have rubbers at the end of them to rub out errors and start again on a clean slate.

It's not a crime to make mistakes, and mistakes do not mean that you have no right to be loved. You can go back to the person you have hurt, apologise and clean up the mess together. Remember that in the span of a lifetime an error is just 'a blink of the eye'.

The earth will still revolve; spring, summer, autumn and winter will arrive and disappear, and the fish will still swim in the sea.

The alternative way, the negative way, is to harbour the hurt, fail to contact the person involved, fester negative emotions and suffer yourself and live with the grudge which will become an obsession for the rest of your life.

Remember, hatred, envy and grudges always affect the person that 'feels' these emotions, not the one that the hatred is directed at. One of the barriers to joy is pent-up grief, sorrow or anger.

'While with an eye made quiet by the power of harmony and the deep power of Joy, we see into the life of things.' *Wordsworth*

'I shall stop pushing a tired body.
I intend to take life at a slower pace, stop worrying ....and start living!'

Reference sources for the following chapters were:
An Area Explained – Colon Health:
Gut Reaction – Gudrun Johnson Vermilion, London.
The Heart of the Matter:
What Doctors Don't Tell You Publication - statistical information.
Cystitis – The Female Complaint: *Green Library*
A Better Understanding of the Brain & It's Not All in the Mind: *Understanding Disease – John Ball.*
Cravings – They Can Be Controlled: Green Library
Evening Primrose Oil: Green Library

also 'The Encyclopaedia of Natural Medicine' – Michael Murray and Joseph Pizzorono.

Alphabetical list of chapters

Also by Ann Gillanders.....

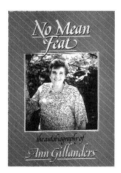

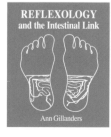
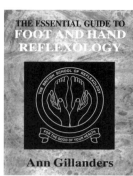
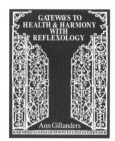

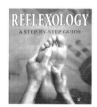